JESUS IS!

WHY LIFE ISN'T FUTILE

JESUS IS!
WHY LIFE ISN'T FUTILE

Knowing Him

Loving Him

Preparing for His Return

"I am the Way, the Truth, and the Life"
-JESUS the CHRIST

A. Arthur Pinno

Xulon Press

Xulon Press
2301 Lucien Way #415
Maitland, FL 32751
407.339.4217
www.xulonpress.com

Unless otherwise indicated, Scripture quotations taken from the Holman Christian
Standard Bible (HCSB). Copyright © 1999, 2000, 2002, 2003, 2009 by Holman Bible
Publishers, Nashville Tennessee. All rights reserved.

Scripture quotations taken from the New American Standard Bible (NASB). Copyright
© 1960, 1962, 1963, 1968, 1971, 1972, 1973, 1975, 1977, 1995 by The Lockman
Foundation. Used by permission. All rights reserved.

Printed and bound in Canada by Houghton Boston Printers, Saskatoon.

ISBN-13: 9781545645765

FRONT COVER

"GOD is pleased when His children work together for that which brings Him glory. The cover photo is an example of that unity of spirit and the result of collective effort. Rick Peterson built the cross out of rough lumber and installed it on the top of a grassy hill in southwestern Saskatchewan. His wife, Joyce, captured the shot against an early morning sky in late March. Dorothy Pinno and son Matt worked to compile and edit the final product. Thanks be to GOD for providing the sunrise and the reason for the hope we have in the cross—His only Son, our Lord and Savior, JESUS CHRIST." -Joyce Peterson

*"I have come so that they may have life
and have it in abundance."*
JESUS, John 10:10

*"Thomas responded to Him, 'My Lord and my God!'
Jesus said, 'Because you have seen Me, you have believed.
Those who believe without seeing are blessed.'"
John 20:28–29*

*"at the name of Jesus every knee will bow —
of those who are in heaven and on earth
and under the earth —
and every tongue should confess
that Jesus Christ is Lord,
to the glory of God the Father."
Philippians 2:10–11*

*"The night is nearly over, and the daylight is near."
Romans 13:12*

"He who testifies about these things says,
'Yes, I am coming quickly.'
Amen! Come, Lord Jesus!
The grace of the Lord Jesus be with all the saints. Amen!"
Revelation 22:20–21

TABLE OF CONTENTS

WHO IS THIS BOOK FOR?

For the glory of JESUS, the CHRIST, the SON of GOD:

Our **One and Only** SAVIOR and GOD, the Beginning and the End, Who entered to bring light and love, died to forgive and save, and is returning in glory to reign forever as Risen LORD and KING!

> *"They said with a loud voice:*
> *The Lamb who was slaughtered is worthy to*
> *receive power and riches and wisdom and*
> *strength and honor and glory and blessing!"*
> *Revelation 5:12*

For sincere followers of JESUS:

Those who love and trust in JESUS, who desire to grow in His grace and knowledge, and whose faith is daily being tested in the sufferings, temptations, mythologies, and persecutions of life in the 21st Century.

> *"So don't throw away your confidence,*
> *which has a great reward. For you need*

endurance, so that after you have done God's will,
you may receive what was promised.
For yet in a very little while,
the Coming One will come and not delay.
But My righteous one will live by faith;
and if he draws back, I have no pleasure in him.
But we are not those who draw back and
are destroyed, but those who have faith and
obtain life." Hebrews 10:35-38

For Generations X, Y, and Z

Given the scientific, social, political, and religious developments of our time, you very possibly may be the last generations before the apocalyptic events of the climax of human history, including the visible return of JESUS, the One and Only CHRIST. In the confusion of these days, turn to JESUS, hold on to His Cross, Resurrection, and Word of mercy and truth, and commit yourselves to His Kingdom work. You will find no better FRIEND, SAVIOR, and COUNSELOR to help and bless you, and to fill your life to overflowing with His grace.

"No one has greater love than this, that
someone would lay down his life for his friends.
You are My friends if you do what I command
you." John 15:13–14

For nominal Christians:

If, because of heritage or culture, you call yourself a Christian, but you have never really come to know JESUS as your SAVIOR and FRIEND or committed your life to listening to Him and following Him, His SPIRIT, and His Word, JESUS loves you and says to you:

"I know your works, that you are neither cold nor hot. I wish that you were cold or hot. So, because you are lukewarm, and neither hot nor cold, I am going to vomit you out of My mouth...<u>As many as I love, I rebuke and discipline. So be committed and repent</u>. Listen! I stand at the door and knock. If anyone hears My voice and opens the door, I will come in to him and have dinner with him, and he with Me." Revelation 3:15–16,19–20

For seekers:

Those who are hungry and thirsty for GOD and for righteousness, forgiveness, peace, truth, love, joy, and hope, and who are open to listening to JESUS and His HOLY SPIRIT.

"Seek the Lord while He may be found; call to Him while He is near. Let the wicked one abandon his way and the sinful one his thoughts; let him return to the Lord, so He may have compassion on him, and to our God, for He will freely forgive." Isaiah 55:6–7

For all people - all sinners:

By creation, we are all brothers and sisters, descendants of Adam and Eve *(Genesis 1 & 2)*. We are all sinners who have fallen from the glory of the eternal GOD and whom the LORD loves and calls to repentance and faith, offering His amazing grace and salvation to all.

"He was in the world, and the world was created through Him, yet the world did not recognize Him. He came to His own, and His own

people did not receive Him. But to all who did receive Him, He gave them the right to be children of God, to those who believe in His name." John 1:10–12

"There is salvation in no one else, for there is no other name under heaven given to people, and we must be saved by it." Acts 4:12

"But now, apart from the law, God's righteousness has been revealed — attested by the Law and the Prophets — that is, God's righteousness through faith in Jesus Christ, to all who believe, since there is no distinction. For all have sinned and fall short of the glory of God. They are justified freely by His grace through the redemption that is in Christ Jesus." Romans 3: 21–24

FOREWORD

P astor A. Arthur Pinno's lavish and extensive book is a feast for the inner life. Forget the many paths to inner peace spouted by many spiritual leaders today. Here is enough to revolutionize a person's mind and life. The author takes the facts of the Christian faith and makes them into an energizing force. He does it by unveiling the life and person of JESUS CHRIST. A faithful presentation of the deeds and words of JESUS together with the proper application of them confirms that JESUS is the Way, the Truth and the Life. I would invite anyone who is looking for an encounter with GOD to read these chapters.

What you will find as you read is that JESUS refuses to be relativized and made one of many enlightened guides to spiritual truth. A sincere person might think that way after hearing about JESUS. However, when you listen to JESUS' words and study His deeds, when you recall the ancient prophecies, and when you give reasonable thought to His crucifixion and resurrection, you will realize that He alone owns the title SON of GOD and humanity's SAVIOR.

Striking to me was to read anew the wonder of JESUS' gift of the Church, the Bride of CHRIST. How illuminating to recognize that the true source of her ridicule is spiritual. CHRIST's

Bride is the community and the life with God for which this age yearns.

Here is an invitation to have your attitude toward the future transformed. Too often the thought of the future of the world breeds despair. Even the brevity of our own lives is a topic to avoid. With the appreciation for the greatness of JESUS and the enormity of His love for us, the fear of the future dissolves into an emotion of happiness, an abiding peace, a note of joy. This is what this book's serious attention to JESUS and His plans will produce.

JESUS CHRIST is the beginning and the end. In JESUS alone we can know GOD and we will have what God defines as abundant and eternal life. Thankfully JESUS IS and was and will be forever.

-Dr. Harald Schoubye, pastor, seminary president, and minister on five continents

This volume is an insightful teaching tool for our daily walk with JESUS as SAVIOR and LORD. I would commend it to everyone, both seeker and believer, teen and adult. All who open its pages will find a blessing and food for the soul. We will be directed again and again on each page, and chapter and line to JESUS—true GOD and true Man.

A. Arthur Pinno sets a good tone for the book in its opening chapters, when he challenges us to remember that *"we live in the conclusion— the conclusion of human history —GOD's conclusion"*. What peace and confidence for the Believer in this—for all of life and for the hour of death and eternity. We live in GOD's conclusion!

At first glance this book seems to be an in-depth adult catechism and it is tempting to think we have heard it all before. Red warning cones need to be posted here keeping us from this error. This volume is much-needed for its solid content and simplicity. It is not a production of an ivory tower -replete with "theological-ese" — understood only by an elite and even then mysterious in places. Instead, it comes from a pastor who has served in congregations for many years and has a pastor's heart for the "flock". Its focus is down-to-earth, it will be understood by all. Its purpose is for the building-up of faith in JESUS as SAVIOR and LORD.

I would also commend this book to you for personal devotions. It focuses the reader on JESUS -who is the center and hope of our lives as Christians. A daily feast for the soul is found in every page and line. Daily devotions are a good discipline for every person and every home—this book will be a powerful tool and gift of GOD for you in these times. GOD bless it to each reader, to your study, and to your prayer life.

-**Pastor Kelly Henning,**
President, Association of Free Lutheran
Congregations—Canada

Some of us who are old enough can recall the images of Billy Graham crusades in the 1950s, evangelism sessions with thousands in attendance. Because the residual Christian worldview has dissipated, it's hard to conceive of such crusades in our present cultural landscape. In **Deuteronomy 8:11**, Moses instructs the people of Israel, ***"Be careful that you don't forget the LORD your GOD by failing to keep His command — the ordinances and statutes — I am giving you today."*** We have a similar situation today in that people have forgotten the LORD their GOD. As the author points out, "A majority of people in the world around us today think JESUS was just a man who lived and died 2000 years ago. They have no idea Who He really Was and Is."

In **Mark 8:27–29**, we have an account of JESUS asking his disciples, ***"Who do people say that I am?"*** We live in a day

JESUS IS! Why life isn't futile

and age when many people if asked such a question would have a blank look in response or present a fanciful notion of who JESUS is, fashioned in their own image. In his book, A. Arthur Pinno will reacquaint a world, desperately in need of a SAVIOR, to who JESUS IS.

-Dr. Ron Voss, Ph.D Chemistry

WITH THANKSGIVING

"Amen! Blessing and glory and wisdom and thanksgiving and honor and power and strength be to our God forever and ever. Amen." Revelation 7:12

We praise You, LORD GOD: FATHER, SON and HOLY SPIRIT, for Who You are and all You have done for us. You are our CREATOR, SAVIOR and COUNSELOR. We thank You for Your constant faithfulness and encouragement in the challenges and opportunities that we experience in this marvelous but fallen world. We praise You for the unimaginable future You are now preparing for all who come to trust in and love You. Thank You for washing away our sin and evil with Your own body and blood, and for transforming us into Your holy people. Thank you for Your amazing grace and truth that carries us in our weaknesses and leads us into Your eternal promised land, the new Heaven and Earth we hunger and thirst for. As You gave Your life to serve us, may we give our lives to serve You and to love and serve others in Your Name. May You bless Your Word proclaimed on these pages to bring some to faith in You and to encourage and strengthen Your people. Through it all, may You be glorified. Amen! May it be so!

"As for the holy people who are in the land, they are the noble ones. All my delight is in them." Psalm 16:3

I have been greatly blessed through the first saints whom I knew, my parents. I had the privileged experience of growing up in a home with a solid foundation. Faith, hope, truth, and love were always co-existent with hard work and perseverance through the trials of life. Paradise it wasn't; a blessing it was. My parents' love and faithfulness to the LORD, to each other, to their children, and to others is deeply etched in my mind and heart. In humble acknowledgment of their own weaknesses and sins they sought to live out the grace and truth of JESUS in their lives, family, congregation, and community through all the trials and testings they encountered. Their autobiography *Looking Up and Walking On* gives testimony to the LORD's faithfulness throughout the horrors of the Second World War, imprisonment, and loss of home and children. Faith incubated and refined by suffering is the faith that is genuine, immovable, and overflowing with thanksgiving and praise. I will be forever grateful to the LORD for loving and faithful Christian parents whom He saved.

For the past thirty-five years my wife Dorothy has been the LORD's gift to me. Her faithfulness, love, patience, and ministry to me, to our children, and to many others has been a joy to experience and observe. Her partnership in life and ministry in our home, in various congregations, and in other nations has been invaluable. She has certainly been my Proverbs 31 blessing. The LORD has also filled our lives to overflowing with the joy of our children, each one with unique strengths and weaknesses, joys and heartaches. Like us, they struggle with sinful natures and the challenges of life in this decaying world. We are thankful that they have the same gracious and patient SAVIOR Who continues to prune and guide their lives and ours. They each have their own adventure of faith in CHRIST to follow with all its challenges and blessings. Though they no longer live in our home, they are always in our hearts and in our prayers. May the LORD help them and us to continue to grow in JESUS, Who WAS, IS and will be coming soon!

Dorothy and I are deeply grateful to the LORD for His many saints who have been part of our lives. We have been privileged to know thousands of believers in various countries and have been encouraged in our faith through them. We are especially grateful to the LORD for the brothers and sisters who have been part of the congregations we have served, and for all of those who have partnered with us in our overseas ministries.

Thirty-six years ago, while serving my first congregations in southern Alberta, I was longing for family and friends who had been such a blessing and encouragement to me. The LORD directed me to His Words to His followers:

> *"And everyone who has left houses, brothers or sisters, father or mother, children, or fields because of My name will receive 100 times more and will inherit eternal life."*
> **Matthew 19:29**

Through the years we've had to say good-bye to friends and family numerous times as the LORD led us from place to place. Through it all He has certainly fulfilled His Word to us. Wherever He has led us, He has filled our lives to overflowing with brothers, sisters, parents, children, houses, and fields. There are far too many to name. To those we are unable to thank in this life, we will express our gratitude in the resurrection life to come. We look forward to eternal fellowship with all the saints in JESUS' majestic and gracious presence, once our journey and work in this world is completed.

Thank you to my brothers, Dr. Harald Schoubye, Pastor Kelly Henning and Dr. Ron Voss, for reviewing *JESUS IS!* and offering helpful suggestions. Your partnership in the LORD's work is a great blessing to me. Special thanks to Dorothy for spending many hours editing these chapters, carefully correcting my many errors, and for being gracious to me during the past thirty-five years.

May the LORD help all of us to humbly pick up our crosses and follow Him in repentance, faith, hope, and love. Amen, come LORD JESUS!

INTRODUCTION

"Sing a new song to the Lord;
sing to the Lord, all the earth.
Sing to Yahweh, praise His name;
proclaim His salvation from day to day.
Declare His glory among the nations,
His wonderful works among all peoples."
Psalm 96:1–3

Amen! It is and will be so eternally!

JESUS IS!

" J ESUS"- "YESHUA"- "YEESOOS" "JESU"- the Name that has been and is being formed by more lips than any other name. Many spew the name of JESUS with contempt, hatred, and rage, even while denying His reality. Simultaneously, many others in every corner of our world lift up His Name in love with prayer, praise, and thanksgiving. There are literally tens of thousands of songs and hymns of praise written for and about JESUS every year in hundreds of languages in every part of our world. How many songs have been or are being written about Molech, Baal, Zeus, Hercules, Allah, Mohammed, Buddha, Krishna, Moses, Peter, Paul, Mary, Julius Caesar, Napoleon,

Lenin, Mao, Hitler, Reagan, Obama, Clinton, Trump, Trudeau, Putin, Merkel, May, or Macron?

While many are being deceived into believing that JESUS is not unusual, just one among many false deities of humanity's evolutionary past, many others in every nation, tribe, and family around our globe are coming to know Him and the joy, peace, and hope that only He can give. Once you know the real, eternal, and historical JESUS, testified to by GOD's HOLY SPIRIT, you will understand why people all over our world are singing and proclaiming His praise and glory above all other names.

JESUS is everything that anyone needs to live a fulfilling life of faith, repentance, holiness, hope, love, peace, and joy, now and for all eternity. JESUS brings everything into proper perspective and removes the veils from the mythologies of every age, including those of the 21st century. He is GOD, SAVIOR, and LORD! He is the constant: *"the same yesterday, today, and forever" (Hebrews 13:8).* He is grace and forgiveness for the past, strength and courage for the present, guidance for the future, and the thrilling anticipation of eternity to come. He is the only source of life, love, truth, mercy, justice, and everything which is good and perfect, even for those who hate His judgments and do not acknowledge His goodness.

> *"For He causes His sun to rise on the evil and the good, and sends rain on the righteous and the unrighteous." Matthew 5:45*

JESUS is the visible expression of GOD's amazing grace and powerful truth. His humble birth, obedient servant life, miraculous ministry, bloodied cross, empty tomb, and coming return stand at the intersection of human history and divine action. He is the Way and the Truth Who came to save people from sin, death, and judgment, and for abundant life in His eternal House and City.

Sin—my sin, your sin, and the fallenness of our human race—has stained our world with suffering and death. **Being separated from GOD by going our own way produces loneliness and a sense of futility, a lack of any goal or purpose to life. GOD's amazing, powerful antidote is JESUS. There's no deeper joy and fulfillment in life than growing in the grace and knowledge of Who JESUS is, of what He has accomplished for us, of what He is doing in Heaven now, and of what He will do when He returns. JESUS said:**

> *"I have come so that they may have life and have it in abundance. I am the good shepherd. The good shepherd lays down his life for the sheep." John 10:10–11*

Living the Conclusion with JESUS!

Regardless of our GPS location, the tint of our skin, the babble proceeding from our vocal chords, the number of houses or acres we may temporarily occupy, or the size and number of our bank accounts, we all share a life on this planet that has a beginning and an end. We have already experienced the beginning of life and, if we aren't anesthetized by the intoxicants in our cultures or blinded by contemporary mythologies, we are aware of the approaching end. Though many stick their heads in the sand and pretend that death only impacts others, the end and the forever-after is near to each of us. We have only so much time and it is running out at light speed. We are all living the conclusion of our lives in this world and very conceivably in the final chapter of human history. For believers this is not something to be feared, but rather to be embraced by faith, looking forward to the eternal future that CHRIST is preparing for us. The conclusion is GOD's conclusion, filled with all His amazing promises for those who trust Him.

No one knows his or her time of exit from this planet, and therefore it is vital to be ready to leave at any time. All airlines issue final calls for passengers to get ready for their departure. The realities of life and the events of the 21st century are final calls from the LORD our GOD, our Creator, for each of us to prepare for our departure from this world by repenting of our sin and turning our hearts to CHRIST and to our neighbors in faith, hope, and love.

As our clay bodies dry up and crumble, our planet shudders, and the nations swarm to the cliff's edge, there is only one Eternal Rock that can support us. His name is JESUS.

> **"In times like these you need a Savior,**
> **In times like these you need an anchor;**
> **Be very sure, be very sure your anchor**
> ** holds and grips the Solid Rock!**
> **This Rock is JESUS, Yes, He's the One;**
> **this Rock is JESUS, the only One!**
> **Be very sure, be very sure your anchor**
> ** holds and grips the Solid Rock."**
> *(Ruth Caye Jones, Copyright 1944, Renewal 1972, Singspiration,*
> *Division of the Zondervan Corp.)*

In times like these we all need His amazing grace and powerful truth to keep us sane, at peace, and invested in His Kingdom. It is crucial for everyone—Christians, secularists, post-modernists, Muslims, Hindus, Buddhists, peasants, philosophers, prime ministers, and presidents—to hear the Name of JESUS the CHRIST, to understand the grace and truth that His Name embodies, and to recognize the impact that He has for our life, death, and eternity.

JESUS prayed on the night before He was crucified:

> *"This is eternal life: that they may know*
> *You, the only true God, and the One You have*

*sent — Jesus Christ...Father, I desire those
You have given Me to be with Me where I am.
Then they will see My glory, which You have
given Me because You loved Me before the
world's foundation.*

*Righteous Father! The world has not
known You. However, I have known You, and
these have known that You sent Me. I made
Your name known to them and will make it
known, so the love You have loved Me with
may be in them and I may be in them."*

John 17:3, 24–26

This is JESUS' prayer. Is this your prayer? Will you say
"Amen"—"may it be so"—to JESUS' prayer?

JESUS IS the ALPHA and OMEGA, the BEGINNING and the END

GOD IS—CHRIST IS—the Beginning and the End of our
world and of our life in this world. In the book **GOD IS! why
evolution isn't**, I sought to focus on the truth given us by GOD's
HOLY SPIRIT in Genesis, and throughout the pages of the Bible,
regarding the beginning of our universe and our life on Earth.
GOD IS! pulled back the veil of the contemporary mythology
of evolution that enslaves much of our world today on a hope-
less path of death and destruction. In an age when many are
blinded to the truth of GOD as our Creator, it is crucial for
us to remember where we came from, Who made us, and
why we are here. Just as the GOD of the Beginning has been
rejected by the leaders and peoples of the nations, so too has
the CHRIST of the End.

The tragic error that many inside and outside the walls of the institutional church make concerning JESUS is to limit Him to a specific period in history—someone who once lived but who is irrelevant in the 21st century. It is no surprise that the designations of BC—*"Before CHRIST"* and AD—*"Anno Domini—In the Year of our LORD"* are being replaced in our contemporary world with BCE—"Before Common Era" and CE—"Common Era". Most of our present planetary administrators no longer see JESUS as the center of history, but merely as a historical religious cult figure that they may give some lip service to but largely ignore. Nothing could be further from the truth.

JESUS, *"the stone that the builders rejected has become the cornerstone" (Matthew 21:42).* A vast majority of school boards, town councils, mayors, legislative assemblies, governors, premiers, prime ministers, presidents, kings, emperors, billionaires, and peasants reject JESUS and His Word as irrelevant to their plans. They run their households, schools, universities, towns, cities, states, provinces, nations, and empires on their own limited and corrupted human perceptions and opinions. They build on the sand of our very limited human understanding rather than the solid rock of JESUS and His teaching. Omitting CHRIST from their foundations, plans, and projects leads ultimately to the collapse of their self-proclaimed accomplishments. The plans of mice and men all eventually crumble. As the Old Testament preacher says: *"'Absolute futility,' says the Teacher. 'Absolute futility. Everything is futile'" (Ecclesiastes 1:2).* This is equally applicable to religious leaders who build their religious empires on their own personal theologies or corporate traditions rather than on the living CHRIST and His Word. Remove JESUS from history and we are left with utter futility. JESUS' life, ministry, death, resurrection, and coming return is at the center of history and infuses human life with meaning and hope. These chapters are focused on some very basic truths concerning JESUS' that

GOD's HOLY SPIRIT has revealed and is proclaiming in all corners of our world today. Only in and through CHRIST and His amazing grace can we begin to taste real peace, joy, and hope.

The Termination of Planet Earth

The last half of this book summarizes the HOLY SPIRIT's Biblical revelation concerning CHRIST's Second Coming and the events on our planet that precede it. Biblically and scientifically the disintegration of the circular rock we temporarily call home is a certainty. There were those around the globe who believed that the end of the ancient Mayan calendar would bring about the end of planet Earth through a cosmic collision with a rogue planet named Nibiru on December 21, 2012. Neither Nibiru, nor huge asteroids, nor global warming, nor another ice age, nor nuclear or chemical warfare will spell the end of the world, although they may impact life on our planet before the end. GOD—CHRIST alone is the End. He who began our amazing universe and world will bring it to its apocalyptic finale in His time. JESUS will step in prior to humanity nuking, overheating, poisoning, or otherwise terminating the planet.

Those who view life through materialistically-focused lenses see the end of the world and our universe as scientifically inevitable, and as the ultimate tragedy. The revelation of GOD's SPIRIT in His Word ushers us into a theater with a very different panoramic vision of the end, one that transforms our entire lives. It empowers us to live victoriously over the folly, ridicule, and persecution of the world, just as it has empowered GOD's people for the past six thousand years. He turns our faith into sight, our defeat into victory, our sorrow into joy, our end into His eternity.

"Besides this, knowing the time, it is already the hour for you to wake up from sleep, for now our salvation is nearer than when we first

> **believed. The night is nearly over, and the day-
> light is near." Romans 13:11–12**

Do you hear what I hear? Do you see what I see? As the HOLY SPIRIT testifies, the conclusion to the world as we know it is preceded by a crescendo of apocalyptic events that shake our globe and expose humanities absurd vanities. Just as our dust bodies experience rapid deterioration as they near their end, so our world is plagued with decay and its corresponding agony as it enters its death throes. The birth pains signaling His return are increasing in intensity and frequency *(Matthew 24:8; Revelation 6)*.

The conclusion of the world is shrouded in some mysteries, but for those who know JESUS as their SAVIOR and LORD, and know the teaching of His SPIRIT, the end will not come as a surprise. As JESUS and the Biblical prophets and apostles taught, the end of the world as we know it will come suddenly and unexpectedly upon the majority of the world's population **(Malachi 3:1; Matthew 24:36–44; 1 Thessalonians 5:1–11; 2 Peter 3:10–13).** Only the Noah-like remnant, who are covered with grace through their faith in CHRIST and His Word, will be prepared and waiting for His return and the sudden conclusion to the present world order and its tyrant antichrist.

Prior to the advent of the antichrist, mini-antichrists will ruin the nations and stain our planet with the blood of the martyrs. As the nations degenerate under the despotic governments of the minor demigods, the stage is being set for the coming of the ultimate antichrist, the Beast of *Revelation 13.* He will come camouflaged as a dynamic man-god savior of our planet. With promises of a new world order of peace, justice, unity, harmony, and salvation, he will lead his global worshippers and followers to their inglorious end. Every individual will decide to either be faithful to CHRIST and His Word and Kingdom, or to join with the masses in cheerleading for the antichrist and his promised utopian fantasy.

For believers in JESUS, as we live through the apocalyptic events gripping, blinding, and enslaving our planet in these last days, we do so, **not** with fear and its reactionary responses of self-preservation, but rather with repentance, faith, hope, and love. Through faith in JESUS, we know that these days of the end will soon be over, and the SON will come with healing power to wipe away all tears and sorrow and usher in a new Heaven and Earth. The crumbling of our nations and the disintegration of our globe will soon pass—nothing to fear for those who are trusting in CHRIST. As JESUS said to His followers before His own crucifixion:

"Your heart must not be troubled. Believe in God; believe also in Me. In My Father's house are many dwelling places; if not, I would have told you. I am going away to prepare a place for you. If I go away and prepare a place for you, I will come back and receive you to Myself, so that where I am you may be also."
John 14:1–3

The End is Better than the Beginning

We are approaching the end, the conclusion of our lives and our planet. However, as it is written, *"The end of a matter is better than its beginning" (Ecclesiastes 7:8).* With JESUS, the end of life in this world and the expiration date of the world itself is even better than its beginning. **JESUS is the End, as He says in *Revelation 22:13,* and therefore *the End* is not something to be avoided, but the Eternal One to be engaged to by faith.** For those who love JESUS, the end refers to the end of the engagement period, ushering us to the altar where the marriage celebration commences. The victorious Bridegroom will come for His Bride.

For the Christian believer, the end of life and the world is not ultimately a focus on events, intrigues, or landscapes, but on the person of JESUS CHRIST: LOVER, CREATOR, SAVIOR, BEST FRIEND, KING, LORD, and GOD. For those who live by faith in CHRIST, the end is a journey through a *"valley"* into the eternal dimension of *"the house of the LORD" (Psalm 23:6),* where GOD IS, CHRIST IS, and life in its fullness and glory is. By faith many have already been engaged to CHRIST, and their new life of love and joy has already begun. Like any engaged couple, we eagerly wait for its coming consummation.

> *"Hallelujah! For the Lord our God, the Almighty, reigns. Let us rejoice and be glad and give the glory to Him, for the marriage of the Lamb has come and His bride has made herself ready."*
> *Revelation 19:6-7*

Do I need to read this book?

Everything we need for life and eternity is given to us in CHRIST and testified to by the HOLY SPIRIT in the Scriptures themselves. All who know the real JESUS and who have the HOLY SPIRIT in their hearts and the Bible on their minds already have everything they need to live a fulfilling life in this world and to know of the eternal life to come.

I am grateful that, by His grace, the LORD has enabled me to write this book as an encouragement and exhortation for all of us to repent and to turn our hearts and thoughts to JESUS our GOD, SAVIOR, and LORD and to the eternal future He is giving us. The basic truths concerning CHRIST, revealed by His HOLY SPIRIT and Word and summarized in these chapters, are foundational for all who sincerely believe in JESUS and desire to follow, love, serve, and honor Him. The revelation concerning the realities of His return and the eternal joy of Heaven are crucial for living a life of repentance, faith, hope, and love during our brief journey in this world.

It is a constant source of perplexity and sorrow for all who love JESUS to hear and see so many individuals, congregations, and denominations calling themselves by JESUS' Name but falling away from faith in Him and His Word or seeking to compromise His message with contemporary mythologies. Those who turn away from their faith in GOD and CHRIST are fulfilling JESUS' prophesy concerning the last days *(Matthew 24:10-11)*. I hope and pray that the testimony of these pages will shine the light of CHRIST to help in the fight to expel the darkness, clarify the confusion, and remove the veils that Satan has created and spread through his subtle and not-so-subtle lies.

The majority of what is written in these pages is merely passing on the revelation of the HOLY SPIRIT concerning the identity, history, and future actions of JESUS. These are basic realities that have been held and proclaimed by the faithful Christian Church over the past 2000 years, as is testified to in the pages of the Bible and by the earliest confessions of the Church. There are some interpretive areas, however, where our present understanding of the Scriptures is clouded. I am a student of JESUS, with much too learn in my head and heart. **I encourage each of you who takes the time to read these chapters to do so with a mindset that carefully examines everything in the light of the testimony of GOD's SPIRIT in His Word.**

For everyone who is open to listening to what GOD, through His SON and HOLY SPIRIT, has revealed concerning JESUS, He has many things to say that are crucial for us to receive.

"GOD has something to say to you,
GOD has something to say to me.
Listen, Listen, pay close attention.
For GOD has something to say."

-Chorus that an engineering grad student from Nigeria shared with fellow students at an Inter-Varsity Christian Fellowship prayer meeting at the University of Saskatchewan, Saskatoon, in the early 1980s.

The Apostle Peter wrote:

"So we have the prophetic word strongly confirmed. You will do well to pay attention to it, as to a lamp shining in a dismal place, until the day dawns and the morning star rises in your hearts." *2 Peter 1:19*

The Morning Star is a reference to CHRIST in His second coming. For our own eternal welfare and the eternal welfare of our family, friends, and neighbors, we need to have the open eyes and ears of a watchman paying careful attention and holding on firmly to the real JESUS revealed in His Word.

Editorial Style

Lastly a word about the editorial style. You will notice that I have capitalized all references to GOD—uppercase for all names of GOD and initial capitals for all pronouns referring to GOD. Further, all Scripture references and quoted verses are in bold and italics to make a clear distinction between all human commentary and the distinctive Word of the LORD. I believe that all interpreters, teachers and preachers of GOD's Word aught always to highlight His Word above their own interpretations, thereby subjecting their interpretations to the actual Word of the HOLY SPIRIT. Although these editorial decisions are not in conformity with the usual grammatical practice, I do so with the desire to exalt and lift up His Name and His Word above all other names and words.

May GOD: FATHER, SON, and HOLY SPIRIT be glorified through us in our generation, perhaps the last generation before His Return.   Amen, come LORD JESUS!

JESUS

Hi Jesus,
It's me again,

I know You told me not to worry,
But all around me
The world is changing in ways I don't understand.
Things are spinning wild and out of control,
And I'm feeling anxious and afraid.

I need You, Jesus.

Your Word says
That I can ask anything in Your name,
And so I'm standing on that promise,
Trusting You to give me
The desires of my heart.

I'm not asking for riches or fame, Jesus—
Not asking for money in the bank
Or personal success,
Or even better circumstances,
Because I've learned
That the comforts and pleasures of this world are fleeting
and deceptive,
And make me prone to
Pride and laziness
And self-indulgent living.

And, Jesus, I'm not seeking signs and wonders—
Demonstrations of Your power—
I'm not asking for another feeding of five thousand
Or water turned to wine,
Or someone's sight restored,
Lest I get captivated by the supernatural
And start pursuing miracles
instead of You.

No Jesus,
My request is simple.
I just want more of You.

I want to sit so close to You
that I can hear Your heart both break
and beat with love
For a crying, dying world.

So close that I can see
The nail marks in Your hands—
Reminders of Your sacrifice.

So close that in Your holy presence,
My doubts and fears all flee,
My faith finds solid footing,
And my peace holds steady and secure.

So close that Your Words of Life and Hope,
Forgiveness and Grace
Wash over me
Like gentle showers—
Cleansing,
Refreshing,
Reviving
My troubled, weary soul.

Grant me this request, Lord.
Grant me more of
You.

Because in You, Jesus,
In You alone,
I have all I really need.

Joyce Peterson

The Greatest Thing in all My Life

The greatest thing in all my life is knowing You;
The greatest thing in all my life is knowing You.
I want to know you more, I want to know You more.
The greatest thing in all my life is knowing You.

The greatest thing in all my life is loving You;
The greatest thing in all my life is loving You.
I want to love you more, I want to love You more.
The greatest thing in all my life is loving You.

The greatest thing in all my life is serving You;
The greatest thing in all my life is serving You.
I want to serve you more, I want to serve You more.
The greatest thing in all my life is serving You.

-Mark D. Pendergrass

PART 1

JESUS IS! OUR HOLY GOD AND SAVIOR

"Christ Jesus, who, although He existed in the form of GOD,
did not regard equality with GOD a thing to be grasped,
but emptied Himself, taking the form of a bond-servant,
and being made in the likeness of men.
Being found in appearance as a man,
He humbled Himself by becoming obedient
to the point of death, even death on a cross.
For this reason also, God highly exalted Him,
and bestowed on Him the name which is above every name,
so that at the name of Jesus every knee will bow,
of those who are in heaven and on earth
and under the earth,
and every tongue confess that Jesus Christ is Lord,
to the glory of God the Father."
Philippians 2:5–11 NASB

CHAPTER 1

THE ONE WE SHOULD ALL BE THINKING, TALKING, AND SINGING ABOUT

Let's Talk about JESUS

Let's talk about JESUS, The KING of KINGS is He!
The LORD of LORDS supreme, Through all eternity.
The Great I AM, the Way, the Truth, the Life, the Door,
Let's talk about JESUS more and more.

Let's talk about JESUS, let all the world proclaim
The power and majesty of such a wondrous name.
The Babe of Bethlehem, the Bright and Morning Star,
Let's sing His praises near and far.

Let's talk about JESUS, the Bread of Life is He,
The SAVIOR of the world, that Man of Galilee.
The Prophet, Priest, and King, the Mighty GOD is He,
The well of Living Water free.

Let's talk about JESUS, the Prince of Peace is He,
The Great Physician too, down through all history.
The Lily pure and white, the Rose of Sharon fair,
The Shepherd of such tender care.

Let's talk about JESUS, the Rock of Ages He,
The Lamb for sinners slain, the Man of Calvary.
The Great Emmanuel, the Word of GOD sublime,
He is our Bridegroom so divine.

Herbert Buffum, 1879-1939

JESUS IS Who He IS!

J ESUS IS and is worthy of our praise, glory, and honor for Who He is, for all that He has done for us and for all He has promised to those who believe in and love Him. Compared to CHRIST and His Word and Kingdom, there really isn't anything else worthy of worship. All of the accomplishments of our human race are mere child's-play in contrast to GOD'S incredible masterpieces of creation and salvation. When people grasp the reality of Who JESUS IS, what He has done for us, and what He promises to us, they will understand why those who know and love Him are always singing and talking about Him.

JESUS IS Who He is! It is vain nonsense to seek to make JESUS into a twenty-first century, culturally-inoffensive relic. We cannot divide JESUS' actions or the characteristics of His nature, keeping what we like and discarding the rest. If we believe in JESUS, we must believe in the totality of Who JESUS IS, what He taught, accomplished, and promised. Anyone who rejects basic truths concerning CHRIST which the HOLY SPIRIT has revealed is being diverted from the historical flesh and blood JESUS to one of many counterfeit saviors that plague the church and world today. **All who repent of their sin and believe in the one and only JESUS Whom the HOLY SPIRIT**

4

and the faithful Church have proclaimed for the past 2000 years will know Him and won't be deceived by the many false prophets or antichrists.

> *"And we know that the Son of God has come and has given us understanding so that we may know the true One. We are in the true One — that is, in His Son Jesus Christ. He is the true God and eternal life. Little children, guard yourselves from idols."* 1 John 5:20–21

JESUS IS our Savior and Faithful Guide for Life and for Eternity

JESUS IS and, ultimately, He is all we need. He is the only path to the abundant and eternal life. The prevailing view in our generation today is that we do not need GOD or CHRIST, that we can manage our world just fine without Him. How well is that working out for our planet on the brink of self-destruction? The attitude that each of us, individually and as a global village, is self-sufficient and has everything needed to live a meaningful, successful, and productive life is blindness spawned by pride. The inhabitants of our global village are like the proverbial lemmings crushing each other in a reckless rush to the cliff's edge. We are a lost and corrupt race, running on empty and incapable of saving ourselves or of fulfilling our identity as His children and friends.

On the cross JESUS prayed: *"Father, forgive them, because they do not know what they are doing" (Luke 23:34)*. The high priest Caiaphas, Governor Pilate, King Herod, and the inhabitants of Jerusalem didn't grasp what they were doing when they crucified JESUS. Neither do the masses and their leaders today. Human understanding alone is a rabbit trail terminating at the fox's den. Each individual and our entire human race desperately needs CHRIST's forgiveness and salvation.

It is written:

> *"The Lord is my shepherd;*
> *there is nothing I lack.*
> *He lets me lie down in green pastures;*
> *He leads me beside quiet waters.*
> *He renews my life;*
> *He leads me along the right paths*
> *for His name's sake.*
> *Even when I go through the darkest valley,*
> *I fear no danger,*
> *for You are with me;*
> *Your rod and Your staff — they comfort me.*
> *You prepare a table before me*
> *in the presence of my enemies;*
> *You anoint my head with oil;*
> *my cup overflows.*
> *Only goodness and faithful love will pursue me*
> *all the days of my life,*
> *and I will dwell in the house of the Lord*
> *as long as I live."*

David, a shepherd boy, ***Psalm 23***

Psalm 23 is preceded by ***Psalm 22,*** a prophecy concerning CHRIST's suffering and death on the cross for us, as well as His resurrection and the mission of His Church. JESUS, the Good Shepherd, laid down His life for His people. He is the ultimate guide Who can lead us victoriously through the maze of life and its conclusion on this shadowy planet. JESUS quoted the first verse of ***Psalm 22*** from the cross as He gave His life in payment for our sin. By quoting the first verse of this Psalm, JESUS was proclaiming that He was fulfilling it on our behalf. Later, in ***Luke 24:44,*** He explains to His disciples that He came to accomplish everything written about Him in the Law, the Prophets, and the Psalms. JESUS is the good and faithful Shepherd Who gave His life for His people. He is the only One Who can guide us through this life, through the valley of death, and into His eternal and dynamic future. JESUS said:

> *"I am the good shepherd. The good shepherd lays down his life for the sheep.... I know My own sheep, and they know Me... My sheep hear My voice, I know them, and they follow Me. I give them eternal life, and they will never perish — ever! No one will snatch them out of My hand." John 10:11–28*

Who's voice are we listening to? The chaotic voices of the world? Our own self-centered and often anxious voice? Or, the voice of JESUS, the Good Shepherd who lay down His life for our eternal blessing?

Do you believe in JESUS the CHRIST?

Dr. Charles Malik, president of the United Nations General Assembly in 1959, said this:

> *"These are great days and what is being decided in them is absolutely historic. But all these things are going to pass, and with them life itself. What, then, is the life that does not pass; what, then, is life eternal: This is the first and last question. I believe that 'this is life eternal, that they might know Thee the only true GOD, and JESUS CHRIST whom Thou has sent.' (John 17:3) ...faith in JESUS CHRIST is the first and last meaning of our life. I do not care who or what you are; I put only one question to you: Do you believe in JESUS CHRIST?"*

7

(McDowell, Josh, *Evidence that Demands a Verdict,* pp 350-351 1972 Campus Crusade for CHRIST International, Arrowhead Springs, San Bernardino, CA: Campus Crusade for CHRIST International; Malik, Charles. "Hope for a World in Crisis." Collegiate Challenge. Vol. 7, No.2, pp 32-35)

Our world and the UN have changed dramatically over the sixty years since Dr. Malik spoke those words, but the question is still the same: Do you believe in JESUS CHRIST?

Most secularists who have heard about JESUS believe that He was a scientifically-unenlightened man who lived and died 2000 years ago, and whose image has been exaggerated and transformed into mythical proportions. Others take it a step higher, professing that He was a great teacher and philosopher, like Buddha or Plato or Confucius. They may read about Him, but since they believe He was just a man, they do not take His words seriously. Some suggest that He was a great prophet like Moses or Elijah, who came with a message from GOD, but they are blind to His identity and deaf to His message. New agers imagine Him as a visitor from another planet or a yogi master who came to shed some new light to help us in our own spiritual evolutionary progression, but again they basically ignore Him. The Church of JESUS CHRIST of the Latter-Day Saints (Mormons) believe that JESUS was one of billions of spirit children of a cosmic god named Elohim. They proclaim that He came into our world, like the rest of us, to learn some lessons and to show us how we can become gods with our own universe and planetary systems, and with more wives than Solomon, to experience eternal sexual ecstasy and populate our own future universes. Jehovah's Witnesses assert that the archangel Michael was incarnated as JESUS and came to testify to Jehovah and give us some advice on how to live as Jehovah's witnesses.

The false conceptions of JESUS are numerous and varied, even within the walls of self-proclaimed Christian churches.

Beware of labels. They are often little more than slick ads, enticing neon lights, or tempting siren voices. Just because someone goes to a church or calls himself a Christian, or, for that matter, an elder, pastor, evangelist, prophet, bishop, or pope, does not make him an authentic follower or servant of JESUS. Hypocrisy and deception are always lurking. Be discerning and read the menu before ingesting the food of any so-called "Christian" churches or organizations. Find out which JESUS they believe in before you contribute your membership dues or tithes, lest you support the spreading of a false image of JESUS. It is written:

> *"Anyone who does not remain in Christ's teaching but goes beyond it, does not have God. The one who remains in that teaching, this one has both the Father and the Son. If anyone comes to you and does not bring this teaching, do not receive him into your home, and don't say, 'Welcome,' to him; for the one who says, 'Welcome,' to him shares in his evil works."* **2 John 9–11**

Take note that these are not the words of some poet or philosopher, but the words of the SPIRIT of CHRIST through the Apostle John. The church was and is plagued with many intellectual or charismatic style teachers who believe that their own insights and teachings are greater than those of CHRIST and His prophets and apostles. JESUS, as well as His servants who have passed on His Word, gave repeated warnings of the false teachers who come in His Name. If we do not test those who come in JESUS' Name by His teaching and that of His prophets and apostles, we are like the child that ignores the warnings about looking both ways before crossing the street. If we disregard the forewarnings of His Word we are opening ourselves and others to much falsehood and evil. **To be able to** test the teachings that are being brought in JESUS' Name, we have to know for ourselves Who JESUS is and what He taught.

The Question

The question is not: Do we believe in some kind of Jesus' image or Christ-like messianic figure or projection? The question is: **Do we believe in JESUS the CHRIST, the SON of the living GOD and humanity's only SAVIOR?** That is a very different question, and it isn't a new one. JESUS posed a similar question to a few of His friends:

> *"When Jesus came to the region of Caesarea Philippi, He asked His disciples, 'Who do people say that the Son of Man is?'*
> *And they said, 'Some say John the Baptist; others, Elijah; still others, Jeremiah or one of the prophets.'*
> *'But you,' He asked them, 'who do you say that I am?'*
> *Simon Peter answered, 'You are the Messiah, the Son of the living God!'*
> *And Jesus responded, 'Simon son of Jonah, you are blessed because flesh and blood did not reveal this to you, but My Father in heaven.'"*
> *Matthew 16:13–17*

C. S. Lewis, an English professor at Cambridge and an agnostic prior to coming to faith in CHRIST, wrote in his book *Mere Christianity*:

> *"I am trying here to prevent anyone saying the really foolish thing that people often say about Him: 'I'm ready to accept Jesus as a great moral teacher, but I don't accept His claim to be GOD.'*

That is the one thing we must not say. A man who was merely a man and said the sort of things JESUS said would not be a great moral teacher. He would either be a lunatic – on a level with a man who says he is a poached egg – or else he would be the Devil of Hell. You must make your choice. Either this man was, and is, the Son of GOD: or else a madman or something worse. You can shut Him up for a fool, you can spit at Him and kill Him as a demon; or you can fall at His feet and call Him Lord and GOD. But let us not come with any patronizing nonsense about His being a great human teacher. He has not left that open to us. He did not intend to."

(Lewis, C.S. *Mere Christianity* 1942, 1943, 1944 William Collins Sons and Co Ltd, Glasgow p 52)

Will the Real JESUS Please Stand Up?

In 1956, when the earth was a little greener and the tube much cleaner, there was a TV program called *"To Tell the Truth"* which lasted for twenty-five seasons. Below is how Wikipedia described "To Tell the Truth":

The show features a panel of four celebrities attempting to correctly identify a described contestant who has an unusual occupation or experience. This central character is accompanied by two impostors who pretend to be the central character. The celebrity panelists question the three contestants; the impostors are allowed to lie but the central character is sworn "to tell the truth". After questioning, the panel attempts to identify which of the three challengers is telling the truth and is thus the central character.

11

Three challengers are introduced, all claiming to be the central character. The announcer typically asks the challengers, who stand side by side, "What is your name, please?" Each challenger then states, "My name is [central character's name]." The celebrity panelists then read along as the host reads aloud a signed <u>affidavit</u> about the central character.

The panelists are each given a period of time to question the challengers. Questions are directed to the challengers by number (Number One, Number Two and Number Three), with the central character sworn to give truthful answers, and the impostors permitted to lie and pretend to be the central character.

After questioning is complete, each member of the panel votes on which of the challengers they believe to be the central character, either by writing the number on a card or holding up a card with the number of their choice, without consulting the other panelists...

Once the votes are cast, the host asks, "Will the real [person's name] please stand up?" The central character then stands, often after some brief playful feinting and false starts among all three challengers."   (Wikipedia, To Tell the Truth, August 1, 2013)

There is a parallel between *"To Tell the Truth"* and the One Who proclaimed that He is *"the Truth" (John 14:6)*. According to JESUS, one of the signs of His return to usher in *"the end of the world as we know it"* is that many false saviors will come claiming to be able to save people and give them the good life. In Part 3 of this book we will focus on the events of the last days and will take a closer look at these counterfeit messiahs, including the beast of Revelation 13.

The church also has its internal false prophets and theologians who use JESUS' name for their own vain purposes, but who proclaim a different savior than the One revealed in the Scriptures *(Acts 20:25–31; 2 Peter 2:1–22; 1 John 2:18–23; Jude 3–25)*. They quote JESUS only when they agree with what He says, and ignore or cover up the salty, bitter, distasteful segments that may be offensive to those they are trying to impress. It is lamentable that so many religious hustlers today are selling false images of JESUS and dispensing cheap grace indulgences to those who reject His Word and teachings. We will take a closer look at these false prophets in the church when we focus on the signs of the last days.

The presence of so many false prophets and saviors in our generation highlights the need for lifting up the whole testimony to JESUS that has been passed on to every generation in His Word. **The real JESUS is standing up and speaking by His SPIRIT in His Word.**

Knowing the Authentic JESUS

While there are a myriad of false saviors seeking to convince others that they are the ones who can guide the world into a human paradise, there is only one genuine CHRIST. How can anyone know the authentic JESUS so they won't be conned by the sham saviors who dominate the nations today? **The only way of knowing the genuine JESUS is by the testimony of the HOLY SPIRIT through the true prophets and apostles in the Holy Scriptures.**

JESUS said to His followers before His crucifixion:

"When the Counselor comes, the One I will send to you from the Father — the Spirit of truth who proceeds from the Father — He will testify about Me. You also will testify, because you have been with Me from the beginning...

Nevertheless, I am telling you the truth. It is for your benefit that I go away, because if I don't go away the Counselor will not come to you. If I go, I will send Him to you. When He comes, He will convict the world about sin, righteousness, and judgment: About sin, because they do not believe in Me; about righteousness, because I am going to the Father and you will no longer see Me; and about judgment, because the ruler of this world has been judged....

When the Spirit of truth comes, He will guide you into all the truth. For He will not speak on His own, but He will speak whatever He hears. He will also declare to you what is to come. He will glorify Me, because He will take from what is Mine and declare it to you." John 15:26–27; 16:7–11,13–14

The Apostle Paul wrote: *"no one can say, 'Jesus is Lord,' except by the Holy Spirit" (1 Corinthians 12:3).* Paul was not implying that people could not say the words "JESUS is LORD", but that they could not say them and truly mean them without the ministry of GOD's SPIRIT in their lives.

JESUS said: *"Not everyone who says to Me, 'Lord, Lord!' will enter the kingdom of heaven, but only the one who does the will of My Father in heaven. On that day many will say to Me,*

> *'Lord, Lord, didn't we prophesy in Your name,*
> *drive out demons in Your name, and do many*
> *miracles in Your name?' Then I will announce*
> *to them, 'I never knew you! Depart from Me,*
> *you lawbreakers!'" Matthew 7: 21–23*

JESUS declared that on the Day of Judgment many false Christians will call Him "LORD", but He will condemn them because they did not know Him or follow His teaching.

What was JESUS really like? There are thousands of imaginary pictures of JESUS and they are all different. The only truth these pictures communicate about CHRIST is that He was a human being Who lived on our planet. About fifteen years ago in Russia, I was shown a photo of a man in Siberia, a former police officer. The photo looked very similar to some popular conceptions of JESUS' appearance. He was claiming to be CHRIST, and many hundreds of people believed in him. He is still living and deceiving people today. *(www.foxnews.com/ world/2017/10/04/meet-siberias-jesus-former traffic-cop-turned-cult-leader.html)*

It is interesting to note that the HOLY SPIRIT does not give us any physical description of JESUS in the New Testament. We are not told how tall He was, how long His hair was, the color of His eyes or skin, or what kind of beard He had. In fact, you can read through the entire Bible and never find any detailed descriptions of the physical appearance of any of the saints, or, for that matter, of others that fill the pages of Biblical history. We know very little of what any of them looked like. We know them in the spirit by their faith or their lack of faith revealed in the words and actions of the portion of their lives that are reported in the Bible. **GOD is not concerned about our outward appearance. His focus is on what is in our hearts.**

> *The LORD tells us* **"Man does not see what the Lord sees, for man sees what is visible, but the Lord sees the heart." 1 Samuel 16:7**
>
> Our generation today is detrimentally preoccupied with physical appearance. People in our cosmetic generation, like the religious leaders of JESUS' time, seek to look attractive on the outside, but inside are filled with greed, pride, lust, self-centeredness, anger, jealousy, and every form of spiritual disease. GOD looks at our hearts and knows the truth that no perfume, make-up, or designer clothes can cover up. GOD knows us well, everything about us: our thoughts, attitudes, words, and actions (Psalm 139:1-6). GOD knows our sin and calls us to acknowledge the evil within our hearts, minds and spirits, and to cry out for His forgiveness and mercy which He pours out through the life-blood of CHRIST
>
> Only JESUS can make us holy, pure, and beautiful.

Although we do not have any physical description of JESUS, the HOLY SPIRIT has preserved and distributed a cosmic-shaking testimony of Who JESUS IS, of what He did during His life in our world, of what He is doing now and what He will do in the near future. If you want to know Who JESUS is, what He did, and what He will do, there is only one reliable source and that is the HOLY SPIRIT's testimony in the Bible.

Our faith is not only in JESUS and what He has done for us, but implicitly we need to trust in the HOLY SPIRIT's testimony to JESUS or we have no way of knowing Him. We believe in CHRIST Alone and Word Alone. Without the HOLY SPIRIT's testimony to JESUS in the Old Testament Law, Prophets, and Psalms, and in the four Gospels and New Testament letters, no one can know Who JESUS is, what He did or taught in the few years He lived in this earthly dimension, what He will do, and what it all means for us. **Praise the LORD that He has inspired and preserved the faithful testimony of the prophets and apostles for us.**

The Testimony of Christians Today

The testimony in word and action of true believers in JESUS, who have the HOLY SPIRIT and His grace and truth in our lives, is a sample or reflection of the SPIRIT's testimony to JESUS in His Word. We are like solar lights. We have no light of our own, but we absorb the light of the SON and then reflect it into the darkness of our world. Every Christian ought to pray and seek to follow CHRIST, and by the power of the HOLY SPIRIT working in us to be a *"little Jesus"* to others. His will is that we would reflect His grace, truth, and salvation to the shadowy world around us.

The LORD graciously enables those who know Him to help others to come to Him. He is able to use us despite all of our failures or shortcomings. Since our sinful, self-centered flesh battles against our born-again spirits, no Christian has complete understanding nor lives the perfect life JESUS lived *(Romans 7:7–25)*. There are also many hollow Christians, Christian in name only, who do not sincerely believe in JESUS or seek to reflect His grace or truth in their thoughts, words, or actions. **Consequently, our understanding of CHRIST is ultimately based not on what other "Christians" may say or do, but on the HOLY SPIRIT's testimony to JESUS in His Word.**

The HOLY SPIRIT gives us a clear testimony to JESUS in the pages of Scripture for all who are open to trusting Him. In the remainder of this section we will listen to five very clear and basic truths that the HOLY SPIRIT has revealed concerning Who JESUS is and what He accomplished for us during His earthly life 2000 years ago.

Pray!

CHAPTER 2
THE ETERNAL GOD

JESUS said:

*"I am the Alpha and the Omega, the First and
the Last, the Beginning and the End."*
Revelation 22:13

Who Is He?

It is not enough to have just heard preachers or other people talking about JESUS. Each of us needs to know Him, talk to Him, listen to Him, and seek to follow Him. Why is it important to know Him? What difference does it make? Why are people all over our world thinking about Him, talking about Him, and singing His praise 2000 years later? Who do you say that He is? Who did He say He was and is?

In some of the last verses of the Bible, the HOLY SPIRIT reveals that JESUS says He is the ALPHA and the OMEGA, the BEGINNING and the END. What does this mean? It means that JESUS is the Eternal GOD, One with the FATHER and the HOLY SPIRIT! He is our Creator, Savior, Counselor, and Judge. This is the testimony of JESUS, of the HOLY SPIRIT, of the prophets and apostles of CHRIST, and of the faithful Christian Church for the past 2000 years.

The Apostle Paul wrote:

"From now on, then, we do not know anyone in a purely human way. Even if we have known Christ in a purely human way, yet now we no longer know Him in this way."
2 Corinthians 5:16

When JESUS lived 2000 years ago, most people thought of Him from an earthly perspective, just another human being among many. They had no understanding of Who He really was. Most people in the world around us today think JESUS was just a man who lived and died many years ago. They have no idea Who He really was and IS.

After JESUS' resurrection, doubting Thomas said to Him:

" 'My Lord and my God!'
Jesus said, 'Because you have seen Me, you have believed. Those who believe without seeing are blessed.'" John 20:28–29

There is only one GOD—JESUS is GOD, in perfect unity with the FATHER and the SPIRIT. **All who come to know and receive JESUS as SAVIOR, LORD, and GOD will be blessed.**

JESUS is GOD and GOD is Triune

The revelation of CHRIST as the GOD-Man propels us into the dynamic reality of the Triune GOD: FATHER, SON, and HOLY SPIRIT. There is no one who completely comprehends this revelation of GOD or of how JESUS could be GOD. The divine nature of CHRIST is not something that can be perfectly theologically defined or explained, but is revealed by His life, words, and actions, and confirmed by the repeated testimony of GOD's SPIRIT. Like all other truth revealed through CHRIST and the HOLY SPIRIT, it is something that we believe and accept, though we acknowledge it is beyond our full grasp. If you insist on completely understanding GOD and His ways before believing in Him, that is impossible, because you are not GOD. GOD calls us through His SON and SPIRIT to come to Him by faith, and He promises that in eternity we will see and understand the whole picture (*1 Corinthians 13:12*).

Some do not find this answer satisfying. They claim to be rational beings that must have complete understanding before they can believe that JESUS is GOD. If that is the space you are in, I have some questions for you. Do you believe in food? Do you eat? Do you know how food is created? Do you have complete comprehension of the process of photosynthesis? Can you elaborate on precisely how plants absorb carbon dioxide and energy from the sun and turn it into food we can eat and oxygen we can breathe? Do you fully understand how the food in our stomachs is digested and then distributed to the trillions of cells in our bodies? Can you explain how the cells open portholes by a complex computerized security system to allow food molecules inside where they are transformed into energy by hundreds of power generators called mitochondria? Can you describe exactly how the mitochondria produce this energy, and then distribute it to empower each cell to perform its many functions that sustain us from moment to moment? Do you understand how all that works? Even though we can't grasp it all, we eat every day. In fact, people have been eating from the beginning without comprehending any of these newly-discovered mysteries.

Do you believe in gravity? Even though no one knows exactly what it is, or what causes it, people have believed in gravity since before the time of Newton, they just didn't call it gravity. It is real; we all believe in it, but we certainly do not understand what it is. Do you believe in sight? Can you explain exactly how you are able to see? How do the images get transferred from your eyes to your brain, and how does your brain process the data it is receiving so that it is interpreted and projected into images you can see in your mind? Where is the program that created our eyes and our brains to see, and our minds to comprehend? Do you believe in time? Do you know what time is? Where does it come from? Why is it relative?

We believe in these realities and countless others, even though no one completely grasps them. There are more questions than answers. The bottom line is that we do not fully comprehend any of the realities of life. How many of us completely understand our wives, husbands, children, parents, brothers, sisters, or friends? Do we believe in them? How many completely understand themselves? Do you know who you are? Do you believe in yourself? We live by faith in every area of life. While we do not, cannot, and will not fully comprehend any of these realities, we believe and live in them.

We may not fully understand the spiritual dynamic of the triune nature of GOD, but we can live in Him. While it is true that $1 + 1 + 1 = 3$, it is also true that $1 \times 1 \times 1 = 1$ and $1 \div 1 \div 1 = 1$. **There is only One GOD in Three Persons, no matter how you multiply or divide Him.** Christian faith in JESUS is based on a higher mathematics than addition.

The Old Testament Revelation of GOD

Our faith in JESUS, as true GOD as well as true man, is not based on complete intellectual comprehension, but on the testimony of CHRIST and His SPIRIT through His prophets and apostles. This testimony that JESUS is GOD begins in the Old Testament. As Augustine of Hippo, an early Christian leader, expressed it: *"The New Testament is in the Old Testament concealed, the Old Testament is in the New Testament revealed."* To put it in another way, the Old Testament is like the seed, and the New Testament is like the plant. This certainly applies to the reality of the triune nature of GOD.

Before turning to the Old Testament testimony concerning the SON of GOD, it is important to grasp the revelation in the Old Testament of the plurality in the oneness or unity of GOD. In the very first verse of GOD's revelation of Himself we read: ***"In the beginning God created the heavens and the earth" (Genesis 1:1).*** GOD reveals Himself as **"GOD"** thirty times in the thirty-one verses of the first chapter. The Hebrew word for GOD in ***Genesis 1*** is a plural form of GOD, transliterated into English as *"Elohim"*. The LORD uses "Elohim", this <u>plural form of His unity more than two thousand times</u> in the Old Testament. Also, in ***Genesis 1***, GOD uses the plural pronouns *"Us"* and *"Our"* referring to His creation of humanity: ***"Let <u>Us</u> make man in <u>Our</u> image, according to <u>Our</u> likeness" (Genesis 1:26).*** However, in the next verse the LORD uses the singular pronouns *"His"* and *"He"* to refer to this same truth:

> ***"So God created man in <u>His</u> own image; <u>He</u> created him in the image of God; <u>He</u> created them male and female." Genesis 1:27***

This seeming paradox of GOD being simultaneously plural and singular continues throughout the Old Testament. GOD uses <u>the singular form</u> *"El" "Eli" "Eloah"* more than <u>three hundred times</u>, and the word *"Yahweh"* translated as ***"the LORD"***, which is also singular, <u>more than five thousand times</u>. "Yahweh" is sometimes used in conjunction with *"Elohim"*- ***"the LORD GOD"***- the singular plural GOD. GOD also refers to Himself continually and repetitively in the Scriptures with the pronouns *"I"*, *"Me"*, *"My"*, *"He"*:

> ***"God replied to Moses, '<u>I</u> AM WHO <u>I</u> AM. This is what you are to say to the Israelites: <u>I</u> AM has sent me to you.'" Exodus 3:14***

"I am the Lord your God... Do not have other gods besides Me." Exodus 20:2-3

The LORD GOD reveals Himself as the singular plural GOD throughout the Old Testament, consistently and repetitively. In contrast to the polytheism that dominated the nations surrounding the Jewish people, Judaism was based on the distinctly revealed truth that there is one eternal GOD, not a multitude of gods. Moses, considered to be the greatest of the Old Testament prophets, received and passed on this truth: *"Listen, Israel: The Lord our God, the Lord is One" (Deuteronomy 6:4).* This truth concerning the oneness of the LORD GOD is deemed to be at the very core of the SPIRIT's revelation of GOD in the Old Testament. Consequently, in the LORD's revelation of Himself in His Word and to His people in the Old Testament, we have this paradox of GOD being both singular and plural at the same time. This corresponds perfectly with the Triune nature of GOD.

The Three Persons of GOD in the Old Testament

The apparent contradiction in the very nature of GOD as simultaneously singular and plural is not without some striking Old Testament hints regarding its resolution. In the Old Testament the HOLY SPIRIT refers to GOD as SPIRIT, as FATHER, and as SON in different settings.

The **SPIRIT of GOD** is referred to over seventy times in the Old Testament:

"the Spirit of God was hovering over the surface of the waters." Genesis 1:2

"Do not banish me from Your presence or take Your Holy Spirit from me." Psalm 51:11

*"'Not by strength or by might, but by <u>My Spirit</u>,'
says the Lord of Hosts." Zechariah 4:6 -*

The HOLY SPIRIT inspired the prophets to write the following testimonies to **GOD as our FATHER**:

*Deuteronomy 32:6; 2 Samuel 7:14; Psalm 68:5;
Psalm 89:26-27; Proverbs 3:12; Isaiah 9:6; Isaiah 63:16;
64:8; Jeremiah 3:19; Malachi 1:6; etc.*

The most intriguing reference to GOD in the Old Testament is to **GOD as the SON,** testified to in the following passages:

*"<u>You are My Son</u>; today I have become Your Father... Pay homage to the Son or He will be angry and you will perish in your rebellion, for His anger may ignite at any moment. All those who take refuge in Him are happy."
Psalm 2:7,12*

*"For a child will be born for us, <u>a son</u> will be given to us, and the government will be on His shoulders. <u>He will be named Wonderful Counselor, Mighty God, Eternal Father, Prince of Peace</u>. The dominion will be vast, and its prosperity will never end. He will reign on the throne of David and over his kingdom, to establish and sustain it with justice and righteousness from now on and forever. The zeal of the Lord of Hosts will accomplish this."
Isaiah 9:6–7*

Neither King David nor any of the kings that descended from him in the Old Testament were ever referred to as Mighty GOD or Eternal FATHER.

There are many other passages in the Old Testament proph-esying various truths concerning JESUS' life, ministry, suffering, death, resurrection, and His return to judge the world. Future chapters will highlight a few of them, but these are the specific ones that pertain to the truth of the triune nature of GOD. These passages in the Old Testament regarding the plural singularity of GOD, and the testimony of the prophets to GOD as FATHER, SON, and HOLY SPIRIT do not present us with a developed understanding of the triune nature of GOD, but they certainly do lay the groundwork, or plant the seeds, of the revelation which JESUS expands and clarifies in His teaching.

JESUS' Self-Identification:

The Old Testament gives hints to open our minds to the triune nature of GOD, but it is through the life and teaching of JESUS that this vibrant reality of GOD is revealed. From the angel Gabriel's words to Mary, announcing JESUS' birth, to the profession of faith of doubting Thomas after JESUS' resurrection, the four Gospel accounts of JESUS' life defy any interpretation other than the truth that JESUS is the SON of GOD, One with the FATHER and the SPIRIT, just as He claimed.

> *"You will conceive and give birth to a son, and you will call His name Jesus.... The Holy Spirit will come upon you, and the power of the Most High will overshadow you. Therefore, <u>the holy One to be born will be called the Son of God.</u>" Luke 1:31,35*

Do not be deceived by those who deny that JESUS claimed to be the SON of GOD, One with the FATHER. JESUS said:

> *"'You are from below,' He told them, 'I am from above. You are of this world; I am not of this*

25

world. Therefore I told you that you will die in
your sins. For if you do not believe that I am
He, you will die in your sins.'
'Who are You?' they questioned.
'Precisely what I've been telling you from the
very beginning'...
So Jesus said to them, 'When you lift up the
Son of Man, then you will know that I am He,
and that I do nothing on My own. But just as
the Father taught Me, I say these things. The
One who sent Me is with Me. He has not left
Me alone, because I always do what pleases
Him... If God were your Father, you would love
Me, because I came from God and I am here.
For I didn't come on My own, but He sent Me.'"
John 8:23–25, 28–29, 42

I was shocked the first time I heard someone, seemingly educated, voice the idea that JESUS never claimed to be GOD's SON or One with GOD. Over the years, and increasingly in the last two decades, this ignorance of JESUS' teaching about Himself is growing, not just in the pagan world, but in so many religious circles of misinformed Christians. All who genuinely listen to JESUS' teaching and preaching will promptly discover Who JESUS claimed to be.

Listed below are truths JESUS said about Himself:

1. *"Don't assume that I came to destroy the Law or*
   the Prophets. I did not come to destroy but to fulfill."
   Matthew 5:17

JESUS spoke repeatedly about coming from Heaven into this world. Only GOD Himself could perfectly understand and fulfill the Law and the Prophets.

2. *"Not everyone who says to Me, 'Lord, Lord!' will enter*
   the kingdom of heaven, but only the one who does

the will of My Father in heaven. On that day many will say to Me, 'Lord, Lord, didn't we prophesy in Your name, drive out demons in Your name, and do many miracles in Your name?' Then I will announce to them, 'I never knew you! Depart from Me, you lawbreakers!'"
Matthew 7:21–23

On the Day of Judgment, people will be calling JESUS 'LORD', the most common Name for GOD in the Old Testament. The Greek word for LORD is "Kyrios", which is also the word used in the Septuagint Greek Translation of the Old Testament for "Yahweh". **Notice** JESUS' claim in these verses to be able to judge people and deny them access to eternal life with Him in Heaven on the basis that He did not know them as faithful followers or servants of His. **Only GOD has the authority to judge and condemn.**

3. *"Therefore, just as the weeds are gathered and burned in the fire, so it will be at the end of the age. The Son of Man will send out His angels, and they will gather from His kingdom everything that causes sin and those guilty of lawlessness. They will throw them into the blazing furnace where there will be weeping and gnashing of teeth. Then the righteous will shine like the sun in their Father's kingdom. Anyone who has ears should listen!"* Matthew 13:40–43

JESUS refers to the angels as *"His angels"* and the Kingdom as *"His Kingdom".* It is perfectly clear in repeated testimony in the Old Testament that the angels are GOD's angels and the Kingdom is GOD's Kingdom (*Genesis 28:12, 32:1; Job 4:18; Psalm 91:11; Psalm 103:19–22; Psalm 148:2).* JESUS' angels are GOD's angels. In His preaching and teaching, JESUS referred to GOD's Kingdom and His Kingdom. They are the same Kingdom of Heaven *(Matthew 16:28; Luke 1:33, 22:30; 2 Timothy 4:1).*

4. JESUS said*: "No one has ascended into heaven except the One who descended from heaven — the Son of Man. Just as Moses lifted up the snake in the wilderness, so the Son of Man must be lifted up, so that everyone who believes in Him will have eternal life... The One who comes from above is above all. The one who is from the earth is earthly and speaks in earthly terms. The One who comes from heaven is above all. He testifies to what He has seen and heard, yet no one accepts His testimony. The one who has accepted His testimony has affirmed that God is true." John 3:13–15, 31–33*

"This is why the Jews began trying all the more to kill Him: Not only was He breaking the Sabbath, but He was even <u>calling God His own Father, making Himself equal with God</u>.Then Jesus replied, 'I assure you: The Son is not able to do anything on His own, but only what He sees the Father doing. <u>For whatever the Father does, the Son also does these things in the same way</u>. For the Father loves the Son and shows Him everything He is doing, and He will show Him greater works than these so that you will be amazed. And just as the Father raises the dead and gives them life, so <u>the Son also gives life to anyone He wants to</u>. The Father, in fact, judges no one but has given <u>all judgment to the Son, so that all people will honor the Son just as they honor the Father. Anyone who does not honor the Son does not honor the Father who sent Him</u>... For just as the Father has life in Himself, so also He has granted to <u>the Son to have life in Himself</u>. And He has granted Him the right to pass judgment, because He is the Son of Man.'" John 5:18–23, 26–27

JESUS made it very clear in repeated testimony that He was the SON of GOD Who came from Heaven, and the Son of Man Who lived in this world. **He has the authority to judge all people. He died for us and has the power to give eternal life to all who truly believe in Him. Further, JESUS here claims that all people should honor Him, worship Him, even as they honor and worship the FATHER.** This is one of the passages that can be shared with Jehovah's Witnesses when they drop by. If anyone cannot worship JESUS as they worship the FATHER, then JESUS says that they are not honoring the FATHER.

5. *"While the Pharisees were together, Jesus questioned them, 'What do you think about the Messiah? Whose Son is He?'*
'David's,' they told Him.
He asked them, 'How is it then that <u>David, inspired by the Spirit, calls Him 'Lord'</u>: The <u>Lord declared to my Lord</u>, 'Sit at My right hand until I put Your enemies under Your feet'? If David calls Him 'Lord,' how then can the Messiah be his Son?' No one was able to answer Him at all, and from that day no one dared to question Him anymore."
                    Matthew 22:41–46

Here JESUS is pointing the religious leaders to the reality that the promised CHRIST or MESSIAH would not only be a descendant of David, but also David's LORD, Who is GOD. **Note** JESUS' clear teaching that David wrote by the inspiration of GOD's HOLY SPIRIT. **People can deny that JESUS is truly GOD only by denying that GOD's Word, the Holy Scriptures, is given to us through the inspiration of GOD's SPIRIT. The devil continually attacks the true testimony of GOD's Word so that people will not believe that JESUS is GOD Who can save us.**

6. *"'If I glorify Myself,' Jesus answered, 'My glory is nothing. <u>My Father</u> — you say about Him, <u>'He is our God'</u> — He is the One who glorifies Me. You've never*

known Him, but I know Him. If I were to say I don't know Him, I would be a liar like you. But I do know Him, and I keep His word. Your father Abraham was overjoyed that he would see My day; he saw it and rejoiced.'

The Jews replied, 'You aren't 50 years old yet, and You've seen Abraham?'
Jesus said to them, 'I assure you:
Before Abraham was, I am.'
At that, they picked up stones to throw at Him.
But Jesus was hidden and went out of the temple complex." John 8:54–59

In defending His ministry against the Jewish religious leaders, not only does He refer to GOD as His FATHER, but states that His FATHER glorifies Him, and that He existed before Abraham. JESUS also uses GOD's Name, *"I AM"*, referring to Himself. *"I AM"*, as previously mentioned, was Yahweh, the central name of GOD in the Old Testament. After JESUS used GOD's name to refer to Himself, we are told that the people threatened to stone Him for blasphemy.

In JESUS' preaching and teaching, there were a number of times when He made statements using the words 'I AM':

"I am the bread of life." John 6:35

"I am the light of the world." John 9:5

"I am the door of the sheep." John 10:7

"I am the good shepherd." John 10:11

"I am the resurrection and the life." John 11:25

"I am the way, the truth, and the life." John 14:6

"I am the true vine." John 15:1

Only GOD Himself is all these realities.
The clearest statements of Jesus applying the name of "I Am" to Himself is when "I am" acts together as a noun, and so the verb "am" has no object. Examples of this are **John 4:26, 8:24,28,58, 13:19, 18:6,8.**
 7. *"Jesus told him, 'I am the way, the truth, and the life. No one comes to the Father except through Me. <u>If you know Me, you will also know My Father. From now on you do know Him and have seen Him</u>.'*

 'Lord,' said Philip, 'show us the Father, and that's enough for us.'
 Jesus said to him, 'Have I been among you all this time without your knowing Me, Philip? <u>The one who has seen Me has seen the Father</u>. How can you say, 'Show us the Father'? Don't you believe that <u>I am in the Father and the Father is in Me</u>? The words I speak to you I do not speak on My own. The Father who lives in Me does His works. <u>Believe Me that I am in the Father and the Father is in Me.</u> Otherwise, believe because of the works themselves.'"
 John 14:6–11

Only those who do not want to hear these words of JESUS can deny His bold statement of His Oneness with the FATHER, and that we can come to the FATHER only through faith in JESUS. **The only way JESUS could say that anyone who has seen Him has seen the FATHER is if He Himself was GOD, One with the FATHER.** In the verses that follow, JESUS also clearly teaches the reality that the HOLY SPIRIT is GOD, One with the FATHER and the SON (*John 14:15–31, 15:26–27, 16:5–15*).

8. *"Now, Father, glorify Me in Your presence with that glory I had with You before the world existed." John 17:5*

In this prayer on the night before His crucifixion, JESUS declares His eternal presence with the FATHER and the glory He received with the FATHER before the creation of the world.

9. *"Then the high priest said to Him, 'By the living God I place You under oath: tell us if You are the Messiah, the Son of God!'*

    'You have said it,' Jesus told him. 'But I tell you, in the future you will see the Son of Man seated at the right hand of the Power and coming on the clouds of heaven.'"   Matthew 26:63–64

JESUS' answer to the high priest Caiaphas concerning His identity as GOD's SON and humanity's SAVIOR was unequivocal, even though He knew it would lead to His being condemned by the religious council.

10. *"Then Pilate went back into the headquarters, summoned Jesus, and said to Him, 'Are You the King of the Jews?'*

    Jesus answered, 'Are you asking this on your own, or have others told you about Me?'

    'I'm not a Jew, am I?' Pilate replied. 'Your own nation and the chief priests handed You over to me. What have You done?'

    'My kingdom is not of this world,' said Jesus. 'If My kingdom were of this world, My servants would fight, so that I wouldn't be handed over to the Jews. As it is, My kingdom does not have its origin here.'"
    John 18:33–36

In His clear testimony before Pilate, JESUS declares that He is the King of His Kingdom, which is not in this world, but in Heaven. In the Old Testament, it is the LORD GOD who alone is KING in Heaven, as it is written:

> *"Lift up your heads, you gates!*
> *Rise up, ancient doors!*
> *Then the King of glory will come in.*
> *Who is this King of glory?*
> *The Lord, strong and mighty,*
> * the Lord, mighty in battle.*
> *Lift up your heads, you gates!*
> *Rise up, ancient doors!*
> *Then the King of glory will come in.*
> *Who is He, this King of glory?*
> *The Lord of Hosts, He is the King of glory."*
> *Psalm 24:7–10*

11. *"Then Jesus came near and said to them, 'All authority has been given to Me in heaven and on earth. Go, therefore, and make disciples of all nations, baptizing them in the name of the Father and of the Son and of the Holy Spirit, teaching them to observe everything I have commanded you. And remember, I am with you always, to the end of the age.'"*
    Matthew 28:18–20

Here JESUS speaks to His followers shortly before His ascension into Heaven. He testifies that He has all authority in Heaven and Earth, which could be true only if He were GOD, One with the FATHER. He commands His people to go to all nations, baptizing people, not in the Name of the FATHER only, but also in the Name of the SON and the HOLY SPIRIT. Lastly, He says that He will always be with His true followers, which only GOD can do through His SPIRIT.

In these and other passages, JESUS teaches us the reality of His complete unity with GOD His FATHER. To be sure, there are other occasions during His ministry where He clearly identifies Himself as the Son of Man and emphasizes His true human nature. We will focus more on this in the next chapter. **JESUS' testimony about Himself, given to us by His SPIRIT in the New Testament, is that He was both true GOD and true man. His testimony is completely validated by the life He lived and by His resurrection from the dead. It will be clear for the whole world at the time of His Return.**

His Miracles and Words

The variety and frequency of the miracles JESUS performed leave no option other than to acknowledge that He is exactly who He claimed to be, the SON of GOD, in perfect unity with GOD His FATHER. Alone, no human being could do any of the incredible miracles that JESUS did. JESUS said, *"What is impossible with men is possible with God" (Luke 18:27).* JESUS did what is impossible for people, but possible for GOD. He healed people who were blind from birth, leprous, paralyzed, or sick with all types of diseases. He even raised people from the dead. These miracles were all part of JESUS' recurring ministry. It is true that with modern medicine, incredible surgeries, and amazing technology today, people are healed of some diseases and handicaps. The difference is that JESUS simply spoke the word or placed His hands on people and they were healed.

Feeding thousands of people with a few loaves and fish, walking on water and calming storms on the sea are acts that only GOD can do. The miracles that characterized JESUS' life testify to His identity as the SON of GOD. The Old Testament prophets did miracles in the LORD's Name, but JESUS' miracles were done with His power. His apostles did miracles in JESUS' Name *(Acts 3:6, 4:29-30, 14:3, 16:18).*

JESUS' words matched His miracles! JESUS' wisdom supersedes that of any man. No one has ever spoken words with so much love, truth, hope, and power in them. From His Sermon on the Mount, near the beginning of His ministry, to His teaching in the Temple before His crucifixion, His words address the greatest needs of the human heart, mind, and spirit. They are like solid rock in contrast to the vain and shifting sand of human thinkers. Whether He was addressing commoners, tax collectors, prostitutes, or the religious or political leaders, His words were like a sword or alternatively like the rebuke or comfort of a mother or father for their naughty or suffering child. His preaching and teaching were beyond any of the great prophets and generated transformation in the lives of anyone who believed them. His words have been relevant to people from all walks of life over the past 2000 years and continue to confront, comfort, and transform individuals all over our world today. His words minister mercy, repentance, love, wisdom, hope, joy, and peace to those who will receive them.

The Testimony of GOD, John the Baptist, and Demons

In addition to the testimony of JESUS' life and teaching regarding His identity as true GOD, we have in the four Gospels the testimony of:

1. **GOD the FATHER:**
   "While he was still speaking, suddenly a bright cloud covered them, and a voice from the cloud said: 'This is My beloved Son. I take delight in Him. Listen to Him!'" Matthew 17:5 (Mark 1:11; Luke 3:21–22; Matthew 3:17, 17:5)

2. **John the Baptist:**
   "And John testified, 'I watched the Spirit descending from heaven like a dove, and He rested on Him. I didn't know Him, but He who

sent me to baptize with water told me, 'The
One you see the Spirit descending and resting
on — He is the One who baptizes with the Holy
Spirit.' I have seen and testified that He is the
Son of God!'" John 1:32–34

3. Even the demons identified CHRIST as GOD's SON and
    unwillingly conceded to His authority:
    "Suddenly they shouted, 'What do You have to
    do with us, Son of God? Have You come here to
    torment us before the time?'" Matthew 8:29

    "Then Jesus rebuked the demon, and it came
    out of him, and from that moment the boy
    was healed." Matthew 17:18.

The Apostles' Testimony

The New Testament is a bold proclamation of Who JESUS
is as true GOD and true man, and what He has already accomplished, is presently completing, and will do for all who sincerely trust in Him:

1. *"In the beginning was the Word, and the Word was*
    with God, and the Word was God. He was with God
    in the beginning. All things were created through Him,
    and apart from Him not one thing was created that
    has been created. Life was in Him, and that life was
    the light of men. That light shines in the darkness, yet
    the darkness did not overcome it."

    John 1:1–5

This is the introduction to CHRIST given by GOD's SPIRIT
through the Apostle John. JESUS is identified, from the beginning to the end of the Gospel of John, as One with GOD the
FATHER from all eternity. He came into our world filled with

GOD's amazing grace and powerful truth for all who would believe in and receive Him. Although Jehovah's Witnesses suggest that the Greek words should be translated as: *"the word was a god"*, the Biblical teaching is that there is only one true GOD, and, therefore, JESUS is GOD. Angels and people are sometimes referred to as sons of GOD, but never as the eternal GOD.

2. *"Paul, a bond-servant of Christ Jesus, called as an apostle, set apart for the gospel of GOD, which He promised beforehand through His prophets in the holy Scriptures, concerning His Son, who was born of a descendant of David according to the flesh, who was declared the Son of God with power by the resurrection from the dead, according to the Spirit of holiness, Jesus Christ our Lord".* **Romans 1:1-4 NASB**

The Gospel of GOD is the Gospel of JESUS CHRIST, the SON of GOD, Who is the crucified and risen LORD.

3. *"Christ Jesus, who, <u>existing in the form of God, did not consider equality with God as something to be used for His own advantage.</u> Instead He emptied Himself by assuming the form of a slave, taking on the likeness of men. And when He had come as a man in His external form, He humbled Himself by becoming obedient to the point of death — even to death on a cross. For this reason God highly exalted Him and gave Him the name that is above every name, so that at the name of Jesus every knee will bow — of those who are in heaven and on earth and under the earth — and every tongue should confess that <u>Jesus Christ is Lord, to the glory of God the Father."</u>* **Philippians 2:5–11**

In these words, the Apostle Paul teaches both the divinity and humanity of JESUS, and makes clear that, according to

GOD's will, all people should bow before Him, to worship and glorify Him. **It is undeniable in the teaching of the prophets in the Old Testament and of CHRIST and His Apostles that only the One true GOD is worthy of being worshipped.** JESUS said to Satan: *"Go away, Satan! For it is written: Worship the Lord your God and serve only Him" (Matthew 4:10).* Twice in Revelation it is stated by the angels that we are not to worship the angels, who are fellow servants of GOD, but rather we are to worship GOD (*Revelation 19:10, 22:8–9*). **Throughout Revelation, however, the angels and the saints are continually worshiping both the FATHER and the SON (***Revelation 1:8,17–18, 4:6–11, 5:6–14, 7:9–17, 11:15–19, 15:1–4, 19:1–10).* Jehovah's Witnesses frequently quote from the book of Revelation, but they are blind to the open worship of CHRIST in unity with the FATHER. **JESUS receives the same praise as the FATHER by the angels and the saints.**

4. *"He is the image of the invisible God, the firstborn over all creation. For everything was created by Him, in heaven and on earth, the visible and the invisible, whether thrones or dominions or rulers or authorities — all things have been created through Him and for Him. He is before all things, and by Him all things hold together. He is also the head of the body, the church; He is the beginning, the firstborn from the dead, so that He might come to have first place in everything. For God was pleased to have all His fullness dwell in Him, and through Him to reconcile everything to Himself by making peace through the blood of His cross — whether things on earth or things in heaven."* **Colossians 1:15–20**

Here the HOLY SPIRIT, through brother Paul, testifies that JESUS, Who spilled His blood on the cross and rose from the dead for us, is the perfect image of the invisible GOD, having the complete fullness of GOD. Additionally, Paul proclaims that everything in Heaven and earth, the physical and the spiritual, were created by CHRIST and for CHRIST. There is no question that in the Old Testament, the world and universe and everything that exists was created by the LORD GOD Almighty.

5. *"<u>The Son is the radiance of God's glory and the exact expression of His nature</u>, sustaining all things by His powerful word. After making purification for sins, He sat down at the right hand of the Majesty on high. So He became higher in rank than the angels, just as the name He inherited is superior to theirs. For to which of the angels did He ever say, You are My Son; today I have become Your Father, or again, I will be His Father, and He will be My Son? When He again brings His firstborn into the world, He says, <u>And all God's angels must worship Him.</u> And about the angels He says: He makes His angels winds, and His servants a fiery flame, but <u>to the Son: Your throne, God, is forever and ever</u>, and the scepter of Your kingdom is a scepter of justice."* Hebrews 1:3–8

Here the HOLY SPIRIT again attests that JESUS is the exact representation of GOD in our world. JESUS' Word is GOD's Word, by which He not only created but maintains our world and universe. Contrary to the Jehovah's Witnesses' teaching that JESUS was the archangel Michael incarnated, the SPIRIT highlights the truth here that **JESUS is not an angel** who came into this world. As in Philippians and Revelation, GOD the FATHER calls all angels to worship CHRIST, even as they worship the FATHER.

6. *"while we wait for the blessed hope and appearing of <u>the glory of our great God and Savior, Jesus Christ</u>. He gave Himself for us to redeem us from all lawlessness and to cleanse for Himself a people for His own possession, eager to do good works."* Titus 2:13–14

> *"Simeon Peter, a bond-servant and apostle of Jesus Christ, To those who have received a faith of the same kind as ours, by <u>the right-</u><u>eousness of our God and Savior, Jesus Christ</u>: Grace and peace be multiplied to you in the knowledge of God and of Jesus our Lord."*
> *2 Peter 1:1–2 NASB*

In these passages Paul and Peter both refer to JESUS as our GOD and SAVIOR. There is only one GOD and SAVIOR. He became JESUS and revealed His grace, truth, Kingdom, and salvation to all who would listen to Him and trust in Him.

JESUS IS the Embodiment of the Living GOD

JESUS was a genuine person like you and I are. He wasn't just a spirit living in a fake human body, as some confused teachers have taught. He was a real flesh-and-blood human being. However, through the life He lived, His words and actions, His miracles and teachings, His suffering, death, resurrection, and ascension, and through the testimony of the HOLY SPIRIT in the New Testament, He has revealed His eternal deity. **His life reveals that He is Who He claimed to be: the eternal SON of GOD, One with GOD the FATHER and the HOLY SPIRIT.**

JESUS is the One Who put each of the galaxies and stars in place and has named them all *(Psalm 147:4, Isaiah 40:26).* He is the One Who originated the genetic code through which He created the innumerable plants, insects, fish, birds, and all the creatures that move above, along, and beneath the ground. He is the Creator of food and of our taste buds. He sustains and daily recreates the beauty of the sunrise and sunset and decorates our world with the majesty of the flora and fauna that surround us. He clothes the lilies *(Matthew 6:28–30).* He is the source of every good in this fallen world.

JESUS is our Creator. He created us in His own image to be like Him. He is the One Who has given us life and filled our lives with blessing after blessing, through no merit of ours, but proceeding completely out of His amazing love and mercy. As it is written: ***"For in Him we live and move and exist" (Acts 17:28).*** JESUS is the One Who created us male and female and instituted the marriage relationship of mutual love and service. He is the Creator of true and faithful sexuality. He is the source of the love for our parents and children, brothers and sisters, and our enemies who despise and hate all who love Him. He became our flesh and blood and taught us about GOD, life, and eternity. He gave His life to save our souls and to give us the abundant and eternal life with Him in His Kingdom.

Together with the FATHER and the SPIRIT, CHRIST fulfills His promises and fills our lives to overflowing with His extravagant love, enfolded in His many blessings. JESUS WAS, IS, and always WILL BE the eternal GOD.

> *"He was in the world, and the world was created through Him, yet the world did not recognize Him. He came to His own, and His own people did not receive Him. But to all who did receive Him, He gave them the right to be children of God, to those who believe in His name, who were born, not of blood, or of the will of the flesh, or of the will of man, but of God. The Word became flesh and took up residence among us. We observed His glory, the glory as the One and Only Son from the Father, full of grace and truth."* **John 1:10–14**

In the Bible, the HOLY SPIRIT testifies that JESUS is GOD. CHRIST Himself proclaimed that He was the SON of GOD in perfect unity with the FATHER. He has all the characteristics of GOD His FATHER. He does exactly what GOD His FATHER does: creates, gives life, forgives sins and judges as only GOD can do. JESUS receives the same worship and praise for the same reasons as GOD the FATHER. Since the HOLY SPIRIT, Who is the ultimate author of the Holy Scriptures, unambiguously reveals JESUS as true GOD and true Man, this is what the true followers and servants of CHRIST have believed and proclaimed since JESUS' ascension into Heaven and will continue to proclaim until He comes.

This is the foundational truth of Christian faith; everything else flows out of this fountain. There is no way of coming to this fountain apart from listening to and accepting the testimony of the HOLY SPIRIT in His Word. No human knowledge alone could ever bring anyone to this faith in JESUS.

This is Who JESUS IS!

Have you received Him into your life as your GOD and SAVIOR and LORD? Do you want to learn more about Who He is and what He has done for you? Are you willing to commit your life to loving, obeying, and serving Him and His Kingdom?

Pray!

CHAPTER 3

OUR PERFECT, LOVING BROTHER

"The Word became flesh and took up residence among us. We observed His glory, the glory as the One and Only Son from the Father, full of grace and truth." John 1:14

GOD Became One of Us

J ESUS, the eternal Son of GOD, became a genuine flesh-and-blood human being living on our planet. Even though JESUS' birth was a uniquely miraculous event through a virgin in whom He was conceived by the wisdom and power of the HOLY SPIRIT, He was completely human. His genetic ancestry is traced all the way back to Abraham, and then to Adam and Eve, who were also miraculously created through the breath of the HOLY SPIRIT *(Matthew 1: 1–17; Luke 3:23–37).*

JESUS was truly human. He was a baby, a child, a teenager, and a young and mature adult. He ate, drank, played, laughed, smiled, talked, listened, walked, ran, and cried. He had friends and family who loved Him, but who were often confused by His mysterious words and actions, particularly after He began

His traveling ministry. After JESUS developed into a teenager, His earthly father is no longer mentioned in the Gospels. It is usually assumed that Joseph died at some point before JESUS began His traveling ministry. As the eldest son, JESUS would then have had the responsibility of assisting his mother.

JESUS grew up in Nazareth, a village unimportant to the rest of the world, and in a subjugated country whose people were oppressed and despised by their Roman conquerors. Although the precise historical circumstances are unique to every individual and age, the basic experiences of life on our planet are common to people of all generations.

JESUS Was the Only Perfect Human

JESUS was like us in every way, except for sin *(Hebrews 4:15).* We are all sinners but CHRIST was conceived in holiness and lived a perfectly holy, sinless, and love-centered life. On one occasion JESUS was asked:

> *"'Teacher, which command in the law is the greatest?'*
> *He said to him, 'Love the Lord your God with all your heart, with all your soul, and with all your mind. This is the greatest and most important command. The second is like it: Love your neighbor as yourself. All the Law and the Prophets depend on these two commands.'" Matthew 22:36–39*

JESUS' words here have profound implications for our life and eternity. They were true then, and they are still true today. This is GOD's will for our lives. **JESUS is the only human being that has completely and perfectly fulfilled these two commandments with all their implications and applications. The rest of us, beginning with our first parents Adam and Eve,**

have fallen fatally short of being the holy loving people that GOD created us to be.

His Childhood

Even as a child, JESUS lived in love and faithfulness to GOD and humanity. The HOLY SPIRIT testifies to only one event in His life between his birth and the beginning of His traveling ministry. This episode happened on a trip with His parents to the Passover celebration in Jerusalem when He was twelve years old.

> *"Every year His parents traveled to Jerusalem for the Passover Festival. When He was* <u>*12 years old,*</u> *they went up according to the custom of the festival. After those days were over, as they were returning, the boy Jesus stayed behind in Jerusalem, but His parents did not know it. Assuming He was in the traveling party, they went a day's journey. Then they began looking for Him among their relatives and friends. When they did not find Him, they returned to Jerusalem to search for Him. After three days, they found Him in the temple complex sitting among the teachers, listening to them and asking them questions. And all those who heard Him were astounded at His understanding and His answers. When His parents saw Him, they were astonished, and His mother said to Him, 'Son, why have You treated us like this? Your father and I have been anxiously searching for You.'*
>
> *'Why were you searching for Me?' He asked them. 'Didn't you know that* <u>*I had to be in My*</u>

__Father's house__?' But they did not understand what He said to them.

Then He went down with them and came to Nazareth and __was obedient to them__. His mother kept all these things in her heart. And __Jesus increased in wisdom and stature, and in favor with God and with people__." Luke 2:41–52

This event in JESUS' life is sometimes misinterpreted as disobedience to His earthly parents, but that is the exact opposite of what this report reveals. It was Mary and Joseph who left Jerusalem without confirming that JESUS was with them, assuming He was with relatives or friends. They were upset when they finally found JESUS three days later and immediately tried to project their guilt onto JESUS, but it was their false assumption and lack of faith and understanding that caused their anxiety.

> It is written: *"Don't worry about anything, but in everything, through prayer and petition with thanksgiving, let your requests be made known to God. And the peace of God, which surpasses every thought, will guard your hearts and minds in Christ Jesus."* Philippians 4:6–7
>
> We often sin against the LORD and others because of our false assumptions. All too often we assume our knowledge or understanding of something or someone is complete and accurate when we don't know all the facts. This creates stress and results in wrong conclusions and inappropriate words and actions. As parents, we sometimes make false assumptions about situations involving our children, resulting in needless anxiety and sinful attitudes and actions. We all need to spend more time on our knees repenting and giving Him our worries, problems, and concerns. He cares for us and our children. Pray for them and commit them to the only One Who can help them. Pray more–worry less.

What this account does reveal is that, even as a child, JESUS loved GOD His FATHER and obeyed GOD's will for His life, which included honoring and obeying His earthly parents. **Love and obedience to GOD His FATHER and love for others, beginning with His earthly parents, was the signature pattern of JESUS' entire life as testified to in the Gospels.**

This account also details for us that, even as a twelve-year-old boy, JESUS had great wisdom and understanding of the Scriptures and no doubt had some interesting conversations with the religious authorities. JESUS probably talked to them about the Messiah and the Passover sacrifice, but we will have to wait until Heaven to learn the details of their conversations.

A Teenager and Young Adult

Our selfish natures are certainly revealed in childhood, but in our youth and young adulthood sin becomes more pronounced and often manifests itself in rebellious and destructive attitudes and actions to ourselves and others. King David wrote:

> *"Remember, Lord, Your compassion and Your faithful love, for they have existed from antiquity.*
> *Do not remember the sins of my youth or my acts of rebellion; in keeping with Your faithful love, remember me because of Your goodness, Lord." Psalm 25: 6–7*

These words are very applicable to all of us, for we have all sinned against GOD and others as children, teenagers, and adults. Even children and teenagers need to repent of their sinful thoughts, words and actions. JESUS, on the other hand, never sinned against GOD or others even in those youthful years. It is possible to imagine JESUS as a cute, obedient, and loving little child, but it takes faith to believe the amazing life He lived during His teen and young adult years, the time when we often go astray. We have only one statement in the Scriptures of JESUS' life as a teenager and young adult: *"And Jesus increased in wisdom and stature, and in favor with God and with people" (Luke 2:52).* In Heaven we will know the incredible details of the LORD's entire life on earth. For now, all we need to know is that even in those turbulent teenage and young adult years He lived in perfect harmony with the will of our FATHER, in perfect love for GOD and others. We praise Him that He lived a perfect life during those years and that He is ready to forgive us for our sinful, selfish ways, including those of our youth.

A Seamless Sinless Life

At the age of thirty, in obedience to His FATHER's will and in preparation for the mission He was sent to complete, JESUS fasted for forty days in the desert. During those days of physical weakness, His obedience and faithfulness to our FATHER was repeatedly attacked and tested by Satan.

>*"Then Jesus was led up by the Spirit into the wilderness to be <u>tempted by the Devil</u>. After He had fasted 40 days and 40 nights, He was hungry. Then the tempter approached Him and said, 'If You are the Son of God, tell these stones to become bread.'*
>
>*But He answered, 'It is written: Man must not live on bread alone but on every word that comes from the mouth of God.'*
>
>*Then the Devil took Him to the holy city, had Him stand on the pinnacle of the temple, and said to Him, 'If You are the Son of God, throw Yourself down. For it is written: He will give His angels orders concerning you, and they will support you with their hands so that you will not strike your foot against a stone.'*
>
>*Jesus told him, 'It is also written: Do not test the Lord your God.'*
>
>*Again, the Devil took Him to a very high mountain and showed Him all the kingdoms of the world and their splendor. And he said to Him, 'I will give You all these things if You will fall down and worship me.'*

> **Then Jesus told him, 'Go away, Satan! For it is
> written: Worship the Lord your God, and serve
> only Him.'" Matthew 4:1–10**

As a true flesh-and-blood human JESUS faced all the common temptations that you and I face in this corrupted, deceitful world. Unlike us, however, JESUS overcame the temptations of the flesh: pride, self-centeredness, and the idolatry of worshiping this world's pleasures and treasures. It is written: *"I have treasured Your word in my heart so that I may not sin against You" (Psalm 119:11).* JESUS is the only One Who fulfilled those words. He overcame Satan's temptations, not only in the desert, but throughout His life, by holding to the truth of the Scriptures.

The desert was not the only place JESUS faced temptations. In *Luke 4:13* (NASB) it is written: *"When the Devil had finished every temptation, he left Him until an opportune time."* Like us, He encountered many temptations to lie, to covet, to lust, to hate, to disobey GOD's commandments and will, and to love Himself more than His FATHER and other people. On every occasion, however, He lived a holy, victorious life of love and faithfulness. It is written:

> *"Therefore, since we have a great high priest
> who has passed through the heavens — Jesus
> the Son of God — let us hold fast to the con-
> fession. <u>For we do not have a high priest who
> is unable to sympathize with our weaknesses,
> but One who has been tested in every way
> as we are, yet without sin. Therefore let us
> approach the throne of grace with boldness,
> so that we may receive mercy and find grace to
> help us at the proper time."</u> Hebrews 4:14–16*

Do Not Project our Human Sinfulness onto JESUS

A Barna poll taken in 2009 asked people who considered themselves to be Christians if they believed that JESUS was sinless. *(www.barna.com/research/barna-survey-examines-changes-in-worldview-among-christians-over-the-past-13-years/)* Approximately one-third of the people who claimed to believe in CHRIST also believed that He probably sinned in His life. We like to project our sinful human failures onto JESUS. We want Him to be a sinner like us so we can excuse or rationalize our sin, thereby removing the need for repentance and faith in CHRIST. **It takes no faith to believe that JESUS was a sinner like all of us, but to believe that He lived a perfectly holy, dedicated life of love to GOD our FATHER and to all people requires faith in Him and in the HOLY SPIRIT's testimony in His Word.** Those who believe that He sinned are either ignorant of the HOLY SPIRIT's clear testimony to the perfect holiness and obedience of CHRIST or they have chosen to ignore and reject that testimony in an attempt to transform Him into just another sinful human being who has no ultimate relevance for their lives.

The bottom line is this: If JESUS sinned He would be no different than any of us and could not forgive us or save us from our sin. If He sinned, His death would have been for His own sin and not for ours. Therefore, He would not be able to save anyone, not even Himself. It is because He was sinless that He could die in our place and take our sin onto His body on the cross. Praise Him that He perfectly fulfilled every part of GOD's Word for all of us. Through our faith in Him He gives us His perfect holiness.

Living for the Pleasures and Treasures

Instead of seeking GOD's Kingdom and righteousness as JESUS did, our human race hungers and thirsts for the plea-sures and treasures of the world and of the flesh. Our sinful, selfish natures, urged on by our warped world and the spiritual forces of evil, tempt us to live for ourselves and for all the stuff that eventually ends up in the garbage dump. **JESUS said: "For what does it profit a man to gain the whole world, and forfeit his soul?" (Mark 8:36 NASB).**

There is a story about a very wealthy man in California who made provision in his will that he would be buried in a new limo with a cigar in his mouth. As a crane lowered the limo containing his body into the grave, someone apparently commented, *"Man, that's living".* No, that is death. **In the end, those focused on themselves and on the toys and desires of this world lose everything, including their soul. Do not be deceived by the temporary pleasures or decaying treasures.**

A Life of Perfect Love

Throughout His life, JESUS loved GOD His FATHER with all His heart, soul, mind, and strength, and He loved others as Himself. Neither the treasures nor pleasures of this fading world diverted Him from His faithfulness and love for GOD or His loving ministry to people. A day or two before His crucifixion, JESUS told His followers:

> *"I will not talk with you much longer, because the ruler of the world is coming. He has no power over Me. On the contrary, I am going away so <u>that the world may know that I love the Father</u>. Just as the Father commanded Me, so I do. Get up; let's leave this place." John 14:30–31*

> *"As the Father has loved Me, I have also loved you. Remain in My love. If you keep My commands you will remain in My love, just as I have kept My Father's commands and remain*

in His love. I have spoken these things to you so that My joy may be in you and your joy may be complete. <u>This is My command: Love one another as I have loved you. No one has greater love than this, that someone would lay down his life for his friends. You are My friends if you do what I command you</u>." John 15:9–14

JESUS didn't verbalize the word "love" as a deception to simply impress people into believing in Him. **JESUS put His love for His FATHER and His love for us into the daily thoughts and actions of His life. It motivated His entire life and led Him to the cross on our behalf.** Many people have heard *John 3:16–18*, but most are not so familiar with its corollary in *1 John 3:16–18*:

"This is how we have come to know love: <u>He laid down His life for us. We should also lay down our lives for our brothers.</u> If anyone has this world's goods and sees his brother in need but closes his eyes to his need — how can God's love reside in him? <u>Little children, we must not love with word or speech, but with truth and action.</u>" 1 John 3:16–18

JESUS didn't love His FATHER and us simply with words, but in *"truth and action"*. In His few years of ministry, He fed the multitudes, gave sight to the blind, enabled the lame to walk and the deaf to hear, healed the sick, freed those who were demon-possessed, restored lepers, and taught all poor, weak sinners who would listen the good news of GOD's forgiveness and eternal Kingdom.

JESUS lived the perfect life of GOD as a genuine flesh-and-blood human being. He understands what this world is like and the temptations and struggles you and I and all people face. He sympathizes with us in our weaknesses and offers His gracious pardon to everyone who comes to Him in sincere repentance, trusting in His promise of salvation.

JESUS is Our Perfect, Loving Brother

It is written:
> *"For in bringing many sons to glory, it was entirely appropriate that God — all things exist for Him and through Him — should make the source of their salvation perfect through sufferings. For the One who sanctifies and those who are sanctified all have one Father. That is why <u>Jesus is not ashamed to call them brothers</u>, saying: I will proclaim Your name to <u>My brothers</u>; I will sing hymns to You in the congregation."* **Hebrews 2:10–12**

JESUS is our Brother Who has done everything to make it possible for us to be His brothers and sisters. JESUS' arms are wide open for you and for me to come to Him each day in faith and repentance, believing in His mercy and seeking His help to live in love and obedience to Him and in love and service to one another.

Pray!

CHAPTER 4

THE ULTIMATE PROPHET, PASTOR, PHYSICIAN, AND PRODUCER OF MIRACLES

"Then Jesus went to all the towns and villages, teaching in their synagogues, preaching the good news of the kingdom, and healing every disease and every sickness."
Matthew 9:35

WDJD

A few years ago, the **WWJD** fad blew through evangelical Christianity. *"What Would JESUS Do?"* was and is a good question that should occupy our thoughts before we ignite our tongues or engage our hands and feet. However, before anyone can know what JESUS **would do**, we need to have some understanding of what He **did**. **WDJD:** "What Did JESUS Do?" has to precede "What Would JESUS Do?". We know that He lived a perfect, holy life of love and obedience to GOD and love and service to others. But what did this mean in terms of His day-to-day life?

In the great mission command that JESUS gave to His followers, He said:

> *"All authority has been given to Me in heaven and on earth. Go, therefore, and <u>make disciples</u> of all nations, <u>baptizing</u> them in the name of the Father and of the Son and of the Holy Spirit, <u>teaching them to observe everything I have commanded you</u>. And remember, I am with you always, to the end of the age."* **Matthew 28:19–20**

To sincerely believe in JESUS means to become His disciple. The easy *"believism"* that is center-stage in nominal Christianity is nothing more than a mirage. Christians are called to discipleship which involves examining our lives in light of Who He is, what He did, taught, and accomplished for us, and what He promises to us, and then committing ourselves to believing and following Him. To believe in JESUS means to believe in the JESUS testified to by the HOLY SPIRIT in the pages of the Bible. We all need to become His students and followers. We are called to follow His teaching, not our own self-centered world views or those of our contemporaries.

To follow Him we need a clear picture of how He lived, and what He did and taught.

The Ultimate Prophet

Speaking to the Jewish people shortly after JESUS' resurrection, the Apostle Peter proclaimed that JESUS was the CHRIST, the Messiah, and the great Prophet that Moses testified GOD would send:

> *"And now, brothers, I know that you did it in ignorance, just as your leaders also did. But*

what God predicted through the mouth of all the prophets — that <u>His Messiah would suffer</u> — He has fulfilled in this way. Therefore repent and turn back, so that your sins may be wiped out, that seasons of refreshing may come from the presence of the Lord, and that He may send <u>Jesus, who has been appointed for you as the Messiah. Heaven must welcome Him until the times of the restoration of all things, which God spoke about by the mouth of His holy prophets from the beginning.</u> Moses said: <u>The Lord your God will raise up for you a Prophet like me from among your brothers. You must listen to Him in everything He will say to you. And everyone who will not listen to that Prophet will be completely cut off from the people.</u>" Acts 3:17–23

JESUS IS the ultimate prophet Who came and spoke GOD's message of grace and truth perfectly to all people and will soon return to restore everything and completely fulfill His Word. **Everyone who does not believe in, listen to, and seek to practice JESUS' teaching will be cut off from His eternal kingdom. So says the LORD.**

Matthew, Mark, Luke, and John provide us with summarized biographies of JESUS' life and ministry. The four Gospels are a condensed travelogue of His preaching, teaching, and healing ministry. One **third** of these Gospels is focused on His suffering, death, and resurrection, which we will highlight in the next couple of chapters, but two-thirds are devoted to revealing His life and ministry.

After His baptism and temptation in the wilderness, JESUS left Nazareth and made His home base in Capernaum, a town on the shores of the Sea of Galilee *(Matthew 4:13)*. From Capernaum He made mission trips to all the cities, towns, and villages in Galilee and Judea, preaching and teaching about the eternal Kingdom of Heaven. Listen to the testimony of the HOLY SPIRIT:

> *"Jesus was going all over Galilee, teaching in their synagogues, preaching the good news of the kingdom, and healing every disease and sickness among the people." Matthew 4:23*

JESUS was the ultimate traveling prophet, preacher, and teacher. Wherever He traveled, He interacted with the whole spectrum of people—little children and youth, men and women on the streets and in churches, religious and political leaders, boozers, prostitutes, criminals, tax collectors, the pious and impious, the sick, demon-possessed, rich and poor, mourners, soldiers, shepherds, carpenters, and fishermen. If you read the four Gospels, you will meet some of these people that JESUS ministered to. Through His preaching, teaching, and personal counsel, He shared a message of grace and truth to those who would listen.

Like the Old Testament prophets and John the Baptist, JESUS was rejected then and is rejected now because of His challenging message. Many came to JESUS because of His healing ministry, but many walked away when they heard His preaching and teaching.

> *"Therefore, when many of His disciples heard this, they said, 'This teaching is hard! Who can accept it?'*
>
> *Jesus, knowing in Himself that His disciples were complaining about this, asked them, 'Does this offend you? Then what if you were to observe the Son of Man ascending to where He was before? The Spirit is the One who gives*

life. The flesh doesn't help at all. The words that I have spoken to you are spirit and are life. But there are some among you who don't believe.' (For Jesus knew from the beginning those who would not believe and the one who would betray Him.) He said, 'This is why I told you that no one can come to Me unless it is granted to him by the Father.'

<u>From that moment many of His disciples turned back and no longer accompanied Him</u>. Therefore Jesus said to the Twelve, 'You don't want to go away too, do you?'

Simon Peter answered, '<u>Lord, who will we go to? You have the words of eternal life</u>. We have come to believe and know that You are <u>the Holy One of God!</u>'" John 6:60–69

A Word to us Preachers

Those of us who are called to preach and teach CHRIST and His Word have been given a holy and blessed calling of which we are not worthy. Our call is to handle His Word humbly and carefully, not subtracting from JESUS' teaching and not adding our own philosophies or private interpretations based on our own personal feelings or private visions or dreams. Self-anointed gnostic teachers are everywhere these days, trusting in their own intelligence and spirituality instead of trusting the teaching of the LORD and His prophets and apostles. The truly anointed ones are those who listen to GOD's Word and faithfully pass it on to those the LORD has made them accountable for. We are to be servants and couriers of JESUS and His Word, passing His grace and truth on to those the LORD gives us opportunity to speak and minister to. As JESUS said to the Apostle Peter in John 21, if we love Him, we are called to feed His sheep with the spiritual nourishment of His Holy Word. If we give people our disputable opinions, rather than the clear water, wine and wholesome food of JESUS and His Word, we will be hindering rather than helping them.

The LORD will hold us accountable for the ministry we carry on in His Name.

Since our generation does not like to be preached to, many preachers have been forced out of congregations and have either left congregational ministry or switched to a career of entertainment— pleasing the itching ears and dry eyes of those who prefer a comfortable recliner to a struggle against sin and a cross to carry. Our sinful nature wants to go our own way. We do not appreciate anyone telling us how we ought to live, or that we need to repent, believe in JESUS, pick up our cross, and follow Him into battle.

If you want to draw a good crowd, promise them healing, prosperity, and a luxurious cruise into heaven. If you want to disperse a crowd, begin to preach and teach the message of JESUS and His cross. People are attracted to miracles and philosophical discussions *(1 Corinthians 1:18–31)* but are offended by words that confront them with sin and unbelief. Unless someone truly believes that JESUS is the Holy One of GOD Who has the words of eternal life, they will probably not stick around to hear His convicting and challenging preaching and teaching.

After listening to JESUS, some left thinking He was demon-possessed or out of His mind. *(John 7:20, 8:48,52)* The world and most religious leaders today view and portray faithful followers of JESUS in the same way. This is exactly what JESUS said would happen:

> *"If the world hates you, understand that it hated Me before it hated you. If you were of the world, the world would love you as its own. However, because you are not of the world, but I have chosen you out of it, the world hates you. Remember the word I spoke to you: 'A slave is not greater than his master.' If they persecuted Me, they will also persecute you. If they kept My word, they will also keep yours. But they will do all these things to you on account of My name, because they don't know the One who sent Me."* John 15:18–21

JESUS Was the Only Perfect Prophet

A prophet's calling from GOD was to faithfully proclaim, in word and deed, GOD's message to those to whom they were sent. JESUS is the only prophet who flawlessly lived and proclaimed the Word of GOD to our world. The other prophets— Noah, Job, Abraham, Jacob, Moses, Joshua, David, Jeremiah, etc.—and all the apostles were sinners whose faith was often weak and who didn't perfectly accomplish the will of GOD. The Biblical record of their lives and ministries reveals that they fell short, as we do, but by GOD's grace were transformed into His saints. They were weak vessels whom the HOLY SPIRIT used for the Glory of GOD and the salvation of His people.

According to JESUS in *Matthew 11:11*, *John the Baptist* was among the greatest of all people, yet even he was weak in faith at times and had doubts:

> *"When John heard in prison what the Messiah was doing, he sent a message by his disciples and asked Him, 'Are You the One who is to come, or should we expect someone else?'"*
> *Matthew 11:2–3*

John the Baptist was a great prophet of GOD who, at the cost of his life, prepared the way for JESUS' ministry. However, like all of us, he fell short of having perfect faith and needed the Word of CHRIST to strengthen him in his time of doubt and weakness. What John did with his doubts we need to do with ours—bring them to CHRIST, Who knows them and will speak to us according to our need.

As stated in the previous chapter, JESUS testified that all the words He spoke came from GOD:

> *"Don't you believe that I am in the Father and the Father is in Me? The words I speak to you I*

> *do not speak on My own. The Father who lives*
> *in Me does His works... The word that you hear*
> *is not Mine but is from the Father who sent*
> *Me."* John 14:10,24
> *(See also: John 3:31–33, 5:19–30, 7:16–18,*
> *8:25–30, 17:6–8,14)*

What Did JESUS Preach and Teach?

What message did JESUS prophesy in the towns and villages He went to?

> *"From then on Jesus began to preach, "Repent,*
> *because the kingdom of heaven has come*
> *near!"" Matthew 4:17*

As the SPIRIT reveals in the four Gospels, JESUS taught and proclaimed the reality of the Kingdom of Heaven and called all people to repentance and faith wherever He went. JESUS was always speaking to people about the reality of Heaven. Tragically the majority of people in our world live as if this world is all there is, with little or no thought concerning the reality of eternity. CHRIST proclaimed the Kingdom of Heaven, the Kingdom of GOD, in all of the towns and villages He covered. It is absolutely crucial that we all understand that our life in this world is just the beginning, and only a small fraction of eternity to come. Although, JESUS also often warned against the reality of the judgment of Hell, it was the Kingdom of Heaven that saturated His thoughts and teaching. He was looking forward to eternity with His people, and desired all people to get ready for His Kingdom which is already present, and will soon come in all of its glory.

To get ready for Heaven we need to repent of our sin. The call to repentance and faith is necessary because we are all sinners, and GOD is holy and loving and desires to forgive and to save through CHRIST. **The call to repentance and faith and the proclamation of GOD's love and forgiveness permeates GOD's Word, just as it saturated JESUS' preaching and teaching ministry. The SPIRIT of CHRIST is bringing this same foundational message of grace and truth to people all over our world today.**

The Kingdom of Heaven is near to us today for three reasons—because we may die at any moment, because CHRIST will soon return to our world, and because GOD's SPIRIT is in our world, revealing CHRIST and calling all people to repentance and faith. Time is short, eternity is near. The time to repent of our sin and turn to CHRIST is now. As the saying goes— "tomorrow may never come".

GOD does not guarantee that any of us will still be living on this planet tomorrow. What He does guarantee through CHRIST is that He will forgive all who sincerely repent of their sin and trust in Him, and that He will give to us an extraordinary eternity with Him in His Kingdom.

In addition to His call to repentance and faith, the LORD's teaching was also overflowing with:

» **the truth that GOD is our Heavenly FATHER Who is holy, just, loving, merciful, and forgiving**
» **parables communicating truths describing the Kingdom of Heaven**
» **the importance of love, truth, righteousness, mercy, and forgiveness in GOD's Kingdom**
» **instructions on what and how to pray**
» **the importance of reaching out and helping those in need**
» **the exhortation to love GOD and our neighbor**
» **the command to leave judgment in GOD's hands**
» **the counsel to not worry or be afraid**
» **the warning about false preachers and teachers and the temptation of money**

» the accountability we have to CHRIST for what we do with His Word and Gospel
» the unity of FATHER, SON, and SPIRIT
» the ministry of the HOLY SPIRIT after JESUS' ascension
» warnings about the reality of the devil and Hell
» etc.

All of JESUS' teaching is crucial for us in living a solid, wholesome and fruitful life, as we wait for our turn to go to Heaven. We all need to continue reading His Word, growing in His grace and knowledge, and practicing more and more of what He taught.

More about JESUS would I know,
More of His grace to others show,
More of His saving fullness see,
More of His love Who died for me
  More, more about JESUS,
  More, more about JESUS;
  More of His saving fullness see,
  More of His love Who died for me!
"*More About JESUS*" Eliza Edmunds Hewitt (1851-1920)

JESUS the Trainer

In addition to His preaching and teaching in various towns and villages, on mountain sides and lakeshores, CHRIST also focused on instructing and training His disciples. These were the ones who followed Him from place to place. JESUS used every opportunity to help these students to grow in faith and to understand Who He was, the mission He was on, and the many realities of GOD's Kingdom. In the four Gospels we read about these students and the intellectual and practical apprenticeship He poured into them. He prepared them to be evangelists to the world and pastors of His needy and growing flock. He equipped them for their future battles and the crosses that they would need to carry for His Kingdom's sake. He prayed for them and taught them to pray with faith and in accordance with GOD's Word (*Matthew 6:5–15; Luke 22:31–32; John 17:1–26, etc.*). He taught, rebuked, corrected, and trained them. They were His beloved, but often befuddled, students who like us, had a lot to learn. Praise JESUS for His patience with all of us who love Him and are seeking to grow in His grace and knowledge to serve Him and others better.

We are called to be students of CHRIST. JESUS came from Heaven to earth to teach us. There is a lot for each of us to learn about GOD, ourselves, this world we are living in, and the realities of death, judgment, salvation and eternal life. He is the Master Teacher and we are the interns. His Word is full of His teaching, given to enlighten us to live a full and abundant life of repentance, faith, hope, and love as we wait for the ultimate coming of His eternal Kingdom. He trains us to be His representatives to our lost and broken world. He gives us His SPIRIT to guide, encourage, and inspire us in our daily walk with Him.

It is not for us to judge CHRIST's teaching, disregarding what we may not like. Since JESUS is GOD's SON and our SAVIOR and LORD, we need to absorb His words into our hearts, minds, and spirits so they will come to permeate our thoughts, words, and actions, and transform our lives. Those who, in their desire for popularity, detract from CHRIST's teaching by picking and choosing the parts they like and discarding or covering up the rest will end up as enemies of JESUS and of His faithful followers, hating and betraying those who trust in JESUS and His Word (*Matthew 24:10*).

A Compassionate Ministry

As JESUS traveled from village to village preaching and teaching, He was also completely committed to ministering to the needs of the people. As was mentioned in the previous chapter, He healed many who were sick with a wide variety of incurable diseases and handicaps—the blind, deaf, leprous, paralyzed, and many who were possessed by evil spirits. He raised at least three people from the dead—a young man, the only son of a widow *(Luke 7:11–17)*; a twelve-year-old girl, the daughter of Jairus, a synagogue leader *(Luke 8:49–56);* and Lazarus, His friend and host in the village of Bethany *(John 11:1–44)*. He miraculously fed thousands of people, calmed a storm at sea, and walked on the Sea of Galilee. His ministry was conducted with great compassion and wisdom, and with the power of the SPIRIT of GOD.

JESUS' ministry of compassion and healing did not, in any way, alter His central message of the need for all people to repent of their sin and believe in Him. Many people came to JESUS for healing but did not follow His call to repent of their sin. It is written:

> *"**Then He proceeded to denounce the towns where most of His miracles were done, because they did not repent:** 'Woe to you, Chorazin! Woe to you, Bethsaida! For if the miracles that were done in you had been done in Tyre and Sidon, they would have repented in sackcloth and ashes long ago! But I tell you, it will be more tolerable for Tyre and Sidon on the day of judgment than for you. And you, Capernaum, will you be exalted to heaven? You will go down to Hades. For if the miracles that were done in you had been done in Sodom, it would have remained until today. But I tell you, it will be more tolerable for the land of Sodom on the day of judgment than for you.'" Matthew 11:20–24*

It is a gracious blessing from GOD to be healed of diseases and experience His miraculous power revealed in numerous ways in our life and world. We all need to be thankful for His many blessings to each of us, including healings and miracles. However, if we do not repent of our sin, these blessings are only temporary, and in the end the LORD will condemn all who have received His blessings but have not repented and followed Him on the path of faith. Better a humble life, with physical handicaps and illnesses, lived in repentance and faith that leads to eternal life with JESUS than a healthy, wealthy, self-righteous life which leads to condemnation. Better to be like Lazarus than the rich man in the account JESUS testified to in *Luke 16:19–31.*

JESUS' daily life was motivated with compassion for all and occupied with pouring His grace and truth into the lives of everyone He met, so that as many as possible would receive His salvation. JESUS said: *"My food is to do the will of Him who sent Me and to finish His work" (John 4:34).* His daily agenda was doing the good, just, and merciful ministry of loving and obeying His FATHER and helping, loving, forgiving, and instructing those He encountered in His traveling ministry.

JESUS' life in this world was amazing, far beyond that of any man.

Billy Sunday, an evangelist for CHRIST, often quoted Thomas De Witt Talmadge, who wrote in 1894:

"JESUS! JESUS! JESUS!

To many, JESUS CHRIST is only the grand subject of a painting,

> *a heroic theme of a pen,*
> *a beautiful form for a statue,*
> *or a thought for a song.*

But to those who have heard His voice,
> *who have felt His pardon,*
> *who have received His benediction,*
> *He is music—light—joy—hope and salvation—*

a friend who never forsakes, lifting you up
when others try to put you down.
There is no name like His.
It is more inspiring than Caesar's,
more musical than Beethoven's
more eloquent than Demosthenes',
more patient than Lincoln's.
The name of JESUS throbs with all life,
weeps with all pathos,
groans with all pains,
stoops with all love.
Who like JESUS can pity a homeless orphan?
Who like JESUS can welcome a wayward prodigal back home?
Who like JESUS can make a drunkard sober?
Who like JESUS can illuminate a cemetery plowed with graves?
Who like JESUS can make a queen unto GOD out of a lost woman of the street?
Who like JESUS can catch the tears of human sorrow in His bowl?
Who like JESUS can kiss away our sorrow?
I struggle for a metaphor with which to express JESUS.
He is not like the bursting forth of an orchestra,
That is too loud and it might be out of tune.
He is not like the sea when lashed by a storm,
That is too boisterous.
He is not like a mountain canopied with snow,
That is too solitary and remote.
He is the Lily of the Valley;
The Rose of Sharon;
A gale of sweet spices from Heaven.
He is our home.

(Sunday, Billy; Praise: Our Songs and Hymns; Compiled by: John W. Peterson & Norman Johnson; Edited by Norman Johnson; 1979 Singspiration, Division of Zondervan Corporation, Grand Rapids, Michigan 49506)

A Short, But Eternally-Fruitful Life

JESUS' life on our blue planet was short, only thirty-three years—thirty-three years of amazing grace and powerful truth for all people. JESUS said that He was *"the way, the truth and the life" (John 14:6).* Anyone who wants to know the way to GOD and the truth and the fullness of life will find it if they are willing to take an honest, open-minded, open-hearted look at JESUS and His life. JESUS said:

> *"Come to Me, all of you who are weary and burdened, and I will give you rest. All of you, take up My yoke and learn from Me, because I am gentle and humble in heart, and you will find rest for yourselves. For My yoke is easy and My burden is light."* Matthew 11:28–30

JESUS said: *"Come to Me" (Matthew 11:28) and "Follow Me!" (John 21:19).* What do you say?
Pray!

CHAPTER 5

OUR CRUCIFIED CHRIST

"Father, forgive them,
because they do not know what they are doing."
Luke 23:34

The Old Testament Prophecies

K ing David, filled with GOD's SPIRIT, prophesied 1000 years before JESUS came:

"My God, my God, why have You forsaken me?...
Many bulls surround me; strong ones of
Bashan encircle me. They open their mouths
against me — lions, mauling and roaring. I
am poured out like water, and all my bones
are disjointed; my heart is like wax, melting
within me. My strength is dried up like baked
clay; my tongue sticks to the roof of my mouth.
You put me into the dust of death. For dogs
have surrounded me; a gang of evildoers has
closed in on me; they pierced my hands and
my feet. I can count all my bones; people look

and stare at me. They divided my garments among themselves, and they cast lots for my clothing." Psalm 22:1,12–18

About three hundred years later the HOLY SPIRIT inspired the prophet Isaiah to write these words:

"Who has believed our message?
And to whom has the arm of the LORD been revealed?...
He was despised and forsaken by men,
A man of sorrows and acquainted with grief;
And like one from whom men hide their face
He was despised, and we did not esteem Him...
But He was pierced through for our transgressions,
He was crushed for our iniquities;
The chastening for our well-being fell upon Him,
And by His scourging we are healed.
All of us like sheep have gone astray,
Each of us has turned to his own way;
But the Lord has caused the iniquity of us all
To fall on Him...
Like a lamb that is led to slaughter...
He was cut off from the land of the living
For the transgression of my people, to whom the stroke was due...
But the Lord was pleased to crush Him, putting Him to grief;
If He would render Himself as a guilt offering,
He will see His offspring."
Isaiah 53:1–10 NASB

The fulfillment of these words is recorded for us in the accounts of JESUS' crucifixion in **Matthew 27, Mark 15, Luke 23, and John 19.**

A Medical Doctor's Description of Death by Crucifixion

Here is Dr. Truman Davis's description of JESUS' crucifixion from a clinical point of view.

The crucifixion began.

> *Jesus was offered wine mixed with myrrh, a mild analgesic, pain-relieving mixture. He refused the drink. Simon was ordered to place the patibulum on the ground, and Jesus was quickly thrown backward, with His shoulders against the wood. The legionnaire felt for the depression at the front of the wrist. He drove a heavy, square wrought-iron nail through the wrist and deep into the wood. Quickly, he moved to the other side and repeated the action, being careful not to pull the arms too tightly, but to allow some flexion and movement. The patibulum was then lifted into place at the top of the stipes, and the titulus reading "Jesus of Nazareth, King of the Jews" was nailed into place.*
>
> *The left foot was pressed backward against the right foot. With both feet extended, toes down, a nail was driven through the arch of each, leaving the knees moderately flexed. The victim was now crucified.*

On the Cross

As Jesus slowly sagged down with more weight on the nails in the wrists, excruciating, fiery pain shot along the fingers and up the arms to explode in the brain. The nails in the wrists were putting pressure on the median nerve, large nerve trunks which traverse the mid-wrist and hand. As He pushed himself upward to avoid this stretching torment, He placed His full weight on the nail through His feet. Again, there was searing agony as the nail tore through the nerves between the metatarsal bones of this feet.

At this point, another phenomenon occurred. As the arms fatigued, great waves of cramps swept over the muscles, knotting them in deep relentless, throbbing pain. With these cramps came the inability to push Himself upward. Hanging by the arm, the pectoral muscles, the large muscles of the chest, were paralyzed and the intercostal muscles, the small muscles between the ribs, were unable to act. Air could be drawn into the lungs but could not be exhaled. Jesus fought to raise Himself in order to get even one short breath. Finally, the carbon dioxide level increased in the lungs and in the blood stream, and the cramps partially subsided.

The Last Words

Spasmodically, He was able to push Himself upward to exhale and bring in life-giving oxygen.

It was undoubtedly during these periods that He uttered the seven short sentences that are recorded.

The first - looking down at the Roman soldiers throwing dice for His seamless garment: "Father, forgive them for they do not know what they do."

The second - to the penitent thief: "Today, thou shalt be with me in Paradise."

The third - looking down at Mary His mother He said: "Woman, behold your son." Then turning to the terrified, grief-stricken adolescent John, the beloved apostle, He said: "Behold your mother".

The fourth cry is from the beginning of Psalm 22:1 "My God, My God, why have You forsaken Me?"

He suffered hours of limitless pain, cycles of twisting, joint-rending cramps, intermittent partial asphyxiation, and searing pain as tissue was torn from His lacerated back from His movement up and down against the rough timbers of the cross. Then another agony began: a deep crushing pain in the chest as the pericardium, the sac surrounding the heart, slowly filled with serum and began to compress the heart.

The prophecy in Psalm 22:14 was being fulfilled: "I am poured out like water, and all my

bones are out of joint, my heart is like wax; it is melted in the midst of my bowels."

The end was rapidly approaching. The loss of tissue fluids had reached a critical level; the compressed heart was struggling to pump heavy, thick, sluggish blood to the tissues, and the tortured lungs were making a frantic effort to inhale small gulps of air. The markedly dehydrated tissues sent their flood of stimuli to the brain. Jesus gasped His fifth cry: "I thirst". Again we read in the prophetic psalm: **"My strength is dried up like a potsherd; my tongue cleaveth to my jaws; and thou has brought me into the dust of death" (Psalm 22:15 KJV).**

A sponge soaked in posca, the cheap, sour wine that was the staple drink of the Roman legionnaires, was lifted to Jesus' lips. His body was now in extremis, and He could feel the chill of death creeping through His tissues. This realization brought forth His sixth word, possibly little more than a tortured whisper: **"It is finished".** *His mission of atonement had been completed. Finally, He could allow His body to die. With one last surge of strength, He once again pressed His torn feet against the nail, straightened His legs, took a deeper breath, and uttered His seventh and last cry:* **"Father, into Your hands I commit My Spirit".**

Death

The common method of ending a crucifixion was by crurifracture, the breaking of the bones of the leg. This prevented the victim from pushing himself upward; the tension could not be relieved from the muscles of the chest, and rapid suffocation occurred. The legs of the two thieves were broken, but when the soldiers approached Jesus, they saw that this was unnecessary.

*Apparently, to make doubly sure of death, the legionnaire drove his lance between the ribs, upward through the pericardium and into the heart. **John 19:34 states, "And immediately there came out blood and water."** Thus there was an escape of watery fluid from the sac surrounding the heart and the blood of the interior of the heart. This is rather conclusive post-mortem evidence that Jesus died, not the usual crucifixion death by suffocation, but of heart failure due to shock and constriction of the heart by fluid in the pericardium.*

(Davis, C. Truman A Physician Analyzes the Crucifixion. From New Wine Magazine, April 1982.

Originally published in Arizona Medicine, March 1965, Arizona Medical Association; http://www.ghaone.org/crucifix.htm June 6, 2015)

He came for us. He lived for us. He taught us. He served us. He died for us.

He Paid for Our Sin

In His life, JESUS is the ultimate example of the person that GOD created each of us to be. In His death, He became our CHRIST, our SAVIOR, our sacrificial High Priest. He came to die in our place. He came to pay for the guilt or debt of our sin. **This is the heart of our common Christian faith, taught by JESUS to His first followers, and passed on through the testimony of the HOLY SPIRIT in the Bible for all to hear. No one can understand our Christian faith without comprehending this truth of JESUS' death on the cross for all our sin.** John the Baptist testified: *"Here is the Lamb of God, who takes away the sin of the world!" (John 1:29).* This is still the testimony of the faithful church of CHRIST to all people. It is written:

"For I passed on to you as <u>most important</u> what I also received:

<u>that Christ died for our sins according to the Scriptures,</u> that He was buried, that He was raised on the third day according to the Scriptures." Apostle Paul, 1 Corinthians 15:3–4

"<u>For Christ also suffered for sins once for all, the righteous for the unrighteous,</u> that He might bring you to God, after being put to death in the fleshly realm but made alive in the spiritual realm." Apostle Peter, 1 Peter 3:18

"If we say, 'We have no sin,' we are deceiving ourselves, and the truth is not in us. If we confess our sins, He is faithful and righteous to forgive us our sins and to cleanse us from all unrighteousness. If we say, 'We don't have any sin,' we make Him a liar, and His word is not in us. My little children, I am writing you these things so that you may not sin. But if anyone does sin, we have an advocate with the Father — <u>Jesus Christ the Righteous One. He Himself is the propitiation for our sins, and not only for ours, but also for those of the whole world."</u>

Apostle John, 1 John 1:8–2:2

Woe to Those Who Cover Up the Cross

JESUS' death on the cross for our sins is of *"first"* importance, as JESUS and His true prophets and apostles all taught.
**Woe to religious leaders who reject this truth by hiding it
under politically-correct theology rather than proclaiming it
loudly and clearly from the pulpits and in the streets!** The
theological revisionists populating many seminaries and pulpits seek to repackage JESUS and the Christian faith to fit into
their own shallow beliefs. They reject the clear testimony of
GOD's SPIRIT to the reality of human sin and CHRIST's atoning
death for our sin. They are the blind leading the blind.

CHRIST's death for our sin is foundational. Those in seminaries and churches who preach a different Gospel need to
repent before it is too late for them and for those who listen
to them. JESUS said it would be better for them to have a large
millstone chained to their neck and be drowned in the depths
of the sea than to lead others, especially the young, away from
Him *(Matthew 18:6).*

Sin Is the Problem

Humanity's **core problem** isn't nuclear weapons, potential
asteroids, global warming, guns, or a lack of money, food, medicine, jobs, housing, or education. My problem, your problem,
our human problem, is sin. The simple three-letter word "sin"
is lacking in people's vocabulary and understanding and pro-
vokes many into angry tirades.

What is sin? <u>Sin is evil.</u> Sin is rebellion against GOD's
"good, pleasing, and perfect will" (Romans 12:2) as testified
to by the HOLY SPIRIT. When convicted of his sin of adultery
and murder, King David confessed to GOD: *"Against You —
You alone — I have sinned and done this evil in Your sight"*

(Psalm 51:4). David's sin of adultery and murder was not only against Bathsheba and her husband Uriah, but against GOD's will for how we are to treat our brothers and sisters. The Ten Commandments were focused on our relationship to GOD and our relationship to others. **All sin is revolt against GOD's Word concerning the responsibilities He has given us in our relationship with Him and with our neighbor.** Sin against other people is ultimately sin against GOD.

Isaiah proclaimed: *"We all went astray like sheep; we all have turned to our own way" (Isaiah 53:6).* Sin is self-centeredness, accompanied by self-pride and arrogance. Sin is idolatry, the worship of this world and anything in it. Sin is lawlessness, being a law unto ourselves, doing what is right in our own eyes, rather than doing the good will of GOD and fulfilling His purposes. It is loving ourselves and doing what pleases our own egos and desires, without any genuine love for GOD or others.

Satan's central attack on the Christian faith in most churches today comes in the form of omitting the HOLY SPIRIT's testimony in His Word to the reality of our sin and our need of JESUS to save us from it. Calling anything a sin is taboo in sophisticated theological circles today. Everything is tolerable except proclaiming the truth regarding humanity's sin and our desperate need of JESUS to rescue us from it and Hell that it leads to. Beware of false apostles and choreographed churches that cover-up the evil of human sin and remove the message of the cross and CHRIST's blood from their beautifully-decorated entertainment centers, where people can have their ears tickled, their minds deceived, and their pockets picked.

Churches used to be called sanctuaries, with the cross at the center. They were **places of safety through the blood of CHRIST,** where people came to confess their sins, and where CHRIST-GOD was **glorified for His mercy.** Now they are often crossless platforms for the promotion and worship of human goodness and promises of health and wealth. *"See no evil, hear no evil"; "no sin to deal with today"; "nothing to see here"; "let's move on to bigger and more positive things"*— obviously no cross is needed today.

A church that no longer preaches the reality of sin and the cross of CHRIST, boldly and clearly, is a counterfeit church that serves up a smorgasbord of self-righteous religion to a sin-soaked and dying world.

The church that doesn't glory in the cross is a church that doesn't know the SAVIOR.

<u>Sins can be sins of commission or omission</u>. As it is written: ***"So it is a sin for the person who knows to do what is good and doesn't do it" (James 4:17).*** We sin against GOD by doing what we ought not to do, but also by not doing what we ought to do. Those who sincerely believe in CHRIST are called and commanded to study His Word, minister to people, help the needy, and bring the Gospel of CHRIST to all people. We sin and fall short of CHRIST's will by failing to do the good we should be doing. **We daily need forgiveness for our sins of commission, but also for our sins of omission. There is no room for boasting or pride in ourselves. *It is written: "The one who boasts must boast in the Lord" (1 Corinthians 1:31).***
We sin in thoughts, attitudes, words, and actions which are contrary to the perfect will of GOD.

> *"Who perceives his unintentional sins? Cleanse me from my hidden faults. Moreover, keep Your servant from willful sins; do not let them rule over me. Then I will be innocent and cleansed from blatant rebellion. May the words of my mouth and the meditation of my heart be acceptable to You, Lord, my rock and my Redeemer."* **Psalm 19:12–14**

JESUS said:

> *"You have heard that it was said to our ancestors, Do not murder, and whoever murders will be subject to judgment. But I tell you, everyone who is angry with his brother will be subject to judgment. And whoever says to his brother, 'Fool!' will be subject to the Sanhedrin. But whoever says, 'You moron!' will be subject to hellfire... You have heard that it was said, Do not commit adultery. But I tell you,*

82

everyone who looks at a woman to lust for her has already committed adultery with her in his heart."   Matthew 5:21–22, 27–28*

He also said:

"I tell you that on the day of judgment people will have to account for every careless word they speak. For by your words you will be acquitted, and by your words you will be condemned." Matthew 12:36–37

Sin is not only what others do, think, or say—it is what we all do, think, or say too much of the time. Not only do we sin, but we all have a sinful nature that desires to sin and tempts us to sin. It is not only Satan that tempts us to sin, but our self-centered, sinful nature leads us into temptation. As it is written:

"No one undergoing a trial should say, 'I am being tempted by God.' For God is not tempted by evil, and He Himself doesn't tempt anyone. But each person is tempted when he is drawn away and enticed by his own evil desires. Then after desire has conceived, it gives birth to sin, and when sin is fully grown, it gives birth to death." James 1:13–15

"For all have sinned and fall short of the glory of God." Romans 3:23

Sin is what GOD says it is.

Sin is not that which doesn't fit in with our plans or philosophy, or the political correctness of societies bullies. Sin is that which goes against GOD's will, as revealed by His SPIRIT through CHRIST and His written Word. It is crucial to understand that GOD's will revealed in His Word is good. As the Apostle Paul wrote:

> *"So then, the law is holy, and the commandment is holy and just and good... For I know that nothing good lives in me, that is, in my flesh. For the desire to do what is good is with me, but there is no ability to do it. For I do not do the good that I want to do, but I practice the evil that I do not want to do. Now if I do what I do not want, I am no longer the one doing it, but it is the sin that lives in me... What a wretched man I am! Who will rescue me from this dying body? I thank God through Jesus Christ our Lord!"   Romans 7:12,18–20,24–25*

GOD's law and commandments revealed in His Word are righteous and good. The LORD <u>does not</u> give us laws and commands because He wants us to be slaves, but because He desires what is best for us—for each of us and for all humanity. **GOD's will for all of us is to become mature children motivated by love and truth**. As our Creator, CHRIST alone knows what will bring blessing to each of us and all people. He also knows those words, attitudes, and actions which will bring the afflictions of confusion, suffering, and death to us. He desires that our lives will be filled with His amazing blessings that He has saturated our world with, **not** with the curses that spring from disobedience to His good and gracious will. His laws and commands are motivated by love. Tragically our sinful, proud, and self-centered nature desires to "do our own thing" and ignores GOD's purposes and warnings, producing the confusion and destructive forces impacting our world today.

Our sinful nature wants to change GOD's will and His Word to align with our own feelings, thoughts, and plans. The age we are living in is pagan or **pre-Christian—prior to the return of CHRIST and the complete coming of His Kingdom.** Most of the thoughts, attitudes, words, and actions CHRIST and the HOLY SPIRIT testify to as being contrary to GOD's will and purposes are portrayed as normal and good in our bizarre world today. Idolatry, lying, greed, cursing, racism, violence, abuse, gluttony, drunkenness, sexual immorality, pornography, homosexuality, lesbianism, the sacrifice of children both born and unborn, hatred of others, dishonoring of parents, and every other form of sin is promoted as liberating and intellectually, emotionally and physically pleasurable *(Psalm 2:1–3; Romans 1:18–32)*. What GOD declares sinful is camouflaged as enlightened and virtuous by the devil, the world, and our own sinful natures. Instead of humbling ourselves, repenting, and committing ourselves to GOD's will, we seek to change His Word to fit our own opinions. JESUS said: *"So if the light within you is darkness — how deep is that darkness" (Matthew 6:23).* The world's wisdom and values result in confusion and the proliferation of evil that saturates our world today. As the prophet Isaiah proclaimed:

> *"Woe to those who call evil good and good evil, who substitute darkness for light and light for darkness, who substitute bitter for sweet and sweet for bitter. Woe to those who are wise in their own opinion and clever in their own sight!" Isaiah 5:20–21*

> *"and whatever is not from faith is sin." Romans 14:23 NASB*

Without believing and trusting the testimony of CHRIST and the HOLY SPIRIT in His Word, no one can understand what is or isn't sin. Without GOD's SPIRIT and Word to enlighten us, all we have is individual self-righteous opinions of what is good and evil. The consequences are tragic. Many in our world are being trampled under the feet of those who are quick to shed the blood of others in self-righteous zeal for their cravings, vain imaginings, and political and religious ideologies *(Romans 3:15).*

Forgiveness From the Cross

JESUS said: "Father, forgive them, because they do not know what they are doing."
Luke 23:34

The LORD GOD, our Creator, is also GOD our Savior. His mercy and forgiveness are revealed repeatedly throughout His Word and made visible in JESUS' death on the cross for our sin—my sin and yours. *"FATHER forgive them"* was a reference not only to the soldiers who crucified Him or the crowd that was mocking Him, but to every sinner. There is no difference between us. We are all sinners, and we all have the same Creator and Savior Who died for each of us. No matter what your sin or my sin against GOD or others may be, JESUS has paid for it with His Holy Body and Blood. As it is written:

"since there is no distinction. For all have sinned and fall short of the glory of God. They are justified freely by His grace through the redemption that is in Christ Jesus. God presented Him as a propitiation through faith in His blood, to demonstrate His righteousness, because in His restraint God passed over the sins previously committed." Romans 3:22–25

The Apostle Paul testified to this reality in terms of his own life:

"This saying is trustworthy and deserving of full acceptance: 'Christ Jesus came into the world to save sinners' — and I am the worst of them. But I received mercy for this reason, so that in me, the worst of them, Christ Jesus might demonstrate His extraordinary patience as an example to those who would believe in Him for eternal life. Now to the King eternal, immortal, invisible, the only God, be honor and glory forever and ever. Amen." 1 Timothy 1:15–17

Brother Paul recognized the depth of his own sin against the LORD and others. He was a blasphemer and persecutor of those who believed in JESUS, but by faith in CHRIST's death on the cross Paul came to understand the LORD's forgiveness and salvation to him. He correctly reasoned that if GOD could forgive him, then He could and would forgive everyone that comes to His cross for mercy.

"Amazing grace! How sweet the sound that saved a wretch like me." John Newton (1725-1807)

JESUS IS the GOD of amazing grace Who saves every wretch that comes to Him for forgiveness. If you don't recognize your wretchedness, then you simply don't know yourself. You need to listen to the HOLY SPIRIT's words of conviction and grace. The Gospel message of CHRIST's forgiveness and salvation is summed up well in the simple words sung in many languages by children and adults around the world today:

"JESUS loves me! this I know, for the Bible tells me so...

JESUS loves me!

He who died Heaven's gate to open wide;
He will wash away my sin,
Let His little child come in.
Yes, JESUS loves me! Yes, JESUS loves me!
Yes, JESUS love me! The Bible tells me so."

- Anna Bartlett Warner, 1827-1915

This is the bottom line and the starting point of Christian faith. JESUS loves us and demonstrated His love through His life in this world and through His death on the cross for us. He took upon Himself the punishment of death that we each deserve, so that we can have our sins washed away and be transformed into holy children of GOD, prepared for eternal life with Him in the new Heaven and Earth.

Proclaiming the Cross to the Ends of the Earth

After His resurrection, JESUS told His disciples:

"He said to them, 'How unwise and slow you are to believe in your hearts all that the prophets have spoken! Didn't the Messiah have to suffer these things and enter into His glory?' Then beginning with Moses and all the Prophets, He interpreted for them the things concerning Himself in all the Scriptures.... Then He told them, 'These are My words that I spoke to you while I was still with you — that every-thing written about Me in the Law of Moses, the Prophets, and the Psalms must be fulfilled.' Then He opened their minds to understand the Scriptures. He also said to them, 'This is what is written: The Messiah would suffer and rise from the dead the third day, and repentance

for forgiveness of sins would be proclaimed in His name to all the nations, beginning at Jerusalem.'" Luke 24:25–27, 44–47

There is hope for you and me and all people because JESUS died for us. Without His death on our behalf, we would all be destined for death and Hell. Praise the LORD that His SPIRIT is present and working all over our world today to bring the good news of CHRIST's death on the cross for our sins to all nations, just as JESUS prophesied. We are living in that day when the HOLY SPIRIT and the faithful redeemed Church are proclaiming and ministering the good news of repentance for our sin and of faith in JESUS' death on the cross for our forgiveness to the ends of the earth. Every day, through the conviction and testimony of the SPIRIT of Truth, thousands scattered across our global village are coming to humbly acknowledge their sin, their lost condition, and their need of JESUS to save them. Praise the LORD for the millions upon millions of people who have come and are coming to know of the LORD's forgiveness and salvation, and who have testified in word and deed—many with their own blood—to the truth of the cross of JESUS.

We are all sinners. The sooner we admit it, confess our sin to GOD, and place our faith in His mercy and grace to us through CHRIST's death on the cross, the sooner we will be forgiven, rescued from sin, death and judgment, and able to help others to come to a new life of faith, hope, and love in JESUS. While many are closing their ears and turning their backs to the message of the cross of CHRIST, many others are listening and being saved.

"My faith has found a resting place—
Not in device or creed;
I trust the Ever living One—
His wounds for me shall plead.
I need no other argument,
I need no other plea;
It is enough that JESUS died,
and that He died for me."

Lidie H. Edmunds (1851-1920)

"Calvary covers it all,
My past with its sin and stain;
My guilt and despair JESUS took on Him there,
And Calvary covers it all."

Ethel Robinson Taylor (died 1950)

Pray!

CHAPTER 6

OUR RESURRECTED LORD

"I am the resurrection and the life.
The one who believes in Me, even if he dies, will live.
Everyone who lives and believes in Me will never
die — ever."
JESUS, John 11:25–26

Gone Away

Gone, gone, gone away,
Just can't get them back there's no way,
'Cause they're gone, gone away,
we just can't 'em back.

Now Marilyn Monroe she had her silver screen,
Martin Luther King had a dream,
John and Bobby and Gandhi and his band,
They're all gone to some other land.

They're all gone, gone, all gone away,
just can't get them back there's no way

'Cause they're gone, they're all gone away,
we just can't get 'em back.

Matthew, Mark and Ann Boleyn
Cain and Abel and Errol Flynn,
Luke and Janis and Jimmy Dean,
Cleopatra and Augustine, Mussolini and Baby
Snoots, Tom Mix and Gable and Captain Cook,
Uncle Amos, O-O-O Funny Man,
all gone to some other land.

They're all gone, gone, all gone away,
just can't them back there's no way
'Cause they're gone, where they're all gone away,
just can't get 'em back.

Forest Lawn, Flanders Field,
Calvary, a Cross Revealed,
Someone dying, crucified
He died, but yet He came alive.
Thank you, thank you JESUS friend,
Living now and livin' then,
And you come, you come, you come to stay,
Here right now and here always.
Thank you, thank you, thank you JESUS
Thank you, thank you LORD,
Thank you, Thank you JESUS,
You've come to stay.
O Thank you LORD, O Thank you LORD,
I want to thank you LORD
Ya, Ya, Ya Thank you JESUS.
  **-Tedd Smith, Russel Music Co., ASCAP, World
Wide Pictures "Time to Run", 1973.**

From Death to Life

H is body was dead. We are all somewhat acquainted with death through observation. We are familiar with the death of people around us, including those whom we have loved and who have been a big part of our lives in this dimension. The fact that JESUS died was not unique. Only GOD knows the exact number of people who have lived and died in this world from the beginning, but it numbers in the tens of billions. All who lived before the twentieth century have died. CHRIST wasn't the first person to die, nor was He the last.

The Romans developed crucifixion as a way of torturing their enemies to death in a way intended to create fear in the populace. Because it was not uncommon for people to be crucified during the Roman era, most would have seen others dying by crucifixion. The fact that CHRIST died by crucifixion was not unusual. What set JESUS apart was that He did not stay dead! On the third day He rose from the dead. **His resurrection sets Him apart from all other people in history—including religious, political, and philosophical leaders—whose bodies have all died and remained dead. JESUS is LORD over death.**

JESUS' resurrection wasn't a mere revival of life, like the resuscitation of someone who was clinically dead for a brief period. His resurrection body was not His former body revived, but a transformation of it into a new, glorified, eternal body. Neither was His resurrection the result of someone else bringing Him back to life. No one else accomplished JESUS' resurrection. He rose from the dead by His own power.

The Promises of the Resurrection Hope

The hope of the resurrection is the fulfillment of GOD's plan for human life. It was already testified to in the book of Job, possibly the oldest book of the Bible.

"I wish that my words were written down,

93

That they were recorded on a scroll
or were inscribed in stone forever
by an iron stylus and lead!
But I know my living Redeemer,
and He will stand on the dust at last.
Even after my skin has been destroyed,
yet I will see God in my flesh.
I will see Him myself; my eyes will look at Him,
and not as a stranger.
My heart longs within me." Job 19:23–27

Job's incredible testimony was written on a scroll and has been preserved for all people to read or hear about. Despite the suffering he endured, through the disease that Satan inflicted on him and the knowledge that one day he would die, he was looking ahead to the wonderful hope of seeing His Redeemer GOD in the flesh, with his own eyes, in his resurrected body. The LORD our GOD has given us an amazing hope despite the sufferings and challenges we face in this present world.

Even before His own death and resurrection, JESUS proclaimed the hope of the resurrection to the people of His generation. As recorded in **Matthew, Mark,** and **Luke**, JESUS engaged in a verbal exchange with the Sadducees, the liberal theologians of His day, who did not believe in the hope of the resurrection of the dead.

"Jesus told them, 'Are you not deceived because
you don't know the Scriptures or the power of
God? For when they rise from the dead, they
neither marry nor are given in marriage but
are like angels in heaven. Now concerning
the dead being raised — haven't you read in
the book of Moses, in the passage about the
burning bush, how God spoke to him: I am

*the God of Abraham and the God of Isaac and
the God of Jacob? He is not God of the dead
but of the living. You are badly deceived.'"*
Mark 12:24–27

On another occasion, when JESUS spoke about the day of
resurrection, He testified:

*"I assure you: An hour is coming, and is now
here, when the dead will hear the voice of the
Son of God, and those who hear will live. For
just as the Father has life in Himself, so also He
has granted to the Son to have life in Himself.
And He has granted Him the right to pass judgment, because He is the Son of Man. Do not
be amazed at this, because a time is coming
when all who are in the graves will hear His
voice and come out — those who have done
good things, to the resurrection of life, but
those who have done wicked things, to the
resurrection of judgment."*
John 5:25–29

The Initial Doubts about the Resurrection

Those who reject JESUS today can do so only because they
deny His resurrection from the dead. If they believed in His
resurrection, they would know that He is GOD, and that everything else His SPIRIT testifies to is true. Unbelief in CHRIST's
resurrection is not new. It was present from the beginning.

In the Gospel accounts it's clear that the resurrection was
astonishing, shocking, and challenging for the first followers
of CHRIST. Despite His teaching concerning His death and resurrection, the disciples were not expecting Him even to die,

let alone rise from the dead. Like many other Jews, they mis-understood the Old Testament testimony and believed that JESUS, the promised Messiah, would use His powers to over-throw the Romans, establish His Kingdom in Israel, and then reign over all the nations of the world from Jerusalem. As His right-hand men, those first disciples believed that they would reign with Him. When He died on the cross their entire vision of the future was pulverized to dust and they sensed that their own lives were in imminent danger. With JESUS' death, their world crumbled around them. All they could do was hide—try to disappear into the woodwork and hope that no one would remember that they had believed in and followed JESUS.

When Mary Magdalene discovered the empty tomb early on the first day of the week and brought news of JESUS' resur-rection to the disciples, the disciples did not believe her **(Mark 16:11; Luke 24:11).** Even after they saw JESUS alive it took a while for the reality of His resurrection to sink into their minds. It is written:

> *"And as they were saying these things, He Himself stood among them. He said to them, 'Peace to you!' But they were startled and ter-rified and thought they were seeing a ghost. 'Why are you troubled?' He asked them. 'And why do doubts arise in your hearts? Look at My hands and My feet, that it is I Myself! Touch Me and see, because a ghost does not have flesh and bones as you can see I have.' Having said this, He showed them His hands and feet. But while they still were amazed and unbelieving because of their joy, He asked them, 'Do you have anything here to eat?' So they gave Him a piece of a broiled fish, and He took it and ate in their presence.*

Then He told them, 'These are My words that I spoke to you while I was still with you — that everything written about Me in the Law of Moses, the Prophets, and the Psalms must be fulfilled.' Then He opened their minds to understand the Scriptures." Luke 24:36–45 (See also: *Matthew 28:16–20; Mark 16:9–14; Luke 24:25–27; John 20:24– 29)*

Doubting Thomas was not the only follower of CHRIST who had problems believing in JESUS' resurrection. All the disciples struggled to believe, even after seeing Him in His resurrection body. The only difference was that Thomas saw JESUS a week later than the other disciples. After Thomas saw CHRIST he clearly understood what JESUS' resurrection meant. His declaration to JESUS was: *"My Lord and my God!" (John 20:28)* He got that right. **JESUS' resurrection means that He is our LORD and our GOD.**

The Resurrection Catalyst

CHRIST's resurrection from the dead not only validates His claim of being One with GOD, but He is also the *"firstfruits"* (*1Corinthians 15:20–23*) or perfected, resurrected prototype for the resurrection of all who sincerely believe and trust in Him. CHRIST, by His power, rose from the dead with a new, resurrected body, and now promises to all who repent of their sin and trust in Him that He will also raise us from the dead and give us a new, eternal, resurrected body like His. This was and is the hope of everyone who has a sincere faith in CHRIST.

JESUS' resurrection from the dead permanently seals the truth of Who He is, of all that He taught, and of His sacrifice on the cross for our sin. He came for us. He died for us. He rose from the dead for us. It is accomplished. The victory over

sin, death, and Hell has been won by CHRIST for all who sincerely trust in Him.

CHRIST's resurrection from the dead establishes the entire truth of His Word and of our faith in Him. Without JESUS' resurrection there would be no Christian faith today. In response to the doubts of some converts in the city of Corinth, the Apostle Paul highlighted the vital importance of CHRIST's resurrection and ours:

> *"Now brothers, I want to clarify for you the gospel I proclaimed to you; you received it and have taken your stand on it. You are also saved by it, if you hold to the message I proclaimed to you — unless you believed for no purpose. For I passed on to you as most important what I also received: that Christ died for our sins according to the Scriptures, that He was buried, that He was raised on the third day according to the Scriptures...*
>
> *And if Christ has not been raised, your faith is worthless; you are still in your sins. Therefore, those who have fallen asleep in Christ have also perished. If we have put our hope in Christ for this life only, we should be pitied more than anyone...Listen! I am telling you a mystery: We will not all fall asleep, but we will all be changed, in a moment, in the blink of an eye, at the last trumpet. For the trumpet will sound, and the dead will be raised incorruptible, and we will be changed. For this corruptible must be clothed with incorruptibility, and this mortal must be clothed with immortality...Therefore, my dear brothers, be steadfast, immovable, always excelling in*

**the Lord's work, knowing that your labor in
the Lord is not in vain."** *1 Corinthians 15:1–4,
17–20, 51–53, 58*

JESUS' resurrection from the dead—and His promise to give
those who believe and trust in Him eternal life in resurrected
bodies—was the catalyst for the spread of the Gospel message
of salvation through CHRIST. It was the knowledge of CHRIST's
resurrection and the promised hope of their own resurrection
that gave the first apostles the faith to proclaim JESUS despite
the persecution and martyrdom they often faced.

**The hope of the resurrection has been the stimulus that
has propelled the Gospel to all nations.** From the beginning there has been tremendous opposition and persecution
from the world and religious authorities to the proclamation
of JESUS. If it were not for JESUS' resurrection victory for His
people, the Christian Church would not have survived. Without
the hope of eternal life in new, resurrected bodies there would
be no reason to believe in JESUS or to be willing to suffer persecution for believing and following Him. **With the help of
GOD's SPIRIT and the knowledge of CHRIST's resurrection victory, no force on earth, nor the devil himself, has been able
to stop those who know and love JESUS from bringing His
Gospel message of His Kingdom and salvation to all peoples.**
During the past 2000 years the testimony to CHRIST's resurrection and ours has spread from village to village, city to city,
country to country.

How Can Anyone Today Really Believe in the Resurrection?

JESUS said to Thomas:

"Because you have seen Me, you have believed.
Those who believe without seeing are blessed."
John 20:29

How is it possible for people today who weren't witnesses to JESUS' life, death, or resurrection to believe in His resurrection when even His closest followers had difficulty believing and grasping it? The unbelievers, or "skeptics" as they like to refer to themselves, say it is only wishful thinking that leads people to believe in JESUS' resurrection. It is true that wishful thinking results in people believing in all kinds of imaginary ideas—evolution, aliens from other planets, power of crystals, reincarnation, mermaids, leprechauns, etc. Human imagination has no limits, particularly when fueled with ignorance and unbelief in the truth.

Faith in the resurrection of CHRIST is not based on human imagination, but on the clear historical testimony of the HOLY SPIRIT through the eyewitness reports of the early apostles, many of whom were martyred for their faith. They died proclaiming the message of CHRIST's death and resurrection to all who would listen. The HOLY SPIRIT brings this testimony to people all over our world today, helping many to know the truth of JESUS, of Who He is and what He has done for us, including the amazing reality of His resurrection from the dead. The account of the resurrection of CHRIST is not some mythological story blowing in the wind, but the culmination of the historical witness to CHRIST woven through the entire Biblical account. **It is only the HOLY SPIRIT's convicting testimony—to the reality of our sin, to our need of CHRIST to save us, and of**

His life, death, and resurrection—that enables an individual to believe and receive Him as SAVIOR and LORD.

CHRIST's resurrection from the dead fits in perfectly with His amazing life and ministry.

> *"Jesus performed many other signs in the presence of His disciples that are not written in this book. But these are written so that you may believe Jesus is the Messiah, the Son of God, and by believing you may have life in His name."* **John 20:30–31**

Through the SPIRIT's witness, people from all walks of life, cultures, races, religious and non-religious backgrounds, young and old, a few rich and many poor are coming into the knowledge of CHRIST, including the knowledge of the resurrection to eternal life. **It is a stunning reality to behold—a clear testimony to the present working of GOD's SPIRIT all over our world.**

How is it possible for anyone to believe in a new resurrected body? As JESUS said: *"What is impossible with men is possible with God!" (Luke 18:27).* Only by trusting in GOD's amazing power and wisdom can anyone believe in the hope of receiving a new, resurrected body. JESUS pointed out to the religious unbelievers of His day, the Sadducees, that they didn't believe in the resurrection because they didn't believe in the infinite power of GOD or the testimony of His Word **(Matthew 22:29).**

From a fallen, human perspective, the resurrection is an impossibility. If human life was only an evolved form of atoms and molecules, with no essential identity beyond the material itself, then there would be no soul in need of a new body. Thus, for the many materialistic skeptics around us, the resurrection is impossible for there is no person to be resurrected. Most people, however, recognize that we are not only flesh and blood, but we have a mind and spirit—a fact that GOD's SPIRIT clearly reveals in His Word. When we die, our bodies return to the dust, but our spirits which GOD created and breathed into us **(Genesis 2:7)** live on, waiting to receive a new, resurrected body to unite with. This will happen to both believers and unbelievers before the Day of Judgment. *(John 5:28–30)*

The promise of GOD, of which CHRIST's resurrection is the beginning, is that He will create new, eternal, human bodies for our eternal spirits to live in. How is that possible? It is no more impossible for GOD to create new, eternal bodies for us than it was for Him to create these bodies in which our spirits now live. These bodies of dust that we are now occupying are amazing beyond all human ability to create or even to comprehend. They are miraculous. No other word can describe them. These present bodies are awesome creations of our infinitely-wise GOD, a fact I highlighted in the book *GOD IS! Why evolution isn't*. If a person is willing to acknowledge the reality of the eternal, infinite GOD, then they should perceive that He could certainly create new eternal bodies for us to live in, after our present bodies have disintegrated back to the dust they were created from. This is what CHRIST has demonstrated for us by His resurrection.

Those who don't believe in JESUS' resurrection, or of the general resurrection of the dead on the last day, are badly mistaken and blinded by their unbelief in GOD, in CHRIST, and in His power and mercy. They live without hope beyond the grave. They are missing out on the fullness of life that He gives now and for all eternity.

Praise Be to GOD—FATHER-SON-HOLY SPIRIT

"Praise the God and Father of our Lord Jesus Christ. According to His great mercy, He has given us a new birth into a living hope through the resurrection of Jesus Christ from the dead

and into an inheritance that is imperishable, uncorrupted, and unfading, kept in heaven for you. You are being protected by God's power through faith for a salvation that is ready to be revealed in the last time. You rejoice in this, though now for a short time you have had to struggle in various trials so that the genuineness of your faith — more valuable than gold, which perishes though refined by fire — may result in praise, glory, and honor at the revelation of Jesus Christ. You love Him, though you have not seen Him. And though not seeing Him now, you believe in Him and rejoice with inexpressible and glorious joy, because you are receiving the goal of your faith, the salvation of your souls." 1 Peter 1:3–9

Throughout our world, every Sunday and every day of the week, millions upon millions of those who trust in JESUS gather together in small and large fellowships, indoors and outdoors, in hospitals, prisons, orphanages, homes, schools, and church buildings to praise GOD—FATHER, SON, and HOLY SPIRIT. We glorify the LORD for the amazing truth of His death and resurrection for us, and the hope, joy, and peace that this gives amid our struggles in this world. After His ascension back into Heaven, JESUS disciples were filled with joy and praise. This joy and praise has continued in the lives of believers for almost 2000 years.

"After worshiping Him, they returned to Jerusalem with great joy. And they were continually in the temple complex praising God." Luke 24:52–53

Despite the ridicule and persecution, more and more people, like the early disciples, are continually worshiping the LORD our GOD for CHRIST's resurrection and for ours. Praise is cascading forth from all points on our globe. Will you join with the holy angels and all the LORD's people on earth in glorifying Him for His amazing grace and powerful resurrection hope?

JESUS loves you and me. He died to forgive us for our sin. He rose from the dead to give us the knowledge of an eternal, resurrected life with Him in His eternal Kingdom. Trust in JESUS, confess your sins to Him, and receive His joy and hope into your heart and mind.

Pray!

PART 2

JESUS IS! IN HEAVEN CONTINUING HIS WORK ON OUR BEHALF

"So when they had come together, they asked Him,
'Lord, are You restoring the kingdom to Israel at this time?'
He said to them,
'It is not for you to know times or periods that the Father
has set by His own authority.
But you will receive power
when the Holy Spirit has come on you,
and you will be My witnesses in Jerusalem,
in all Judea and Samaria, and to the ends of the earth.'
After He had said this,
He was taken up as they were watching,
and a cloud took Him out of their sight.
While He was going, they were gazing into heaven,
and suddenly two men in white clothes stood by them.
They said, 'Men of Galilee,
why do you stand looking up into heaven?
This Jesus, who has been taken from you into heaven,
will come in the same way
that you have seen Him going into heaven.'"
Acts 1:6–11

CHAPTER 7

OUR INTERCEDER

*"Therefore, since we have a great high priest who has
passed through the heavens — Jesus the Son of God —
let us hold fast to the confession.
For we do not have a high priest who is unable
to sympathize with our weaknesses,
but One who has been tested in every way as we are,
yet without sin.
Therefore let us approach the throne of grace with boldness,
so that we may receive mercy and find grace
to help us at the proper time."
Hebrews 4:14–16*

What Now?

JESUS came into our world as a human being. He lived the
perfect life of love and obedience. He died on the cross
for our sin. He rose from the dead to destroy the power of
death and give us the knowledge of the resurrection to eternal
life. He left this world and returned to Heaven. He came, He
conquered, He left. **But why did He go?** Why did He choose
not to stay with us in this chaotic world and to begin to build

His eternal Kingdom with His resurrection power? This is what His first disciples wanted and were expecting. GOD's thoughts and plans are higher—and always better— than ours (*Isaiah 55:8-9*).

Before His death, resurrection, and ascension back to Heaven, JESUS taught His followers that He would be leaving them, what He would be doing while He was gone, and what He wanted them to do before He would return. Here is part of JESUS' teaching in this area:

"If you love Me, you will keep My commands. And I will ask the Father, and He will give you another Counselor to be with you forever. He is the Spirit of truth. The world is unable to receive Him because it doesn't see Him or know Him. But you do know Him, because He remains with you and will be in you. I will not leave you as orphans; I am coming to you....

But the Helper, the Holy Spirit, whom the Father will send in My name, He will teach you all things, and bring to your remembrance all that I said to you. Peace I leave with you; My peace I give to you; not as the world gives do I give to you. Do not let your heart be troubled, nor let it be fearful...

When the Counselor comes, the One I will send to you from the Father — the Spirit of truth who proceeds from the Father — He will testify about Me. You also will testify, because you have been with Me from the beginning...

But now I am going away to Him who sent Me, and not one of you asks Me, 'Where are

You going?' Yet, because I have spoken these things to you, sorrow has filled your heart. Nevertheless, I am telling you the truth. It is for your benefit that I go away, because if I don't go away the Counselor will not come to you. If I go, I will send Him to you. When He comes, He will convict the world about sin, righteousness, and judgment...

I still have many things to tell you, but you can't bear them now. When the Spirit of truth comes, He will guide you into all the truth. For He will not speak on His own, but He will speak whatever He hears. He will also declare to you what is to come. He will glorify Me, because He will take from what is Mine and declare it to you. Everything the Father has is Mine. This is why I told you that He takes from what is Mine and will declare it to you."

John 14:15–18; 15:26–27; 16:5–8, 12–14

It's important to understand that even though His followers would no longer be able to see or touch His resurrected body in this life, He did not abandon them or us. He was leaving them so that His HOLY SPIRIT would come to be with them and live in them. His HOLY SPIRIT would teach, guide, and empower them to be His witnesses to our world. In His resurrected physical body JESUS could be in only one place at a time, which would not allow Him to be with His faithful followers everywhere in our world. His HOLY SPIRIT, working in the spiritual dimension, is with all His followers all the time.

CHRIST carefully explains this to His disciples before His crucifixion in *John 14–16*. GOD the FATHER had a plan, and JESUS was fulfilling the plan. He came and completed His mission of living the perfect life of love, sacrificing His body on a cross for our sin, and winning the victory over death through His resurrection. With His work here completed, He needed to leave so that the HOLY SPIRIT could come and live with—and in—His faithful followers, and through them bring the message of CHRIST and His salvation to all nations.

The Mission Age

JESUS' instructions to His followers regarding the work they were to do after He left them are summed up in what is called the Great Commission:

> *"Then Jesus came near and said to them, 'All authority has been given to Me in heaven and on earth. Go, therefore, and make disciples of all nations, baptizing them in the name of the Father and of the Son and of the Holy Spirit, teaching them to observe everything I have commanded you. And remember, I am with you always, to the end of the age.'"*
> *Matthew 28:18–20*
> *(Matthew 24:13–14, 45–51, 25:14–46; Mark 16:15–20; Luke 24:45–49; Acts 1:1–11)*

For nearly 2000 years, the HOLY SPIRIT and the Bride, the faithful church, have been bringing this good news of CHRIST and His forgiveness and eternal life to all peoples and to the ends of the earth. This can be best characterized as the mission age, which has been a cleansing, preserving stream through the Roman Age, Dark Ages, Middle Ages, Industrial Age, and our present Information Age. Through the ages, by the presence and ministry of GOD's HOLY SPIRIT, the good news of JESUS and His salvation and Kingdom has gone from Jerusalem, through Israel, Samaria, and to the ends of the earth. It has been a phenomenal and miraculous expansion of the LORD's Kingdom into all the kingdoms of this world, from one village, town, city, and country to another.

The devil and his demonic and human agents of chaos have not been able to stop the growth of the LORD's Kingdom on our planet *(John 1:5)*. Satan's strategy of creating confusion in the church through a myriad of false, gnostic teachings and through the persecution of JESUS' faithful followers hasn't derailed the steady advancement of the Gospel in every direction. The good news of JESUS' life, death, and resurrection has been like a tide of living water that washes over every continent, bringing many lost souls into His abundant and eternal life.

A thousand years before JESUS' first coming, through His servant David, the HOLY SPIRIT announced:

> *"All the ends of the earth*
> *will remember and turn to the Lord.*
> *All the families of the nations*
> *will bow down before You,*
> *for kingship belongs to the Lord;*
> *He rules over the nations.*
> *All who prosper on earth will eat and bow down;*
> *all those who go down to the dust*
> *will kneel before Him —*
> *even the one who cannot preserve his life.*
> *Their descendants will serve Him;*
> *the next generation will be told about the Lord.*
> *They will come and tell a people yet to be born*
> *about His righteousness — what He has done."*
> *Psalm 22:27–31*

The battle for souls is not diminishing. It is intensifying worldwide in preparation for the LORD's second coming. JESUS said:

*"This good news of the kingdom will be pro-
claimed in all the world as a testimony to
all nations. And then the end will come."
Matthew 24:14*

**The LORD calls all who sincerely believe in and love Him
to commit to helping to fulfill this mission as we wait for His
return.** We will look more closely at this incredible mission in
the last chapter of Part 3.

JESUS is Praying for Us

While believers, inspired by GOD's SPIRIT, are engaged in
the Great Commission, what is JESUS doing? What has He
been doing since He returned to Heaven?

In *John 17* the HOLY SPIRIT has preserved for us the prayer
JESUS prayed the evening before He was arrested. This prayer
contains many of the essential elements of JESUS' continuing
intercession for all who sincerely believe in Him. His prayer
was that:

➢ He would be glorified through the salvation of people—
  verses 1–5
➢ we would believe in Him and hold to His Word, be sanctified by His Word, dedicated to doing His will—verses
  6–8, 17–19
➢ we would be protected from the evil one and his many
  lies—verses 9–16
➢ we would live in His love aFTnd in unity with Him and
  all sincere believers—verses 20–23, 25–26
➢ we would be with Him in His eternal Kingdom to experience His love and see His glory— verses 3 & 24

CHRIST prayed for everyone who would believe in Him.
He prayed:

"I pray not only for these, but also for those who believe in Me through their message." (John 17:20)

This is a powerful prayer that all who sincerely trust in JESUS can join Him in praying. Since He ascended into Heaven, He continues to speak to GOD our FATHER on our behalf. The HOLY SPIRIT testifies:

"Who is the one who condemns? Christ Jesus is the One who died, but even more, has been raised; He also is at the right hand of God and intercedes for us." Romans 8:34

"Therefore, He is always able to save those who come to God through Him, since He always lives to intercede for them." Hebrews 7:25

"My little children, I am writing you these things so that you may not sin. But if anyone does sin, we have an advocate with the Father — Jesus Christ the Righteous One. He Himself is the propitiation for our sins, and not only for ours, but also for those of the whole world." 1 John 2:1–2

Repeatedly in His Word, the SPIRIT testifies that CHRIST is at the FATHER's Right Hand, speaking on our behalf. He is there for us. We are all weak and vulnerable in this fallen, confused world. All of us need CHRIST's intercession on our behalf. As the African American spiritual says: *"It's me, it's me, it's me O LORD, standing in the need of prayer."* Without CHRIST we would have no way to approach the FATHER, since none of us is righteous in and of ourselves. Every time we pray, we enter GOD's presence with JESUS in front of us. We can approach

GOD in prayer only in and through CHRIST's invitation and sac-rifice for us—His blood covering our sin and His righteousness radiating in us.

It is the SPIRIT of CHRIST in us that cries out, *"Abba! Father!" (Romans 8:15; Galatians 4:6)* for ourselves and for others. As the followers of JESUS, we are repeatedly encouraged to pray for ourselves and others, even those who mistreat us. This is good and pleasing to GOD. We are being like CHRIST when we pray for each other, for He is continually praying for all of us.

CHRIST prays for us even when we fail Him. JESUS said to Peter on the night when He was arrested:

> *"Simon, Simon, look out! Satan has asked to sift you like wheat. But I have prayed for you that your faith may not fail. And you, when you have turned back, strengthen your brothers."*
> *Luke 22:31–32*

Just as CHRIST prayed for Simon Peter, so He is interceding for all who believe in Him, even when our faith is small and failing. **Take time to thank JESUS for His continual advocacy on your behalf.**
Pray!

CHAPTER 8

THE GREAT ARCHITECT AND CREATOR OF THE ETERNAL HOME FOR HIS BRIDE

JESUS said:

"Your heart must not be troubled.
Believe in God; believe also in Me.
In My Father's house are many dwelling places;
if not, I would have told you.
I am going away to prepare a place for you.
If I go away and prepare a place for you,
I will come back and receive you to Myself,
so that where I am you may be also."
John 14:1–3

JESUS IS Praying and Working at the Same Time

JESUS is praying and working for us in Heaven. Praying and working always go together. What is JESUS working at in Heaven? His mind and heart are focused not only on

115

the spreading of His Kingdom on Earth but on creating a new Heaven and a new Earth, an eternal home for His people.

My understanding of the background to JESUS words in **John 14:1–3** is that He used an analogy from the marriage customs of His generation. In that day, after becoming engaged, a bridegroom would typically leave his fiancé and begin to build a home for his bride and himself on his father's land. This home was often attached to his father's house. Until he returned, the bride waited, prepared, and longed for his coming. The groom worked diligently and enthusiastically to complete the home for his bride. When the home was finished the groom would excitedly return for his bride, at which time they would be married and live—united in love—in their new home.

In a delightful thread of revelation running through the Old and New Testaments, the HOLY SPIRIT speaks about GOD/CHRIST as the bridegroom and His faithful people as His bride. Here are a few Old Testament references to this analogy— **Song of Solomon; Isaiah 54:5, 62:5; Jeremiah 2:2, 3:14–20, 31:32; Ezekiel 16:32; Hosea 2:1–16.** In the Old Testament GOD was the Husband and Lover. In the New Testament JESUS is the Bridegroom.

JESUS, the Enthusiastic Groom

In the New Testament, John the Baptist, the prophet sent by GOD to prepare the way for the coming of CHRIST, testified to CHRIST as the Bridegroom:

> *"No one can receive a single thing unless it's given to him from heaven. You yourselves can testify that I said, 'I am not the Messiah, but I've been sent ahead of Him.' He who has the bride is the groom. But the groom's friend, who stands by and listens for him, rejoices greatly at the groom's voice. So this joy of*

mine is complete. He must increase, but I must decrease.'" (John 3:27–30)

> If only we who call ourselves friends and servants of CHRIST today would have this same humble attitude of John the Baptist. Our ministry should always be to point others to JESUS, so that, as His servants and friends, we fade into the background and JESUS the bridegroom becomes the focus. People should be coming to their local congregations or parishes to hear more and more about JESUS. People don't have to know our name or who we are. They need to know the name of JESUS, Who He is, and what He has done for them and for all of us.
>
> LORD, forgive us for seeking to draw attention to ourselves rather than encouraging others to focus on You. LORD, help us to become less that You might become greater.

JESUS used this analogy of a bride and bridegroom several times to express His relationship to His followers:

> *"Jesus said to them, 'Can the wedding guests be sad while the groom is with them? The time will come when the groom will be taken away from them, and then they will fast.'"*
> *Matthew 9:15*

To illustrate what GOD's Kingdom is like, JESUS tells the parable of a king who gave a wedding feast for his son (*Matthew 22:1–14*). He also uses the illustration of ten virgin bridesmaids waiting for the bridegroom to come to celebrate the wedding as a parallel to His followers waiting for His return to our world (**Matthew 25:1–13**).

The Apostle Paul clearly understood this parallel of CHRIST and His bride, the church, as he teaches on the husband and wife relationship in **Ephesians 5:22–33**. He carefully explains how husbands should love their wives sacrificially as CHRIST loved and died for His Bride, the Church. On her part, the wife should love, respect, and obey her husband as the church should love, respect, and obey CHRIST. *(As an aside here, don't be commanding or demanding of your husband or wife to perfectly fulfil the LORD's instructions on their responsibilities in marriage. We often fail each other and need to forgive each other as JESUS forgives us (Colossians 3:13). Rather, focus your attention on being the husband or wife that GOD has called you to be. This is the most important key to a blessed marriage.)*

The verses that seal this parallel are found in the HOLY SPIRIT's testimony in **Revelation** where it is written:

> *"Then I heard something like the voice of a vast multitude, like the sound of cascading waters, and like the rumbling of loud thunder, saying: Hallelujah, because our Lord God, the Almighty, has begun to reign!*
> *Let us be glad, rejoice, and give Him glory, because the marriage of the Lamb has come, and His wife has prepared herself.*
> *She was given fine linen to wear, bright and pure. For the fine linen represents the righteous acts of the saints.*
> *Then he said to me, 'Write: Those invited to the marriage feast of the Lamb are fortunate!'"*
> ***Revelation 19:6–9***

In the very last chapter of the Bible, the faithful Church is referred to as the Bride of CHRIST— *"Both the Spirit and the bride say, 'Come!'" (Revelation 22:17).* How many people will accept GOD's invitation to come to faith in CHRIST, be saved, and participate in the wedding celebration in Heaven? Only GOD knows the exact number, but we are told by the SPIRIT that it will be a multitude of people from every *"nation, tribe, people, and language" (Revelation 7:9).* A remnant from nations down through history will come together into a multitude of saved people, and into the arms of CHRIST. Then the consummation celebration of CHRIST with His Holy Bride will commence and never end.

JESUS is the excited, enthusiastic Bridegroom that can hardly wait for the time when He can be married and bring His Bride, His saved and holy people, into the eternal paradise that He is preparing for us.

The Construction Phase

Forty days after His resurrection, JESUS ascended into Heaven, to the Home of His FATHER, where He is creating or constructing an eternal home paradise for His Bride, His faithful people. The LORD has been working as the architect, engineer, and builder of our eternal home. No one can fully comprehend the dynamic splendor of this new Heaven and Earth. It will be an eternal wonder that dwarfs the wonders of our present universe and world. As His SPIRIT testifies, the reality of this new Heaven and Earth which JESUS is busy creating for us now will surpass anything that we can presently imagine *(1 Corinthians 2:9).* The last two chapters of Revelation give us a glimpse into this new, abundant, and eternal life.

"Then I saw a new heaven and a new earth, for the first heaven and the first earth had passed away, and the sea no longer existed. I also saw

> *the Holy City, new Jerusalem, coming down out of heaven from God, prepared like a bride adorned for her husband.*
> *Then I heard a loud voice from the throne: Look! God's dwelling is with humanity, and He will live with them.*
> *They will be His people, and God Himself will be with them and be their God.*
> *He will wipe away every tear from their eyes. Death will no longer exist; grief, crying, and pain will exist no longer, because the previous things have passed away. Then the One seated on the throne said, 'Look! I am making everything new.' He also said, 'Write, because these words are faithful and true.'"*
> **Revelation 21:1-5**

I encourage you to read through the last two chapters of the Bible prayerfully, allowing the SPIRIT of JESUS to fill your mind with the vision of this incredible new paradise that He is constructing for us. There is no need to argue over the interpretation of how literal or symbolic the description is—the reality will be exceedingly greater than these words describe. It will be grander than golden streets and precious jewel crystals. It is the Holy City with the perfect Garden.

The beauty of this new Heaven and Earth is only an outward indication of the glory of the loving and honoring relationship that GOD—FATHER-SON-HOLY SPIRIT— has with His people, and that we will have with all the other citizens of His Kingdom— our brothers and sisters and our spiritual angel relatives. It is the complete fulfillment of JESUS' prayer for us in *John 17*.

The new Heaven and Earth is the holy and eternal Kingdom where JESUS, the KING of KINGS, reigns in love and righteousness, and His citizens live in love and obedience to their KING.

He fills us with joy in His presence, and with eternal pleasures from His right hand *(Psalm 16:11).* Here we will spend eternity in our resurrected bodies, experiencing the wonders of His love, the fellowship of the saints and angels, and the fulfillment of loving and serving Him and each other.

CHRIST created our present world and universe in all its glory in six days, to last for at least 6000 years. For 2000 years He has been creating our forever-after home. As I highlighted in *GOD IS! why evolution isn't*, our present world and universe are an awesome creation overflowing with a googolplex of miraculous realities. Nevertheless, as the saying goes—**"we ain't seen nothin yet"**. For it is written:

> *"What eye did not see and ear did not hear,*
> *and what never entered the human mind —*
> *God prepared this for those who love Him."*
> *1 Corinthians 2:9*

We wait with eager expectation for the End, to be held in the arms of CHRIST, and to see His glory in the eternal home He is creating for those who love Him. JESUS prayed:

> *"Father, I desire those You have given Me to be*
> *with Me where I am.*
> *Then they will see My glory, which You have*
> *given Me because You loved Me before the*
> *world's foundation."* *John 17:24*

JESUS' prayer will soon be fulfilled. Amen!

Pray!

PART 3
JESUS IS! THE RETURNING KING OF KINGS AND LORD OF LORDS

"And He has a name written on His robe and on His thigh:
KING OF KINGS AND LORD OF LORDS."
Revelation 19:16

CHAPTER 9

COMING SOON, READY OR NOT

"He who testifies about these things says,
'Yes, I am coming quickly.'
Amen! Come, Lord Jesus!
The grace of the Lord Jesus be with all the saints. Amen."
Revelation 22:20-21

Mysteries and Revelations

There have been widely different interpretations of some aspects of JESUS' return, such as the timing or number of Raptures, the identity of the Antichrist, etc. As with JESUS' first coming, we won't know all the details until they are upon us. We need to be awake, waiting and watching, seeking the help of GOD's SPIRIT to discern these events as they develop around us.

The LORD has not given me a special vision or revelation concerning His coming return. However, to you and me and all who will read and listen, He has given all the information we need in His Word to prepare us for His coming. Most people make a lot of preparations to get ready for company. JESUS

125

isn't just a brother and a friend, He is also our KING and LORD. It is crucial for all of us to be prepared. The basic promise and outline of JESUS' return is firmly set forth in His Word. My hope and prayer is that these basic truths of CHRIST's coming will be clearly presented in this section, and that we will all get ready for His return.

There are many mysteries concerning JESUS' return. I'm not going to try to explain those mysteries, but rather to share what the LORD has clearly revealed in His Word, as proclaimed through the prophets, apostles, and the faithful church over the past 2000 years. I do not consider myself an expert on the LORD's Second Coming. I am a disciple or student of CHRIST, seeking to learn more and more about JESUS, including His return, and seeking to pass on these basic truths to others as the LORD enables me. No matter how many years we may have believed in and followed JESUS, we remain His disciples, with much more to learn. **Praise the LORD for His patience with all of us.**

Wait for the LORD

"Wait for the Lord; be strong and courageous. Wait for the Lord." Psalm 27:14

"I wait for Yahweh;
I wait and put my hope in His word.
I wait for the Lord
more than watchmen for the morning —
more than watchmen for the morning."
Psalm 130:5–6

I first began to think about JESUS' return when I was a teenager. There was much I did not comprehend then and much that I still don't comprehend now—but I knew that nothing could be better for sincere believers than CHRIST coming back

126

to put an end to the evil in our world and establish His righteous, just, and loving Kingdom. Like all true believers, I have been waiting for His return since I first learned about it. We know that the timing of His return is not up to us. His plan is perfect, so we patiently and eagerly wait.

Pursuing GOD's Will While We Wait

Waiting isn't sitting around twiddling our thumbs. Waiting is pursuing GOD's gracious will for our lives. Since no one knows the exact date of the LORD's return, all true believers live by faith that His return is drawing near and seek His purposes for each day. As we wait for the LORD, we seek to fulfill our GOD-given responsibilities to our families, our congregations, our communities, and our global village.

For many, especially young adults, this includes seeking the LORD's direction on marriage and family. The Apostle Paul wrote so clearly on this matter some 2000 years ago. It is best for all believers to listen and pray through these words the HOLY SPIRIT gave:

> *" Now concerning virgins I have no command of the Lord, but I give an opinion as one who by the mercy of the Lord is trustworthy. I think then that this is good in view of the present distress, that it is good for a man to remain as he is. Are you bound to a wife? Do not seek to be released. Are you released from a wife? Do not seek a wife. But if you marry, you have not sinned; and if a virgin marries, she has not sinned. Yet such will have trouble in this life, and I am trying to spare you." 1 Corinthians 7:25-28 (NASB)*

As a young adult believer, I was willing to be *"a bachelor until the rapture"*, if that was the LORD's will. At the same time, I hoped to be able to meet some wonderful gal and raise a family—if the LORD's return wasn't going to happen for a while. I know that many young adult CHRIST-followers today have similar thoughts and dreams regarding this world and the return of JESUS. On the one hand, you desire the LORD to return to end the incredible chaos and evil in our world, but on the other hand, you desire the opportunity to experience the blessings of marriage and family. Life in our world has many blessings, but also many sorrows. If the LORD returns in our time, it will be to spare those who believe in Him from the sorrows that would come if He did not return.

Although marriage and family are a tremendous blessing, they are not necessary to have a fulfilling life in CHRIST. JESUS, not our spouse or children, is the source of the abundant and eternal life. Whether we are married or single, the LORD should occupy the center of our lives, and nothing can surpass His will for us now and in His Kingdom to come. His desire is to fill our lives with eternal blessings beyond comprehension, and that can only be fulfilled when He comes.

We wait for JESUS to return and for the abundant and eternal life with Him and all the saints in His coming glorious Kingdom. In the meantime, our lives as followers of JESUS are filled with being faithful wives, husbands, mothers, fathers, brothers, sisters, employees or employers, and sharers of His grace and truth. Life in JESUS is overflowing for all, single or married, who will walk with Him into His eternal future.

Repent for the End is Near!

As a teenager, I saw a man at a bus depot in Edmonton, Alberta, Canada, carrying a sign that read: *"Repent, for the end is near!"* Most of us have seen that kind of sign somewhere, or at least in some Hollywood movie where the message was scoffed at. I don't know what is in the hearts and minds of those who hold those cardboard signs, or what kind of impact those signs have on those passing by. I don't pass judgment on the sign-bearers, but I hope that they have done what their signs say, so they are prepared for the end through personal faith and trust in CHRIST. The message is true regarding our lives in this world, but it misses the focus of JESUS' words— ***"Repent, because the kingdom of heaven has come near!"*** *(Matthew 4:17).* It is best for all of us, including those holding up signs, to live repentant, humble lives, sharing GOD's grace and truth with others, even as we look forward to the eternal future with Him. We need to live our lives here in the light of JESUS' eternal Kingdom, which is already present by faith, and which will soon come in all its completeness and visibility.

The end of our life in this world is near. Life is short. Death and Hades or Heaven are only one breath away. The conclusion of our world is also drawing near. The writing on the wall is coming into focus even as the world's leaders take the role of cheerleaders for the coming antichrist and his global empire. We all need to repent and get prepared because the LORD is coming soon.

I'll be Back

Arnold Schwarzenegger gained worldwide fame through the *Terminator* movies with his phrase: *"I'll be back!"* Those words were meant to encourage those he had come to save, and to be a warning to his enemies. It was part of the script— he would return and put an end to the evil forces who were seeking to destroy and enslave people. It is tragic that so many are fascinated with the Hollywood mythologies of our generation, but miss the truth concerning our real Savior. As it is written, ***"They will turn away from hearing the truth and will turn aside to myths" (2 Timothy 4:4).***

JESUS is the only Savior of people, and the only Terminator of all evil. He came into our world to rescue the enslaved and dying from the evil powers of sin, death, and the devil. When He left our world some 2000 years ago, He made the promise that one day He would return, not only to rescue His people but also to bring His judgment on the evil rebellion against Him and His Kingdom. **His promise was and is a tremendous encouragement for those who believe in Him, but also a clear warning to the world and its leaders that He will soon come and deal with them.** It is written:

> *"So now, kings, be wise; receive instruction,*
> *you judges of the earth.*
> *Serve the Lord with reverential awe and*
> *rejoice with trembling.*
> *Pay homage to the Son or He will be angry and*
> *you will perish in your rebellion,*
> *for His anger may ignite at any moment.*
> *All those who take refuge in Him are happy!"*
> *Psalm 2:10–12*

When JESUS returns, His wrath will flare up and consume the enemies of His people and Kingdom. These words of CHRIST, and of His prophets and apostles are both sweet and bitter—sweet for those who believe in Him, love Him, and are waiting for Him to come, but bitter for those who reject Him and live in the delusion that He isn't coming back. We choose whether JESUS' return will be bitter or sweet.

If Those Days Were Not Cut Short, No one Would Survive

For the first time in recorded human history, humanity has the technological capability of destroying most life forms on our planet, particularly human life. The latest scientific

Frankensteinian experiments—to create black holes, alter the human genome, create hybrid human-animal combinations (Chimeras), and develop more powerful weapons of mass extinction— are just the tip of the iceberg of the potential for humanity's self-destruction. During my lifetime, some of the loudest voices warning of the end of the world have come from within the scientific community. The Doomsday Clock is never far from twelve midnight.

Over the past 50 years, our planet has gone through a series of fears for the end:

◊ **in the 1960s it was the potential for global nuclear destruction**

◊ **in the 1970s it was the coming of an ice age and a population explosion**

◊ **in the 1980s it was AIDS and other plagues that were agents of mass death**

◊ **in the 1990s it was the depletion of the ozone layer and being fried by the sun**

◊ **in the 2000s it was fears of global warming and rising oceans**

◊ **and the 2010s have seen a return to global hostilities, worldwide terrorism, and the incitement of a new world war waged with nuclear, chemical, biological, laser, and EMP (electromagnetic pulse) weapons**

All these potential doomsday events have generated fear among the masses.

A few lonely voices out there have been willing to point out that the greatest threats to human life come from the scientific and technological "advances" themselves. There is no greater threat to humanity than the development of human technology which, though neutral, is capable of destroying human life and is often manipulated to that end. Separated from GOD, the heart of man is self-destructive. Sooner or later, all human knowledge is used for arrogant destructive purposes.

From 1984-2008, thousands of top scientists and engineers from all parts of our world collaborated to construct the largest machine in the world. The CERN Collider is approximately twenty-seven kilometers long and had an initial cost of about ten billion dollars. It was constructed approximately one hundred and seventy-five meters below ground along the border between Switzerland and France, just a short distance from Geneva. It was designed to perform experiments on the basic particles of the universe by propelling them at just under the speed of light to collide with each other. Some of their recent experiments included trying to discover parallel universes and creating miniature black holes. Although many scientists are excited by the information gained from these experiments, at least a few secular physicists and others have expressed concerns over the potential danger these experiments pose for our planet and the very structure of the universe itself. The late Dr. Stephen Hawking, considered the world's leading physicist, expressed some grave concerns regarding some of these experiments—

> "The Higgs potential has the worrisome feature that it might become megastable at energies above 100bn giga-electron-volts (GeV). This could mean that the universe could undergo catastrophic vacuum decay, with a bubble of the true vacuum expanding at the speed of light. This could happen at any time and we wouldn't see it coming." Dr. Stephen Hawking
> (Stephen Hawking Says 'God Particle' Could Wipe Out the UniverseBy Kelly Dickerson, Staff Writer | September 8, 2014 02:21pm ET www.livescience.com/47737-stephen-hawking-higgs-boson-universe-doomsday)

It is also noteworthy that the statue in front of the CERN headquarters is of Lord Shiva, the Hindu god of the cycle of creation and destruction. He is dancing on the body of a baby. (www.quora.com/ Why-is-there-a-Shiva-god-of-destruction-statue-on-CERNs-front-lawn)

Whether it is by way of the CERN collider or through nuclear, chemical, biological, or other doomsday weapons being developed, the reality is that, for the first time in history, people have developed the technological ability to destroy much, if not all, of this incredible world that GOD created for us. As followers of JESUS, we do not have to be afraid that humanity will destroy itself, for CHRIST has made it clear that He will intervene before that happens. JESUS said:

> *"For at that time there will be great tribulation, the kind that hasn't taken place from the beginning of the world until now and never will again! Unless those days were limited, no one would survive. But those days will be limited because of the elect." Matthew 24:21–22*

Humanity is on the cliff's edge of self-annihilation. It is difficult to imagine a clearer fulfillment of these words than the situation developing on our planet today. **The global events of our generation ought to be trumpet blasts calling everyone to repent of our sin and turn our hearts to GOD and to one another.** It is crucial to remember that the LORD maintains this world—it will not be destroyed by anything humanity does. He Himself will bring His judgment on our world before people are able to destroy it. **Our world will not end with a whimper or a bang— but by His judgment.**

While some of the world's scientific and political leaders see the writing on the wall and are engaged in a frantic, albeit misguided, effort to gather humanity into a global society to solve the crises our human race is in, much of the church has appallingly hushed up the clear warnings, promises, and testimony of CHRIST and the HOLY SPIRIT to His return. Without the return of CHRIST to look forward to, the world is left without any hope except to turn to the antichrist and his delusional humanistic utopia. Praise the LORD that He will intervene before humanity destroys itself.

While our world rushes headlong towards self-destruction, it is crucial for all who believe in JESUS to understand His promises and warnings regarding His second coming, and to prepare ourselves and others for the LORD's soon return. JESUS said: **"Therefore be alert, since you don't know what day your Lord is coming" (Matthew 24:42).**

Whether we are ready or not, JESUS is coming soon! Blessed are those who hear the message of the LORD's soon return and take it to heart!

Pray!

CHAPTER 10
THE FULFILLMENT OF THE PROMISES AND WARNINGS

"As God is faithful,
our message to you is not Yes and no.'
For the Son of God, Jesus Christ,
who was preached among you by us...
did not become 'Yes and no';
on the contrary, a final 'Yes' has come in Him.
For every one of God's promises is 'Yes' in Him.
Therefore, the 'Amen' is also spoken through Him by us for
God's glory."
2 Corinthians 1:18–20

The Promise Keeper

C HRIST's return is the ultimate confirmation of His iden-tity and the complete fulfillment of the teachings and promises of His Word. JESUS said that He would completely fulfill GOD's Word, and it will happen soon. Everyone who knows JESUS knows that He keeps His promises, unlike the sham saviors of this world. **At the very core of the nature of GOD is His faithfulness to His Word and His people. He is**

135

trustworthy, and His Word is true. As it is written*: "**Lord, Your word is forever; it is firmly fixed in heaven" (Psalm 119:89).** Nothing can prevent GOD from accomplishing every teaching and promise in His Word. It is a solid rock to build our lives on, and a guide to prepare us for His return and the coming of His eternal Kingdom. As JESUS said:

> *"For I assure you: Until heaven and earth pass away, not the smallest letter or one stroke of a letter will pass from the law until all things are accomplished."* **Matthew 5:18**

GOD—the FATHER, SON, and HOLY SPIRIT—has promised that JESUS is coming again. GOD is faithful and has the infinite power to fulfill all the promises that He has made.

JESUS' return will be a surprise for the world—but for those who have believed in Him and trusted His Word and promises, it will be the time when our faith will become sight and our joy immeasurable. JESUS said to His followers:

> *"So you also have sorrow now. But I will see you again. Your hearts will rejoice, and no one will rob you of your joy."* John 16:22

The Old Testament Prophesies of CHRIST's Return

In this chapter we are focusing on the promises and warnings of His return which flow through His Word. Even in the Old Testament, many of the promises or prophesies of CHRIST's coming to our world refer to what the New Testament identifies as His Second Coming.

Many prophesies, such as this passage from Isaiah, point to both His first and second coming:

"For a child will be born for us, a son will be given to us, and the government will be on His shoulders. He will be named Wonderful Counselor, Mighty God, Eternal Father, Prince of Peace. The dominion will be vast, and its prosperity will never end. He will reign on the throne of David and over his kingdom, to establish and sustain it with justice and righteousness from now on and forever. The zeal of the Lord of Hosts will accomplish this."
Isaiah 9:6–7

These verses are usually associated with Christmas and the celebration of JESUS' birth. Since then His kingdom has grown and spread, so that people in all nations are coming to know JESUS as their Wonderful Counselor, Mighty GOD, Everlasting FATHER, and Prince of Peace. The complete fulfillment of this passage will come only when JESUS returns, and His reign and government are established over all peoples.

There are many Psalms that point to CHRIST: *Psalms 2, 21, 22, 23, 31:5, 45:6–7, 69:9, 69:21, 72, 89:19–29, 110, 118:13–29, etc.* These Psalms are partially fulfilled in JESUS' first coming but will not be completely fulfilled until His return. *Psalm 96* proclaims the LORD's message of creation, salvation, and His coming to judge the world in His righteousness and truth:

"Let the heavens be glad and the earth rejoice;
let the sea and all that fills it resound.
Let the fields and everything in them exult.
Then all the trees of the forest will shout for
joy before the Lord, for He is coming —
for He is coming to judge the earth.
He will judge the world with righteousness
and the peoples with His faithfulness."
Psalm 96:11–13

The Day of the LORD

From the beginning of the Old Testament, the LORD's faithful servants proclaimed the Day when the LORD would come to judge the entire world. Enoch, who lived in the seventh generation after Adam *(Genesis 5)* and while Adam was still living, proclaimed the LORD's coming to judge the world for its evil:

> *"And Enoch, in the seventh generation from Adam, prophesied about them:*
> *'Look! The Lord comes with thousands of His holy ones to execute judgment on all and to convict them of all their ungodly acts that they have done in an ungodly way, and of all the harsh things ungodly sinners have said against Him.'" Jude 14–15*

The prophet Daniel also received significant visions or dreams from the LORD pertaining to historical events before the LORD's first and second comings to our world *(Daniel 7–12).* Zechariah and Malachi, the last two prophets in the Old Testament, testified to the second coming of CHRIST with these words:

> *"A day of the Lord is coming when your plunder will be divided in your presence... On that day His feet will stand on the Mount of Olives, which faces Jerusalem on the east. The Mount of Olives will be split in half from east to west, forming a huge valley, so that half the mountain will move to the north and half to the south... On that day there will be no light; the sunlight and moonlight will diminish. It will be a day known only to Yahweh, without day or*

night, but there will be light at evening. On that day living water will flow out from Jerusalem, half of it toward the eastern sea and the other half toward the western sea, in summer and winter alike. On that day Yahweh will become King over all the earth — Yahweh alone, and His name alone." Zechariah 14:1,4,6–9

"'See, I am going to send My messenger, and he will clear the way before Me. Then the Lord you seek will suddenly come to His temple, the Messenger of the covenant you desire — see, He is coming,' says the Lord of Hosts. But who can endure the day of His coming? And who will be able to stand when He appears? For He will be like a refiner's fire and like cleansing lye. He will be like a refiner and purifier of silver...

'For indeed, the day is coming, burning like a furnace, when all the arrogant and everyone who commits wickedness will become stubble. The coming day will consume them,' says the Lord of Hosts, 'not leaving them root or branches. But for you who fear My name, the sun of righteousness will rise with healing in its wings, and you will go out and playfully jump like calves from the stall.'"
Malachi 3:1–3, 4:1–2

The "He" Who is coming is JESUS, Who is the LORD Almighty. Zechariah's and Malachi's prophecies focus on the coming of the Day of the LORD, which is testified to by many Old Testament prophets including Isaiah, Ezekiel, Joel, Amos, Obadiah, and Zephaniah. In the Old Testament, the Day of the LORD referred to the time of the LORD's judgment on the world, which is partially fulfilled in past historical events, but will be totally accomplished on that great Day when CHRIST will descend with His holy ones, the angels of Heaven and the saints who have lived before us *(1 Thessalonians 4:13–18).*

The Second Coming of JESUS is Revealed and Concealed in the Old Testament

Since many Old Testament Messianic prophecies focus on JESUS' second coming rather than His first coming, there was much confusion regarding His first coming. The Jewish scholars and people did not perceive that there would be two comings of the Messiah, one to bring salvation and one to bring His judgment on the world and to establish His Eternal Kingdom. In His wisdom, GOD revealed—but also concealed—this truth in the Old Testament.

When we approach the city of Calgary from the east, the Rockies appear to be right behind the city. In reality these incredibly huge mountains are about sixty miles (one hundred kilometers) beyond the city. It was similar for the prophets given foresight into the future coming of JESUS. Their glimpse of the future cross and empty tomb was overshadowed by their vision of CHRIST's glorious eternal reign in power after it. They saw this as one picture and did not realize there would be a significant period of time between these events. This only becomes clear in the teaching of CHRIST through His Apostles.

The New Testament Promises of CHRIST'S Return

The testimony of CHRIST and His Apostles in the New Testament connects the dots for us, so we understand that the Day of the LORD spoken of in the Old Testament is referring to the Day of JESUS' return. The seed concerning JESUS' second coming had been cultivated and sown in the Old Testament, but it is only through CHRIST and His Apostles that the plant begins to germinate and develop.

There are over three hundred references to JESUS' return in the New Testament, some of which we will mention in future chapters. It is lamentable that so many churches and people who call themselves by CHRIST's name no longer believe in the second coming of CHRIST in His resurrected, glorified body. **Only the willfully blind or deceived could miss the LORD's promise of His return.**

Some of the realities JESUS focused on in teaching His disciples during the week before His crucifixion were the promises, signs, and warnings of His final coming to our world. ***Matthew 24–25, Mark 13, Luke 21, and parts of John 14–17*** are concentrated on the truth of His return to our world. CHRIST spoke clearly to His followers concerning His departure from this world and promised that at some point He would return to be with them forever. The disciples did not understand these words of JESUS until after His resurrection and ascension back into Heaven.

The Rapture—Rising to Meet JESUS in the Clouds

JESUS said:

> *"Then the sign of the Son of Man will appear in the sky, and then all the peoples of the earth will mourn; and they will see the Son of Man coming on the clouds of heaven with power and great glory. He will send out His angels with a loud trumpet, and they will gather His elect from the four winds, from one end of the sky to the other." Matthew 24:30–31*

Part of the promise of JESUS' return is the rapture of the saints to meet Him in the sky. The faithful believers will be lifted or "beamed up" to meet JESUS in the clouds when He returns. The Apostle Paul also testified to this reality:

> *"Since we believe that Jesus died and rose again, in the same way God will bring with Him those who have fallen asleep through Jesus. For we say this to you by a revelation from the Lord: We who are still alive at the Lord's coming will certainly have no advantage over those who have fallen asleep. For the Lord Himself will descend from heaven with a shout, with the archangel's voice, and with the trumpet of God, and the dead in Christ will rise first. Then we who are still alive will be caught up together with them in the clouds to meet the Lord in the air and so we will always be with the Lord. Therefore encourage one another with these words."*
>
> *1 Thessalonians 4:14–18*

> *"Listen! I am telling you a mystery: We will not all fall asleep, <u>but we will all be changed, in a moment, in the blink of an eye, at the last trumpet. For the trumpet will sound, and the dead will be raised incorruptible, and we will be changed.</u> For this corruptible must be clothed with incorruptibility, and this mortal must be clothed with immortality. When this corruptible is clothed with incorruptibility, and this mortal is clothed with immortality, then the saying that is written will take place:*
>
> *Death has been swallowed up in victory. Death, where is your victory? Death, where is your sting?*

Now the sting of death is sin, and the power of sin is the law. But thanks be to God, who gives us the victory through our Lord Jesus Christ!"
1 Corinthians 15:51–57

That will be quite the incredible experience for the saints who come with CHRIST— and for the faithful who are living in our world at that time. The Rapture is the miraculous event promised by CHRIST and His Apostles—when He gives new resurrected bodies to all true believers living in the world and raises them to meet Him and the angels and saints in the sky. It is interesting to note that science fiction fans have no problem believing that, at some point in the future, objects and people will be teleported through space by humanity's scientific knowledge, but most do not believe that GOD can suspend gravity or teleport people to meet Him in the clouds. They foolishly believe that humanity's intelligence and power are greater than GOD's. They do not know GOD, His Word, or His infinite power. **His promise is sure. Wait for it.**

My understanding from the Word of the LORD is that the rapture of His people will take place at the sounding of the last and seventh trumpet (*1 Corinthians 15:51–52*; *Revelation 11:15–19)*, immediately before the angels begin to pour out the seven bowls of wrath onto the global empire of the antichrist. Nevertheless, I acknowledge that other faithful followers and servants of the LORD believe that the rapture will take place earlier. We can all rest in Him and His perfect plan. GOD has the power and wisdom to fulfill every Word He declares.

While believers may disagree on the exact timing there is no doubt that the HOLY SPIRIT has revealed the truth of the rapture to us. There is no excuse for believers in JESUS not to know about the rapture or believe in it. JESUS is coming back soon, and when He does, those who are faithfully waiting for Him will be the first to see Him in His glory, with the holy angels and the multitude of the saints that have preceded them.

"What a day that will be
when my JESUS I shall see,
And I look upon His face –
the One who saved me by His grace"
- Jim Hill, 1955

What the Mockers Choose Not to Understand

The Apostle Peter also wrote unambiguously concerning the LORD's return and the scoffers who would mock His second coming—

"First, be aware of this: <u>Scoffers will come in the last days to scoff, living according to their own desires</u>, saying, 'Where is the promise of His coming? Ever since the fathers fell asleep, all things continue as they have been since the beginning of creation.' They willfully ignore this: Long ago the heavens and the earth were brought about from water and through water by the word of God. Through these waters the world of that time perished when it was flooded. But by the same word, the present heavens and earth are stored up for fire, being kept until the day of judgment and destruction of ungodly men. Dear friends, don't let this one thing escape you: <u>With the Lord one day is like a thousand years, and a thousand years like one day. The Lord does not delay His promise, as some understand delay, but is patient with you, not wanting any to perish but all to come to repentance.</u>" 2 Peter 3:3–9

I want to highlight two truths, declared here by the HOLY SPIRIT through the Apostle Peter, regarding JESUS' promise to return to our world:

> ➤ **Firstly, we need to understand that *"time"* for the LORD in eternity is different from our experience of time in our present world.** When the LORD says in the last verses of Revelation that He is coming soon (***Revelation 22:20***), He is speaking from the Biblical perspective of *"soon"*, not that of a three-year-old child. GOD is not being slow, just patient with our world, giving opportunity for people down through history to repent and believe. **Praise the LORD for His amazing patience with our fallen world**. If JESUS had returned when His first followers were waiting for Him to come, the people who have lived and died through faith in Him during the past 1900 years, including us, would never have existed or received eternal life through Him.

> ➤ **Secondly, we all need to remember what the scoffers deliberately forget. GOD created the world and universe through the power of His Word, and He will bring it to an end according to His Word.** Scoffers are those who do not believe that what the LORD says in the Bible is true. They choose not to believe that GOD created our world or that GOD's SON came into our world 2000 years ago to be our Savior, and therefore, they certainly do not expect Him to come back. To scoffers, JESUS is just a dead man, not their Creator or Savior or Risen LORD. They are blind and deaf and refuse to consider the truth concerning who JESUS is, what He did, and what He will do in the future.

Tragically, many church preachers these days, who preach and teach for money and the approval of people, join the world in scoffing at JESUS' return. They know the promise of

145

His return, but they choose not to believe that He is really coming back again. They are like the servants in JESUS' parable who quit believing that their lord was going to return and began to live like those who didn't know their lord *(Matthew 24:45–51)*. Their end is not a "better place".

The LORD tells us that He has not returned to our world yet because He is patient and giving people time to repent and come to faith in Him. How much longer will His patience with our world last? How much more time will He give before He comes to judge the living and the dead? Time is rapidly running out for our increasingly bizarre degenerate world. The HOLY SPIRIT calls both the world and the Church to get ready to meet Him.

The Final Word of Revelation

In the last book in His Word, all twenty-two chapters are focused on the LORD's return and the events that happen before and after His return. Revelation opens with these words, which we should plant deeply in our minds and hearts—

> *"The Revelation of Jesus Christ, which God gave Him to show to His bond-servants, the things which must soon take place; and He sent and communicated it by His angel to His bond-servant John, who testified to the word of God and to the testimony of Jesus Christ, even to all that he saw. Blessed is he who reads and those who hear the words of the prophecy, and heed the things which are written in it; for the time is near." Revelation 1:1–3 (NASB)*

GOD gives great blessing to those who read and meditate on His many promises and teachings regarding His return. Only those who read and believe in His promised return will be waiting for Him and carrying out the various aspects of the work of His Kingdom when He comes.

Even though the book of Revelation is filled with much symbolism or imagery—for which knowledge of other parts of the Bible is helpful—its basic message is a clear testimony to CHRIST and His return. For those who do not know JESUS as their Crucified SAVIOR and Risen LORD, the book of Revelation often produces foreboding and fear. For those who love Him, it is a message of comfort and incredible hope.

> Revelation is not a negative book, as many perceive it to be, but a book of eternal hope and joy. In its verses we are given glimpses of where human history is headed and how CHRIST will intervene to bring His people into His eternal paradise. The hope and joy of Revelation is not found in humanity overcoming sin and evil and creating a humanistic utopia on Earth, as the antichrist will deceptively proclaim, but in the reality that before the human race completely destroys itself JESUS will return and end the reign of evil. Just as JESUS was the only One able to save us from our sin, so He alone can put an end to evil in our world and usher in His Promised Kingdom.

"Amen! Come LORD JESUS!" Revelation 22:20

In response to CHRIST's promise of His soon return, all who sincerely believe in JESUS and love Him respond by calling Him to come. **By faith in CHRIST, in Who He Is, what He has already done for us, and what He promises to those who**

believe in Him, His people are waiting and praying for Him to come as soon as possible. No one knows the day or hour when JESUS is going to fulfill His promise to return—but He has given His people an abundance of promises regarding His Second Coming and He has given the world plenty of warnings. Soon the promises and warnings will all be fulfilled.

    Pray!

CHAPTER 11
ISRAEL'S KING

"Pilate also had a sign lettered and put on the cross.
The inscription was:
JESUS THE NAZARENE THE KING OF THE JEWS."
John 19:19

"But to Israel He says:
'All day long I have spread out My hands
to a disobedient and defiant people'...
So that you will not be conceited, brothers,
I do not want you to be unaware of this mystery:
A partial hardening has come to Israel
until the full number of the Gentiles has come in.
And in this way all Israel will be saved, as it is written:
The Liberator will come from Zion;
He will turn away godlessness from Jacob.
And this will be My covenant with them
when I take away their sins."
Romans 10:21, 11:25–27

Israel, O Israel

The momentous events transpiring in the country of Israel today are signs pointing to the LORD's soon return. The history and present existence of Israel are clear indicators testifying to the amazing plan of GOD. GOD's preservation of the Jewish people and the re-emergence of the nation of Israel— after almost 2600 years of being oppressed and scattered throughout the nations of the world— are remarkable by any standards. For those with spiritual eyes to see, these signs are miraculous.

There is much debate among sincere Christian believers regarding Israel and its role in the prophesies pertaining to JESUS' return. Many books have been written in this area, and I encourage everyone to carefully study the Scriptures and the prophesies in this area. David R. Barnhart's latest book, *Living in the Times of the Signs,* has abundant, up-to-date information on the fulfillment of various prophecies related to the LORD's return, including much involving Israel.

In today's apocalyptic times, take careful note of the events transpiring in the country of Israel. Pray that the people of Israel will recognize JESUS as their Messiah—and receive Him as LORD in their lives.

LORD of All Nations

It is written:

> *"From one man He has made every nationality to live over the whole earth and has determined their appointed times and the boundaries of where they live. He did this so they might seek God, and perhaps they might reach out and find Him, though He is not far from each one of us. For in Him we live and move*

**and exist, as even some of your own poets
have said, 'For we are also His offspring.'"
Acts 17:26–28**

This year—2018—is the seventieth anniversary of the
re-establishment of the nation of Israel. Ever since Israel
proclaimed its Declaration of Independence on May 14, 1948,
there has been an ongoing physical, spiritual, and moral
struggle between the Palestinians, Muslims and the people
of Israel over this tiny piece of real estate in the Middle
East. Israel is the focus of much of the world's attention in
our present generation, and the object of intense spiritual
hatred on the part of numerous people in all nations. This has
been expressed in frequent wars, intifadas, terrorist attacks,
boycotts, and countless UN resolutions.

Before we jump into the dispute over Israel, it is
important to begin closer to home. My country of temporary
residence is Canada. Who does Canada belong to? Does it
belong to us? The Queen? The First Nations peoples? The
English? The French? The immigrants from many countries
who have now made Canada their temporary home? How
far back do we go? Who or what determines ownership of a
piece of land? Military might? The United Nations? Money?
Is possession nine-tenths of the law of ownership? Who
establishes and enforces the law of ownership? Who decides
what is right or just?

The above questions are as relevant to Israel or Palestine
as they are to Canada, or any other part of the world. How far
back in history should we go in our attempt to unravel the mystery of who has the right to this little chunk of rock?

Who owns the land? GOD does! It is written: **"The earth
and everything in it, the world and its inhabitants, belong to
the Lord" (Psalm 24:1).** As the Creator of our world, it belongs
to Him. In His sovereignty He can give it to whom He chooses—
when He chooses. It is His to give.

Our lives in this world are short. We never really own any land; we are simply tenants who live on it for a few fleeting years. The nations of the world are constantly fighting over little pieces of land they can possess for only a few brief moments. Land in this world is a temporary gift for our present blessing, but our hope is in the eternal land which the LORD has promised to all who trust in Him. As Scripture says of Abraham:

> *"By faith he stayed as a foreigner in the land of promise, living in tents with Isaac and Jacob, co-heirs of the same promise. For he was looking forward to the city that has foundations, whose architect and builder is God."*
> *Hebrews 11:9–10*

The Covenant with Abraham and His Descendants

After the global flood, GOD called and led Abraham to the land He had chosen and promised to give to him and to his descendants, the land we call Israel *(Genesis 12)*. Abraham had two sons. The first son, Ishmael, was conceived as a result of Abraham's unbelief. Ishmael became the father of the Arab peoples, which include the Palestinians. The second son, Isaac, was conceived by Abraham's faith in GOD's promise *(Hebrews 11:11)*. Isaac was the father of Jacob, whose name GOD changed to Israel. The descendants of Israel and the descendants of Ishmael both claim to be the rightful heirs of this land that GOD promised to Abraham and his descendants. Through Moses, and then through Joshua, GOD made it clear that He gave this tiny piece of real estate to the Twelve Tribes of Israel, the descendants of Jacob. **It is crucial to note, however, that the LORD did not leave the descendants of Ishmael homeless, but gave them the entire remainder of the Middle East. The area which God gave the descendants of Ishmael is more than two hundred times the size of Israel and contains**

vast resources of oil and gas (_Genesis 21:8-21_). Here are the approximate sizes of these nations:
    Israel - 21,000 square kilometers
    Saudi Arabia - 2,150,000 square kilometers
    Iran – 1,650,000 square kilometers
    Iraq - 437,000 square kilometers
    Syria - 185,000 square kilometers
    Jordan – 90,000 square kilometers

GOD's Historical Covenant with Israel Was Not Unconditional

The LORD's gift of this tiny piece of land as the inheritance to the descendants of Jacob was part of His covenant with them, and it was conditional according to the terms of the covenant. Through Moses, and other Old Testament prophets, GOD warned Israel repeatedly that if they were unfaithful to Him and became like the idol-worshiping nations around them, He would allow other nations to drive them out and possess the land. Before they even entered the Promised Land, Moses declared to the people of Israel:

> *"See, today I have set before you life and prosperity, death and adversity. For I am commanding you today to love the Lord your God, to walk in His ways, and to keep His commands, statutes, and ordinances, so that you may live and multiply, and the Lord your God may bless you in the land you are entering to possess. But if your heart turns away and you do not listen and you are led astray to bow down to other gods and worship them, I tell you today that you will certainly perish and will not live long in the land you are entering to possess across the Jordan. I call heaven and earth as*

> *witnesses against you today that I have set*
> *before you life and death, blessing and curse.*
> *Choose life so that you and your descendants*
> *may live, love the Lord your God, obey Him,*
> *and remain faithful to Him. For He is your life,*
> *and He will prolong your life in the land the*
> *Lord swore to give to your fathers Abraham,*
> *Isaac, and Jacob." Deuteronomy 30:15–20*

Here is another warning given by Moses, and echoed by other prophets as well:

> *"Then the Lord will scatter you among all peo-*
> *ples from one end of the earth to the other, and*
> *there you will worship other gods, of wood and*
> *stone, which neither you nor your fathers have*
> *known. You will find no peace among those*
> *nations, and there will be no resting place*
> *for the sole of your foot. There the Lord will*
> *give you a trembling heart, failing eyes, and*
> *a despondent spirit." Deuteronomy 28:64–65*
> *(See also Deuteronomy 4:27; Nehemiah 1:8;*
> *Psalm 44:11, 106:27; Jeremiah 9:16, 30:11;*
> *Ezekiel 5:10, 12:15, 20:23, 22:15, 36:19;*
> *Zechariah 7:14, 10:9; etc.)*

The people of Israel did govern the land periodically for a few hundred years from about 1300– 600 BC. With the passing of time, and the hardening of their hearts, they rebelled against the LORD and His Word by adopting the worship of idols and the evil practices of the pagan nations surrounding them. The LORD, Who is always faithful to His Word, removed His protection and allowed their enemies to dominate them. For the last 2600 years, the descendants of Israel have lived as servants of foreign occupiers in Israel or as exiles scattered throughout the nations of the world. GOD's words have certainly been literally fulfilled in the history of the Jewish people.

GOD's Plans for Israel Today

Miraculously—after 2600 years of being in exile or being dominated by alien powers— the descendants of Israel, according to the LORD's sovereign will, were reestablished in the land the LORD promised to Abraham. Never in world history has a nation, conquered and scattered among all nations, maintained its identity and become re-established 2600 years later. This is a clear sign of the sovereign will of GOD and the truth of His Word.

Here are just a couple of the many Old Testament prophesies that foretell the re-gathering of the Jewish people to Israel:

"This is what the Lord God says: Though I sent them far away among the nations and scattered them among the countries, yet for a little while I have been a sanctuary for them in the countries where they have gone...I will gather you from the peoples and assemble you from the countries where you have been scattered, and I will give you the land of Israel." Ezekiel 11:16–17

"For the Israelites must live many days without king or prince, without sacrifice or sacred pillar, and without ephod or household idols. Afterward, the people of Israel will return and seek the Lord their God and David their king. They will come with awe to the Lord and to His goodness in the last days." Hosea 3:4–5

JESUS IS! Why life isn't futile

*(See also Psalm 107:2–3; Isaiah 11:10–12,
66:8; Jeremiah 23:3–6, 30:3–4, 31:8; Ezekiel
20:34, 36:24–35; Joel 3:1–3; etc.)*

GOD's warning to the people of Israel that they would be scattered to the ends of the earth has been fulfilled—now His promise to gather them from the ends of the earth and bring them back to Israel is in the process of being accomplished. Jewish people are facing increasing oppression and persecution in all nations of the world. Every year more Jewish people are driven by fear, or by yearning for their own homeland, to return to Israel from all the countries in which they had settled. It's estimated that more than forty percent of Jewish people in our world have already returned to Israel in the first seventy years of its existence. More are on their way. CHRIST always keeps His promises—even when, because of humanity's sin, these promises take a few thousand years to be fulfilled.

The People of Israel Continue to Fulfill GOD's Word

Many believe that the return of Jacob's descendants to Israel fulfills JESUS' words regarding the fig tree in Matthew 24. In speaking of the events of His return, JESUS said:

"Now learn this parable from the fig tree: As soon as its branch becomes tender and sprouts leaves, you know that summer is near. In the same way, when you see all these things, recognize that He is near — at the door! I assure you: This generation will certainly not pass away until all these things take place. Heaven and earth will pass away, but My words will never pass away." Matthew 24:32–35

The LORD's reference to the fig tree in speaking about the timing of His return is notable. In the Old Testament the fig tree was associated with the nation of Israel *(Deuteronomy 8:8; Isaiah 9:10; Hosea 9:10)*. Accordingly, these words of JESUS have been interpreted to mean that the generation that sees the budding of the nation of Israel after its dormancy will not pass away before all the prophesies concerning His return are fulfilled. Therefore, many believe that JESUS will return to our world within a generation after 1948, the year the nation of Israel budded again after being dormant for 2600 years. If this is the proper interpretation of JESUS' words, then our generation will be witnesses of all the events leading to His return. A generation is anywhere from seventy to one hundred twenty years.

It is important to recognize that this is an interpretation, not a clear teaching of His Word. Even though it appears to be a probable explanation, it is not the only way these words can be understood. It is also possible that CHRIST is using the fig tree, which was common then, to illustrate that the generation that sees the beginning of the events of the very last days will not pass away before His return. The bottom line is that, since no one fully understands all the details of the LORD's return, all who truly believe in Him should always live in the anticipation of His coming. Whether in reference to Israel or to the other signs JESUS spoke about, the fig tree certainly appears to be budding—pointing all of us to His soon return.

It is obvious that the people of Israel did not receive the land back on account of their returning to the LORD and His Word. Israel was re-established in 1948 as a secular nation, and many of its citizens are atheistic or agnostic, with no commitment to being the LORD's people or obeying His Word. **GOD has once again given the Jewish people this piece of land, not because they are more noble or righteous than the Palestinian people, but to fulfill His promises and the**

prophesies of His Word pertaining to Israel's future in conjunction with the second coming of CHRIST.

It's no accident that Israel is the center of attention in our world today. The following Scriptures all make it clear that Israel and Jerusalem will be the focus of many events occurring in the last days before CHRIST's return:

> ➢ JESUS' reference to *"the abomination that causes desolation" (Matthew 24:15)* that will take place in the Holy Place in Jerusalem
> ➢ the lesson from the fig tree *(Matthew 24:32–35)*
> ➢ the Apostles' testimony to the antichrist's declaration of godhood in the Temple (*2 Thessalonians 2:4*)
> ➢ the two Witnesses' testimony to CHRIST in the Holy City *(Revelation 11:1-12)*

JESUS is Israel's MESSIAH KING

In His mercy, the LORD is bringing Jacob's physical descendants back to Israel in the last days to lead them back to Himself. It is crucial for the physical descendants of Abraham to come to know JESUS as their Passover Lamb and their Messiah King, and to receive His SPIRIT into their lives. For 2000 years most Jewish people have rejected JESUS as their Savior and King. In the last days, as Israel becomes the focus of the world's antagonism, a remnant of Jewish people will hear the Gospel, turn their hearts to the LORD, and receive JESUS as their Savior *(Romans 11:25-32)*. This is already occurring but will increase dramatically during the reign of the antichrist.

JESUS and His prophets and apostles taught that Jewish people, like all other peoples, must repent and believe in JESUS' death and resurrection—for the forgiveness of their sin and to receive the gift of eternal life with Him. Lamentably, many theologians, pastors, priests, bishops, and various organizations falsely teach that Jewish people do not need to be converted to faith in JESUS as their Messiah to receive eternal salvation. Many are being deceived by this twisting of GOD's Word.

GOD's SPIRIT makes it clear that, with respect to sin and the need of salvation, there is no distinction between Jewish people and Gentiles. We have all sinned against the LORD and one another, and we all need to repent of our sin and receive JESUS into our lives as our Crucified Savior, Risen LORD, and Returning King. Jews are not more holy or righteous than Gentiles and cannot be saved by obedience to the Mosaic Law, because not even the rabbis keep it perfectly *(Romans 2:1–3:31)*. The Jewish people need JESUS' forgiveness and salvation as much as all others.

Everywhere JESUS went, He called all people to repentance and faith, and most of His preaching was to His Jewish kin, the physical descendants of Abraham through Jacob. To the Jewish people of His generation JESUS proclaimed:

> *"You are from below...I am from above. You are of this world; I am not of this world. Therefore I told you that you will die in your sins. For if you do not believe that I am He, you will die in your sins." John 8:23–24*

JESUS said to His chosen Apostles after His resurrection:

> *"This is what is written: The Messiah would suffer and rise from the dead the third day, and repentance for forgiveness of sins would be proclaimed in His name to all the nations, beginning at Jerusalem." Luke 24:46–47*

Notice that JESUS proclaimed that the preaching of the Gospel, calling all people to repentance and faith in Him, would begin in Jerusalem, in Israel, and then extend to all nations.

JESUS' apostles followed His example and instructions and called all Jews and Gentiles alike to repentance and faith everywhere they went. The first testimony to CHRIST, following His ascension, was given in Jerusalem to mostly Jewish people by the Apostle Peter on the Day of Pentecost. Brother Peter proclaimed JESUS' death and resurrection and called them to repent and believe in CHRIST *(Acts 2:14–41)*.

Similarly, the Apostle Paul testified:

> *"I testified to both Jews and Greeks about repentance toward God and faith in our Lord Jesus." Acts 20:21*

> *"For I am not ashamed of the gospel, because it is God's power for salvation to everyone who believes, first to the Jew, and also to the Greek. For in it God's righteousness is revealed from faith to faith, just as it is written: The righteous will live by faith." Romans 1:16–17*

JESUS is the only way of salvation for Jewish people. Religious leaders who deny the need of the descendants of Jacob to repent and embrace JESUS as their Passover Lamb and Messiah King are false prophets, a snare to all who follow them. Only the blood of CHRIST can cleanse and bring salvation. Praise the LORD for all the Jewish people who humble themselves and kneel at the cross of JESUS, accepting Him as their Crucified Savior, Risen LORD, and Returning King. These are exciting days in the land of Israel as more and more people are receiving CHRIST into their lives.

KING and LORD for Jews, Muslims, and All Peoples

Amid the confusion and violence in these last days, many Jews, Muslims, and Palestinians in the Middle East are turning their hearts to GOD and coming to know of His salvation through His Son JESUS. There are thousands of Muslims every year, in countries all over our world, who are coming to know CHRIST as their Savior, LORD, and GOD. Through dreams, visions, the clear testimony of GOD's Word, and the witness of believers, many are coming to trust in Him. According to ministries reaching out to Muslims all over our world, more Muslims are coming to faith in the LORD today than at any other time in history.

This is still the day of salvation. GOD wills that people from all nations should come to know JESUS as their GOD and LORD and receive the abundant and eternal life that He gives to all who trust in Him. Praise the LORD that amid the injustices and evils of humanity, His HOLY SPIRIT and His faithful people are bringing the knowledge of CHRIST to all nations for the salvation of many souls, including Jews and Palestinians!

Pray that the people of Israel and Jerusalem, Jews and Palestinians alike, would come to know JESUS, the only real Prince of Peace, Who will soon come to bring His ultimate justice to all nations of the world.

Pray!

CHAPTER 12
THE SIGN GIVER

"Now concerning that day and hour no one knows — neither the angels in heaven, nor the Son — except the Father only. As the days of Noah were, so the coming of the Son of Man will be. For in those days before the flood they were eating and drinking, marrying and giving in marriage, until the day Noah boarded the ark. They didn't know until the flood came and swept them all away. So this is the way the coming of the Son of Man will be: Then two men will be in the field: one will be taken and one left. Two women will be grinding at the mill: one will be taken and one left. Therefore be alert, since you don't know what day your Lord is coming. But know this: If the home-owner had known what time the thief was coming, he would have stayed alert and not let his house be broken into. This is why you also must be ready, because the Son of Man is coming at an hour you do not expect." JESUS, Matthew 24: 36–44

"About the times and the seasons: Brothers, you do not need anything to be written to you. For you yourselves know very well that the Day of the Lord will come just like a thief in the night. When they say, 'Peace and security,' then sudden destruction comes on them, like labor pains come on a pregnant woman, and they will not escape. But you, brothers, are not in the dark, for this day to overtake you like a thief. For you are all sons of light and sons of the day. We do not belong to the night or the darkness. So then, we must not sleep, like the rest, but we must stay awake and be serious."

Apostle Paul, 1 Thessalonians 5:1–6

No One Knows When

JESUS said that no one knows the exact date or hour of His return. Therefore, we all need to stay awake, waiting and watching for His return. It's a waste of time to pay attention to all the date setters out there who believe they have figured out exactly when JESUS is coming back. They are right that He is coming back, but wrong about exactly when. Like the boy who cried wolf, they bring the truth into disrepute and encourage the scoffers. They hinder people from taking JESUS' return seriously. GOD has clearly revealed, by His SPIRIT, that we are neither to add our own private interpretations to His Word nor subtract from what He has testified to *(2 Peter 1:19–21; Revelation 22:18–19).* We are to proclaim His Word as He has given it to us. It does not include a date or hour of His coming.

In *Matthew 24,* JESUS said that the days of His return would be like the days of Noah. What were those days like? According to the HOLY SPIRIT's historical testimony in *Genesis 6,* the world of that day was turning its back to GOD, worshiping idols (including the Nephilim, the world leaders at that time) and engaging in rampant sexual immorality and violence. I cannot think of any three words which more adequately describe world affairs today than these—rampant idolatry, immorality, and violence. JESUS referred to the days of Noah to highlight the truth that since the populace and their leaders had turned away from GOD, they didn't realize that their world would suddenly be destroyed by the global flood as a consequence of their evil.

Noah, a righteous man who trusted in the LORD, was the only sincere believer left in his generation. He was a prophet who preached to the people around him *(2 Peter 2:5)*, but instead of listening, they scoffed. They had no excuse for not being ready for the flood. Noah had warned them for many years, and I suspect that the LORD had given them other signs as well. Though they had been warned, their unbelief kept them oblivious to the imminent flood that would destroy them all. They were going about their lives, ignorant of GOD and of the nearness of death and destruction. Ditto for our world today.

No Excuse

People today have no legitimate excuse for ignorance about JESUS' return and His coming judgment. The testimony to His second coming is being proclaimed throughout our world today through personal witness, the internet, TV, radio, pamphlets, and books. In addition, all the apocalyptic human and planetary events over the last century are signs that ought to cause every thinking person to humbly seek GOD.

Statistically, approximately two billion people in our world are labelled as Christians. Tragically, many of them do not believe in or proclaim CHRIST's second coming to their families and communities. It's very strange that so many who call themselves Christian believers—even pastors, priests, or bishops—are not wanting, waiting, or praying for JESUS to come, even as JESUS taught us to pray. **The LORD is returning for those who believe that He died for them and that He is coming again. They are waiting for Him to come and are seeking to live their lives in harmony with the truth of His return.**

> *"so also the Messiah, having been offered once to bear the sins of many, will appear a second time, not to bear sin, but to bring salvation to those who are waiting for Him." Hebrews 9:28*

It's logical for people who don't believe JESUS is GOD's SON and our SAVIOR to disregard His coming return, and therefore be surprised by His second coming. On the other hand, it's foolish for individuals who claim to believe in JESUS to be caught off guard by His return. During my early years of ministry, I was rather shocked to learn that not only are there individuals calling themselves Christians who no longer believe in JESUS' second coming, but whole denominations that no longer believe, preach, or teach their people about His return. This is simply bizarre. How can anyone say they believe in JESUS yet not believe His clear testimony to His second coming? Do they believe that JESUS rose from the dead and ascended into Heaven? Why do they not believe or want JESUS to come back? Tragically, like the rebellious servants in the parable about His return (**Matthew 24:45-51**), they do not really believe in Him and have not been listening to or practicing His Word in their daily lives.

As it was in the days of Noah, so it is in our world and in many churches today. Despite all the promises and warnings the vast majority will not be ready and waiting for JESUS. As JESUS said: *"when the Son of Man comes, will He find that faith on earth?" (Luke 18:8).*

The Signs of the Last Days

Although we cannot know the date or hour of JESUS' return, He has commanded us to watch and wait and be aware of the signs that will indicate His approaching return. We are living in incredible days when the signals of JESUS' return are increasing all over our world.

It's important to remember that, Biblically, the *"last days"* *(Acts 2:17; 2 Timothy 3:1; Hebrews 1:2; James 5:3; 2 Peter 3:3)* began following JESUS' ascension into Heaven approximately two thousand years ago and will end with His return.

World history can be divided into four main sections:
1. **The Beginning: creation to the flood**
2. **The Old Testament Covenant: the flood until the first coming of CHRIST—the history of Israel**
3. **The first advent of CHRIST, including His ministry, suffering, death, resurrection, and ascension**
4. **The Last Days—the New Covenant: Begins with the receiving of the HOLY SPIRIT at Pentecost and concludes when the mission of the Church is completed and JESUS returns**

> *"And it will be in the last days, says God, that I will pour out My Spirit on all humanity; then your sons and your daughters will prophesy, your young men will see visions, and your old men will dream dreams." Acts 2:17*

To prophesy in the New Testament age means to give testimony to CHRIST and His Word and Gospel— *"because the testimony about Jesus is the spirit of prophecy" (Revelation 19:10).* JESUS taught that the HOLY SPIRIT has been given to us to enable us to testify to and glorify CHRIST in our world, to help everyone to come to repentance and faith in JESUS *(John*

15:26–27, 16:5–15; Acts 1:8). We will focus on this mission of the LORD's Church in chapter 19.

Buckle Your Seat Belts

Buckle your seat belts to JESUS and His Word, for the journey is going to get much rougher. As we get closer to JESUS' return, the signs increase in frequency and intensity. In *Matthew 24, Mark 13, Luke 21, and Revelation,* JESUS speaks of signs occurring in three areas that describe the last days and preface His Second Coming:

- ❖ **World affairs**
- ❖ **Effects in nature**
- ❖ **The Mission of the faithful Church to proclaim the Gospel of salvation through faith in JESUS CHRIST.**

World Affairs

One category of signs that JESUS told us would point to His return relates to the activities of the world of unbelievers, the things we see, hear, and read about in the media. The signals being broadcast around the globe today include the worship of false messiah leaders and celebrities of the nations, false prophets, escalation in wars, famines, plagues, idolatry, violence, immorality, persecution of believers, and all other fruits of humanity's rebellion against the will and commandments of GOD. These signs have been present since humanity's fall into sin and are therefore not unique to the last days before CHRIST's return. **JESUS said that these symptoms are like birth pains *(Matthew 24:8).* They will increase in number and intensity as human history advances towards its climax of total rebellion by the nations against their CREATOR, SAVIOR and LORD.**
 No objective observer of our world today can deny the dramatic increase in all these realities over the past century.

Of course, many prefer to stick their heads in the sand and pretend things aren't getting worse. They gullibly believe the world, despite some problems, is evolving into a better place as humans throw off the restraining cords or chains of the commandments of Biblical Christianity *(Psalm 2:3).* Nothing could be further from the truth! Satan's specialty is making people blind to the truth in front of them.

When a woman is in labor, there may be times when the contractions stop briefly, but then the contractions begin again, often with greater intensity than before. This continues until the child is born. Similarly, with the signs of the events in world history, there may be slight improvements for a period, and it may seem that JESUS' coming is not near. But then the symptoms return with even greater intensity, producing more pain for more people in more places.

The remainder of this section will focus on these signs that are exponentially increasing today, fulfilling JESUS' testimony to the last days before His return. As our brother Paul wrote:

> *"Besides this, knowing the time, <u>it is already the hour for you to wake up from sleep, for now our salvation is nearer than when we first believed</u>. <u>The night is nearly over, and the daylight is near,</u> so let us discard the deeds of darkness and put on the armor of light."*
> *Romans 13:11–12*

Pray!

CHAPTER 13

THE EXPOSER OF
THE IMPOSTERS

**"Then Jesus replied to them:
'Watch out that no one deceives you.
For many will come in My name, saying,
'I am the Messiah,' and they will deceive many....
Many false prophets will rise up and deceive many.'"
Matthew 24:4, 11**

Why?

One of the great curses on humanity through the ages has been the proliferation of false saviors and sooth-sayers who divert people from their CREATOR and SAVIOR, and from GOD's gracious purposes for human life. Since the time of humanity's fall, people have been deflected away from GOD and His Word by counterfeit messiahs and religious leaders who cleverly camouflage the darkness of their own wisdom as light. The deception began in the garden with Satan's lies about GOD and has continued through human charlatans mas-querading as messengers of enlightenment or progress. In this chapter we are paying attention to the LORD's warnings concerning these antichrist spirits that dominate our world today.

Before we focus on the antichrists and false prophets, it is important to understand why GOD allows them to operate in our world. Why did GOD allow Satan to tempt our first parents, and then, through antichrists and false prophets, to deceive others down through history? It is written:

> *"If a prophet or someone who has dreams arises among you and proclaims a sign or wonder to you, and that sign or wonder he has promised you comes about, but he says, 'Let us follow other gods,' which you have not known, 'and let us worship them,' do not listen to that prophet's words or to that dreamer. For the Lord your God is testing you to know whether you love the Lord your God with all your heart and all your soul. You must follow the Lord your God and fear Him. You must keep His commands and listen to His voice; you must worship Him and remain faithful to Him." Deuteronomy 13:1–4*

Antichrists and false religious leaders are a clear test of our faith. Throughout Old and New Testament times, political and religious leaders conspired together to mislead the people of their generation away from the LORD and His Word and into every kind of falsehood and evil. The LORD allowed the faith of people to be tested in this way. False saviors and deceptive prophets sift our hearts, minds, and spirits to reveal what we truly place our faith or trust in. Do we really trust in and love GOD and His SON JESUS and His Kingdom, or do we love the pleasures, treasures, and idols of this world?

Antichrists Everywhere

In JESUS' answer to His followers' question regarding what signs would indicate His coming and the end of the age, the very first omen He mentioned was the presence of many false messiahs or antichrists *(Matthew 24:4)*. He repeats that warning a few verses later, just before He speaks of the last events before His return—

> **"If anyone tells you then, 'Look, here is the Messiah!' or, 'Over here!' do not believe it! False messiahs and false prophets will arise and perform great signs and wonders to lead astray, if possible, even the elect. Take note: I have told you in advance. So if they tell you, 'Look, He's in the wilderness!' don't go out; 'Look, He's in the inner rooms!' do not believe it. For as the lightning comes from the east and flashes as far as the west, so will be the coming of the Son of Man." Matthew 24:23–27**

The Apostle John also gave clear warning concerning the antichrists in the world:

> *"Children, it is the last hour. And as you have heard, 'Antichrist is coming,' even now many antichrists have come ... I have not written to you because you don't know the truth, but because you do know it, and because no lie comes from the truth. Who is the liar, if not the one who denies that Jesus is the Messiah? This one is the antichrist: the one who denies the Father and the Son. No one who denies the Son can have the Father; he who confesses the Son has the Father as well." 1 John 2:18–23*

"This is how you know the Spirit of God: Every spirit who confesses that Jesus Christ has come in the flesh is from God. <u>But every spirit who does not confess Jesus is not from God. This is the spirit of the antichrist; you have heard that he is coming, and he is already in the world now.</u>" 1 John 4:2–3

"For many deceivers have gone out into the world, those who do not acknowledge Jesus Christ as coming in the flesh. <u>This is the deceiver and the antichrist.</u>" 2 John 7

The title "CHRIST" is the Greek word for messiah or savior. False messiahs or antichrists are false saviors. **They reject the truth that JESUS IS GOD's SON and humanity's one and only SAVIOR Who came from Heaven. They deny JESUS and seek to take His place.** They try to persuade people to support, and even worship them and their religious, philosophical, and political ideology. Though they are themselves sinful people, they promise to lead others to a utopia in this world—and perhaps in the next.

JESUS proclaimed that He was *"the way, the truth, and the life" (John 14:6),* Who could give people a full, satisfying, and eternal life if they followed Him *(John 10:10).* The false saviors or antichrists proclaim this same assurance to those who will follow them. They project that they have some exceptional abilities, often combined with intellectual and spiritual powers, which enable them to bring wealth, power, peace, and pleasure to those who follow them. They are self-deceived and proficient at deceiving others.

Those who do not know the real JESUS as their SAVIOR and LORD are often seeking for some great human leader to arise and lead them to a promised land where they can indulge their fleshly appetites and live without the commandments of GOD.

*"Why do the nations rebel
and the peoples plot in vain?
The kings of the earth take their stand,
and the rulers conspire together
against the Lord and His Anointed One:
'Let us tear off their chains
and free ourselves from their restraints!'"
Psalm 2:1–3*

Most of the worlds leaders down through history have been antichrist leaders. This includes not only the political and military leaders, but also intellectual, business, religious, and cultural leaders. Instead of guiding people to believe and follow the teachings of the LORD, bringing harmony and blessing to their nations, they make up their own laws and rules that are often contrary to GOD's will. They may initially seem lamb-like and kind in their schemes for their utopian societies, but in the end they inevitably turn to the use of dictatorial force at the point of a sword or a gun to persuade people to obey and follow them. Their laws and rules, based on their own sinful and limited understanding, are often in direct conflict with the words of JESUS and His prophets and apostles, resulting in great persecution of the LORD's faithful people.

Although most of the leaders of the nations have been antichrist in their spirits, the LORD'S clear teaching is that we are to give human leaders what is theirs, and to obey all the laws except for those that are clearly contrary to the will and commandments of GOD *(Matthew 22:21; Acts 4:18–21; Romans 13:1–7)*. We ought to give them the proper respect and obedience whenever we can, but we are to avoid worshiping them or placing our ultimate trust or confidence in them, for they will never be able to usher in CHRIST's Kingdom.

*"It is better to take refuge in the Lord
than to trust in man.*

It is better to take refuge in the Lord
than to trust in nobles." Psalm 118:8–9

Recognizing the Counterfeit Saviors

The only way to recognize false saviors is to know the real JESUS and His teaching. Without knowing and listening to JESUS, people will not even be aware that there are antichrists. Only those who walk and talk with JESUS in their daily lives, who listen to His SPIRIT in His Word, and who are seeking to put the teaching of His Word into practice in their lives will be able to recognize the antichrists who seek to lead them away from obedience to CHRIST. It is similar to the situation of identical twins. Only their parents, siblings, and friends who have a close relationship with them can tell them apart. They may look similar, but their spirit, beliefs, and attitudes will identify them. Some of the antichrists who come will quote Scripture and pretend to be good shepherds who really care for the sheep and want to save our nation and planet, but they will be thieves and murderers who have only come *"to steal and to kill and to destroy" (John 10:10).* Do you know JESUS and His Word well enough that you will recognize the deceptive voices of the sham saviors?

JESUS said:

"The doorkeeper opens it for him, and the sheep hear his voice. He calls his own sheep by name and leads them out. When he has brought all his own outside, he goes ahead of them. <u>The sheep follow him because they recognize his voice. They will never follow a stranger; instead they will run away from him, because they don't recognize the voice of strangers</u>... I am the good shepherd. <u>I know</u>

*__My own sheep, and they know Me,__ as the
Father knows Me, and I know the Father. __I lay
down My life for the sheep... My sheep hear
My voice, I know them, and they follow Me.__
I give them eternal life, and they will never
perish — ever! No one will snatch them out of
My hand."* John 10:3–5, 14–15, 27–28

When people know the real JESUS and listen to His voice,
they will never be deceived by any antichrist because they
are watching out for those who will try to deceive them, just
as JESUS warned them to do. Those who do not heed JESUS'
words of warning concerning the antichrists are not listening
to His voice. They will easily be deceived by one or another of
the antichrists who come camouflaged as shepherds or angels
of light. Those who know CHRIST will not be deceived—either
by the little antichrists or the final and ultimate antichrist who
will come before JESUS returns. Chapter 16 and 17 will focus
specifically on the ultimate antichrist beast who will come camouflaged as a lamb who "loves" the world and wants to save it.

Wolves in Sheep's Clothing

*JESUS said: "Then many will take offense,
betray one another and hate one another.
Many false prophets will rise up and deceive
many... false prophets will arise and perform
great signs and wonders to lead astray, if possible, even the elect." Matthew 24:10–11,24*

A babel of voices fills the airwaves, broadcasting every
imaginable falsehood to the world and infiltrating many of
the "Christian" churches. Rather than listening to GOD's SPIRIT
in His Word, many prefer the soothing opiates and tempting
voices emanating from many pulpits, stages, and media outlets.

In addition to the false messiahs that will appear in the nations, JESUS warns us about the many false prophets who will appear in the church and in the religions of the world in the last days, like weeds in a planted field *(Matthew 13:24–30, 36–43)*. They will lead people away from faith in CHRIST and into many false teachings and activities, including worship of and allegiance to false saviors. Their self-anointed teachings will result in many people rejecting CHRIST and His Word and hating each other.

True prophets are those who have been called by GOD's SPIRIT, who listen to what GOD's SPIRIT says in His Word, and then faithfully proclaim that message to the people to whom the LORD sends them. False prophets are those who use GOD's—JESUS'—the HOLY SPIRIT's name in vain to preach or teach their own feelings, dreams, visions, and views instead of the truths of GOD's Word. They claim to be servants of GOD, but don't listen to what CHRIST and His SPIRIT have said. They imitate the popular political and spiritual messages of the world or other false prophets or make up their own messages which they then proclaim to those with ears that desire to be entertained or *"tickled" (2 Timothy 4:3)*.

Sitting on a mountainside, near the beginning of His ministry, JESUS warned those who believe in Him about spiritual wolves that camouflage themselves in sheep's clothing:

> *"Beware of false prophets who come to you in sheep's clothing but inwardly are ravaging wolves. You'll recognize them by their fruit."*
> **Matthew 7:15–16**

Are you one of JESUS' sheep, or a wolf in sheep's clothing? This question is not rhetorical but is directed to each of us for our critical consideration. We all need to examine our hearts, minds, and spirits to see if we are true believers in CHRIST and His Word, or if we have replaced Him with our own 20th or 21st century fashionable opinions. May the HOLY SPIRIT of

GOD reveal the truth of our own hearts and minds and expose what is false. As it is written: *"Search me, God, and know my heart; test me and know my concerns" (Psalm 139:23).* This has eternal ramifications—not just for us but for those within our influence whom GOD will hold us accountable for.

JESUS said:

> *"But whoever causes the downfall of one of these little ones who believe in Me — it would be better for him if a heavy millstone were hung around his neck and he were drowned in the depths of the sea!" Matthew 18:6*

This is an especially critical question for all who believe that they have been called by CHRIST to shepherd His people. If we claim to be anointed by His SPIRIT to feed His sheep and to care for His lambs, we need to be wise and faithful. Listen to JESUS' words which He spoke and will speak again on the day of judgment:

> *"Not everyone who says to Me, 'Lord, Lord!' will enter the kingdom of heaven, but only the one who does the will of My Father in heaven. On that day many will say to Me, 'Lord, Lord, didn't we prophesy in Your name, drive out demons in Your name, and do many miracles in Your name?' Then I will announce to them, 'I never knew you! Depart from Me, you law-breakers!'" Matthew 7:21–23*

There are many wolves in Christian churches today. This should not shock you. It isn't new! Spiritual wolves have been around from the beginning, preying on careless individuals and helpless lambs handed over to them by those who pay no attention to the LORD's warnings. It is tragic that so many

Christian believers are giving their children into the hands of false teachers, not only in public institutions, but also in numerous so-called Christian churches, schools, and colleges. Youth attending these institutions are being indoctrinated in the mythologies of our age—evolutionism, humanism, new age spirituality, false religious unity, sexual promiscuity, gender confusion—and often face abuse and scoffing at the teachings of CHRIST and His prophets and apostles. These false teachers, preachers, philosophers, theologians, and church bureaucrats often denigrate those who still believe in the historical Biblical accounts and teachings. Beware of those who no longer believe the history and principles that GOD's SPIRIT has testified to in His Word.

Unbelief in Biblical History

In the book *GOD IS! why evolution isn't*, I warned of the dangers of theistic evolution that has invaded the Christian church over the past one hundred fifty years. The mythology of evolution is now spreading like a terminal cancer in most evangelical churches—through many of their seminaries, colleges, and Bible Schools. Because of their belief in the contemporary mythology of evolution, many no longer believe that:
  ➤ Adam and Eve were real historical people
  ➤ GOD instituted marriage between a man and a woman
  ➤ the world was "very good" without disease, violence, suffering, and death before Adam and Eve fell into unbelief and sin
  ➤ the world of Noah's day was destroyed through a global flood.

Although they do not proclaim it very loudly, most theistic evolutionists believe that JESUS and His prophets and apostles were simply presenting the false understanding of their scientifically-ignorant contemporaries. They know that

JESUS clearly affirmed the historical reality of Adam and Eve (*Matthew 19:4–6, 23:34–35*), and of the flood of Noah's Day (*Matthew 24:37–39*). They know that JESUS and His apostles affirmed the authority and historical testimony of the prophets repeatedly in their many quotes from the Old Testament. They know what JESUS and His prophets and apostles believed and taught about these events. Therefore, by rejecting the truths that JESUS and His apostles testified to, they are claiming that their understanding of the Old Testament is superior to CHRIST's understanding.

Theistic evolution is just one of the many false teachings that has crept into the church. Numerous entertaining, progressive, and popular preachers in self-proclaimed "Christian" churches today contradict various clear teachings of CHRIST and His SPIRIT in His Word, even while they are quoting the Bible. In addition to the rejection of the SPIRIT's testimony to creation and the flood, many also reject His testimony to:

- the Tower of Babel
- the account of Sodom and Gomorrah
- the exodus
- the crossing of the Red Sea
- the receiving of the Ten Commandments
- David's battle with Goliath
- the miracles of the Old Testament prophets
- the teaching on the sanctify of life, sexual morality and the family
- the prophecies predicting future events
- the virgin birth
- the miracles of CHRIST
- His, and our, bodily resurrection
- the identity of JESUS as GOD
- JESUS' teaching on the way of salvation through faith in Him
- the LORD's testimony to the reality of Hades and Gehenna or Hell

⬇His teaching concerning His coming return and the reality of the new Heaven and Earth

⬇etc.

In a growing segment of churches today, every clear teaching that the Church has received from CHRIST and His prophets and apostles is being rejected and replaced by other ideas more compatible with the world's philosophies and values. We need less sophisticated philosophers and theologians who no longer believe the Biblical accounts but propagate their own ideas and the myths of our fallen world. We need more children of GOD, children of simple trust and faith in CHRIST and His Word. As JESUS said:

> *"I praise You, Father, Lord of heaven and earth, because You have hidden these things from the wise and learned and revealed them to infants. Yes, Father, because this was Your good pleasure." Matthew 11:25–26*

Amen!

The Warnings of the Faithful Apostles

The Apostle Paul, in his last words to the leaders of the church at Ephesus, gave this warning:

> *"I testified to both Jews and Greeks about repentance toward God and faith in our Lord Jesus... And now I know that none of you will ever see my face again — everyone I went about preaching the kingdom to. Therefore I testify to you this day that I am innocent of everyone's blood, for I did not shrink back from*

> *<u>declaring to you the whole plan of God. Be on</u>*
> *<u>guard for yourselves and for all the flock that</u>*
> *<u>the Holy Spirit has appointed you to as over-</u>*
> *<u>seers, to shepherd the church of God, which</u>*
> *<u>He purchased with His own blood. I know that</u>*
> *<u>after my departure savage wolves will come in</u>*
> *<u>among you, not sparing the flock. And men will</u>*
> *<u>rise up from your own number with deviant</u>*
> *<u>doctrines to lure the disciples into following</u>*
> *<u>them. Therefore be on the alert</u>, remembering*
> *that night and day for three years I did not*
> *stop warning each one of you with tears. And*
> *now I commit you to God and to the message*
> *of His grace, which is able to build you up and*
> *to give you an inheritance among all who are*
> *sanctified." Acts 20:21,25–32*

Notice that many of these false prophets or wolves develop right within the church itself. Initially they believed the truths of GOD's Word, but then they began to distort those truths and draw people away from the wisdom of CHRIST to follow their new, enlightened, progressive teachings. The early church was plagued by false teachers and preachers called Gnostics. Gnostics believed their own knowledge and spiritual experience superseded the testimonies of the prophets and apostles in GOD's Word. They proclaimed that the SPIRIT of GOD had given them greater wisdom and insight than those first followers of JESUS.

It is written:

> *"Dear friends, do not believe every spirit, but*
> *test the spirits to determine if they are from*
> *God, because many false prophets have gone*
> *out into the world. This is how you know the*
> *Spirit of God: Every spirit who confesses that*

Jesus Christ has come in the flesh is from God. But every spirit who does not confess Jesus is not from God. This is the spirit of the antichrist; you have heard that he is coming, and he is already in the world now. You are from God, little children, and you have conquered them, because the One who is in you is greater than the one who is in the world. They are from the world. Therefore what they say is from the world, and the world listens to them. We are from God. Anyone who knows God listens to us; anyone who is not from God does not listen to us. From this we know the Spirit of truth and the spirit of deception.

Dear friends, let us love one another, because love is from God, and everyone who loves has been born of God and knows God. The one who does not love does not know God, because God is love. God's love was revealed among us in this way: God sent His One and Only Son into the world so that we might live through Him." 1 John 4:1–9

The HOLY SPIRIT, through the Apostle John, gave three clear tests for assessing the testimonies of those who claim to represent GOD—

1. **Verse 1–3**: Are they giving a clear testimony to JESUS as GOD's SON and humanity's one and only SAVIOR Who came in the flesh? Are they encouraging people to repent of their sin and to trust in JESUS, in Who He is, in what He taught and did for us on the cross and in His resurrection, and what He will do when He comes—or are they using JESUS' Name, calling themselves Christians, to attract people's attention to their

philosophy, theology, or spirituality and to garner financial support for their lavish lifestyle? Are they pointing people to JESUS or to themselves or some other false prophet or antichrist?

2. **Verse 5–6:** Do they acknowledge the authority and teaching of the prophets and apostles of CHRIST in His Word so that they listen to and pass on these teachings — or do they twist or ignore the teaching of JESUS and His prophets and apostles, and instead promote ideas, values, and philosophies that are popular with the world?

3. **Verse 7–8:** Do they minister with a spirit of love that desires the salvation and blessing of GOD through CHRIST on those they are ministering to? Do they share the blessings GOD has given them to enable others to come to faith in CHRIST and to honor JESUS with their lives— or do they hoard their wealth, build their mansions on earth, and manipulate the sheeple?

Applying these three tests will identify the false prophets, who have invaded the church since the time of CHRIST. Lamentably, most people ignore these tests in favor of what their itching ears want to hear— the ideas which the antichrists and false prophets are experts at delivering. **Do not be afraid to test everyone who comes in the Name of JESUS or GOD. Every true servant of JESUS CHRIST will be thankful for those who will test their message by the clear teachings of GOD's Word.** It is written:

> *"The people here were more open-minded than those in Thessalonica, since they welcomed the message with eagerness and examined the Scriptures daily to see if these things were so." Acts 17:11*

The HOLY SPIRIT commends the Bereans for both their openness to listening to the testimony of Paul and for testing it by the Scriptures. **We should always <u>be willing and eager</u> to listen to those who come in JESUS' Name with a word or message for us, but it is crucial to test the message by the SPIRIT of CHRIST and the teachings of the Bible. This includes testing our own understanding by the Scriptures themselves.** As the Apostle Paul wrote to Timothy:

> *"Pay close attention to your life and your teaching; persevere in these things, for by doing this you will save both yourself and your hearers."* **1 Timothy 4:16**

False prophets are motivated by love, not for the LORD our GOD, His Word, or His people, but for prosperity, possessions, power, pleasures, and popularity. As the HOLY SPIRIT says through Jude:

> *"Dear friends, although I was eager to write you about the salvation we share, I found it necessary to write and exhort you to contend for the faith that was delivered to the saints once for all. For some men, who were designated for this judgment long ago, have come in by stealth; <u>they are ungodly, turning the grace of our God into promiscuity and denying Jesus Christ, our only Master and Lord</u>... But you, dear friends, remember what was predicted by the apostles of our Lord Jesus Christ; they told you, 'In the end time there will be scoffers walking according to their own ungodly desires.' <u>These people create divisions and are unbelievers, not having the Spirit.</u>" Jude 3–4,17–19*

Like JESUS, His faithful apostles were always calling the believers to test everything and to remain faithful to CHRIST and His Word and Kingdom. Anything contrary to the testimony of the LORD and His SPIRIT in the Scriptures will be rejected by those who are wise and discerning. Our discernment is not to be based on our intuition or our feelings concerning the speaker. Most who attend churches today want to be entertained, not convicted. Whether or not a speaker has an entertaining and captivating style or makes us feel good about ourselves is irrelevant. **What counts is whether the message is in harmony with the teachings of JESUS and His prophets and apostles. Does the message call people to repentance from sin and to a living faith in CHRIST and His Word—or is it just scratching the itching ears and inspiring laughter?**

Legions of Phony Preachers, Teachers, and Spiritual Entertainers

As has been the case down through history, false prophets are dominant today on our planet and often within Christian churches and denominations. There are legions of phony spiritual leaders and teachers who have camouflaged themselves in Christian words and spirituality and have infiltrated churches of all flavors and colors.

I conclude this chapter with just one example of the slippery teachings of some of these false spiritual leaders and of the masses of people that are following them—

'I Kissed a Girl'—Katy Perry Speaks About Transcendental Meditation at Vatican Conference
By Heather Clark on May 15, 2018

Pop singer Katheryn Hudson, who goes by the stage name Katy Perry and is known for her lesbian experimentation song "I Kissed a Girl," recently spoke on transcendental meditation alongside her mentor at the Vatican's "Unite to Cure" conference. Her appearance, along with others, such as Deepak Chopra and Dr. Mehmet Oz, have raised concern about ongoing ecumenism at the Vatican in joining together all kinds of beliefs and practices under one banner.

"Bobby was able to teach me meditation in India," Hudson told those gathered during the talk entitled "Impacting Children's Health Through Meditation Globally." "The stillness that I found is beyond anything I've ever experienced."

"It's helped a lot with my anxiety. Instead of having to turn to [a] prescription, I've been able to turn to this," she said. "It helps incredibly with jet lag … and for all the Italians, it helps with the hangovers."

Hudson asserted during the talk that meditation is not a religion but is simply "taking care of one's temple."

"I was raised in a Christian household," Hudson outlined, noting that her parents, who identify as evangelists, were present at the talk. "I was raised around the idea that our body is a temple. And I think if our body is truly a temple, we must take care of it mind, body and soul. And this takes care of your mind."

"I notice when I meditate that my whole brain kind of opens up—it kind of feels like a halo is ignited above my head," she continued. "And it's like I'm clearing out the cobwebs of my neuropathways and finding new neuropathways to ignite."

Hudson said that transcendental meditation has also helped her creativity as a musical artist, "especially when I come out of it."

Her mentor, Bob Roth, praised Hudson, stating that "100 million people really trust" the pop singer, and said that she had helped others get into meditation because of her influence.

"600,000 young kids have learned to meditate, and a lot of it because of your words," Roth stated. "No exaggeration, you have saved thousands and thousands of lives."

"Words are very powerful," Hudson replied. "God created the world with words."

The pop singer also met Roman Catholic leader Jorge Bergoglio, known as Pope Francis, during her visit and tweeted, "Honored to be in the presence of His Holiness @franciscus' compassionate heart and inclusivity."

The event was billed as a global health care initiative and presented by the Vatican's Pontifical Council for Culture, the Stem for Life Foundation, the Cura Foundation and the STOQ Foundation. It featured several doctors and health care leaders, including New Age figure Deepak Chopra, and was moderated by CNN's medical correspondent Dr. Sanjay Gupta, a Hindu; talk show host Dr. Mehmet Oz, a Muslim; CBS correspondent Max Gomez, and journalist Meredith Vieira.

While the Vatican's three-day conference was attended by priests, biotech representatives and celebrities alike, Mike Gendron of Proclaiming the Gospel Ministries told Christian News Network that he found both the allowance of a presentation on transcendental meditation and the ecumenical speakers' list to be troubling.

"We can only wonder why Katy Perry was invited to a Vatican conference and an audience with the pope," he said. "Perry pontificated about the benefits of TM from the very chair that Pope Francis often communicates his messages. In both cases, their 'wisdom of this world is foolishness before God' (1 Cor. 3:19)."

As previously reported, Hudson, a former Contemporary Christian Music (CCM) artist, spoke at a Human Rights Campaign gala in March 2017 and was presented with a homosexual advocacy award. She pointed to her 2008 hit song "I Kissed a Girl" during her speech as she told those gathered that "I did more than that." Her remark generated both cheers and applause from attendees.

Hudson also made headlines in 2016 when she donated $10,000 to the abortion and contraception giant Planned Parenthood out of fear that the organization might be defunded by the Trump administration.

"Planned Parenthood educated me on my body and my reproductive health, so that I could focus on my dreams and using my voice until I knew the timing was right for me to make a plan to have a family," she wrote on social media. "Without this education, I may have had a different life path."

Gendron said that he believed that the allowance of Roth and Hudson's talk on transcendental meditation, along with the other aforementioned speakers, further evidenced Bergoglio's desire to unite all religions and beliefs.

"He is aggressively pursuing his ecumenical agenda for religious unity and not anything to stand in his way. Clearly part of his strategy for a global religion is to cast the net into all of society and unite the world through highly influential people," he opined.

"What better way to suppress the doctrinal differences that divide religions than to promote the ungodly Hindu practice of TM. The practice is embraced by atheists, agnostics and people from a variety of religious affiliations," Gendron stated. "The process opens the mind to the spiritual realm such that any thought can enter. God's word gives a resolute warning to

such devilish practices. We are to take every thought captive to the obedience of Christ so that we can destroy speculations and every lofty thing raised up against the knowledge of God (2 Cor. 10:5)."

According to reports, transcendental meditation was first made popular in the 1950's by Hindu guru Mahesh Prasad Varma, also known as Maharishi Mahesh Yogi. He learned the technique from Indian Hindu leader Swami Brahmananda Saraswati, of whom he was a follower, and named his efforts the Spiritual Regeneration Movement. Secular artists such as the Beatles are stated to have been taught by Varma.

(www.christiannews.net/2018/05/15/i-kissed-a-girl-katy-perry-speaks-about-transcendental-meditation-at-vatican-conference)

Although this conference, camouflaged as uniting the world to help cure illnesses, took place at the Vatican, the false teachings presented there are prevalent everywhere in our world and in churches of every stripe. Whether falsehoods come dressed as scantily-clad pop stars or fancifully-robed church leaders, they are equally destructive. As it is written:
"test all things. Hold on to what is good.
Stay away from every kind of evil"
(1 Thessalonians 5:21–22).

The days of the false prophets and teachers are numbered, but in these last days before CHRIST's return, their numbers are legion. CHRIST has given us clear warnings and ways of testing these false teachers. Be on guard for yourself, your children, grandchildren, and the fellowship of believers you are part of.
Pray!

CHAPTER 14

THE CONSEQUENCES
OF IMPOSTERS

*"There is a way that seems right to a man,
but its end is the way to death."*
Proverbs 14:12

Warning: Antichrists and False Prophets are a Leading Cause of Death

L ike Hitler, Stallin, and Mao, all antichrists and false
prophets promise the good life, but they lead individuals,
nations, and—in the last days—the entire world, to destruction. The annals of history are filled with the testimony of
the great evils that overcame nations as they followed their
political and religious leaders into the depths of suffering and
death. In this chapter we will highlight many of the consequences in the last days of following these counterfeit saviors
and imitation prophets. These are the signs that saturate the
news in our generation today.

Wars, Rumors of Wars, and Famines

JESUS said:
> *" You are going to hear of wars and rumors of wars. See that you are not alarmed, because these things must take place, but the end is not yet. For nation will rise up against nation, and kingdom against kingdom. There will be famines and earthquakes in various places."*
> *Matthew 24:6–7*

In Revelation we read:

> *When He opened the fourth seal, I heard the voice of the fourth living creature say, 'Come!' And I looked, and there was a pale green horse. The horseman on it was named Death, and Hades was following after him. Authority was given to them over a fourth of the earth, to kill by the sword, by famine, by plague, and by the wild animals of the earth." Revelation 6:7–8*

Violence and war have characterized our world since people began to listen to the deceptive voices of evil rather than to the voice of GOD's SPIRIT. It began with Cain's murder of his brother Abel. With the arrival of tribes and kingdoms, individual violence grew into rebellions and wars involving mass destruction of human life. These were inspired and led by the demigod antichrists and false prophets of the world. Although a few wars have been necessary to defend against and stop the aggressive evils that have proliferated in some nations, these are the exception and not the rule.

Where there is war, there is poverty and famine. Many, perhaps most, famines are the result of the tactics and consequences of war. The starvation of people is a weapon of war that has been used repeatedly down through history. Wherever wars are being fought, people often do not have the financial resources or time or security to grow their own food to survive. People in every generation have either gone through wars and famines themselves or heard of them in other parts of the world. While hordes of people are deceived into blaming GOD for these horrors, the truth is that war, poverty, and famine are consequences of living contrary to GOD's Word and gracious purposes by worshiping idols and following antichrist political and religious leaders.

War permeates the affairs of our world. Over sixty countries are at war today, and over seven hundred internal civil battles are being fought by various guerrilla, terrorist, separatist militias, and cartels. (www.warsintheworld.com August 5, 2016) Here is a list of significant wars and their death tolls since the end of the Second World War:

1946-49: Chinese civil war (1.2 million)

1946-49: Greek civil war (50,000)

1946-54: France-Vietnam war (600,000)

1947: Partition of India and Pakistan (1 million)

1947: Taiwan's uprising against the Kuomintang (30,000)

1948-1958: Colombian civil war (250,000)

1948-1973: Arab-Israeli wars (70,000)

1949: Indian Muslims vs Hindus (20,000)

1949-50: Mainland China vs Tibet (1,200,000)

1950-53: Korean war (3 million)

1952-59: Kenya's Mau Mau insurrection (20,000)

1954-62: French-Algerian war (368,000)

1958-61: Mao's "Great Leap Forward" (38 million)

1960-90: South Africa vs Africa National Congress (?)

1960-96: Guatemala's civil war (200,000)

1961-98: Indonesia vs West Papua/Irian (100,000)

1961-2003: Kurds vs Iraq (180,000)

1962-75: Mozambique Frelimo vs Portugal (10,000)

1962-75: Angolan FNLA & MPLA vs Portugal (50,000)

1964-73: USA-Vietnam war (3 million)

1965: second India-Pakistan war over Kashmir

1965-66: Indonesian civil war (250,000)

1966-69: Mao's "Cultural Revolution" (11 million)

1966: Colombia's civil war (31,000)

1967-70: Nigeria-Biafra civil war (800,000)

1968-80: Rhodesia's civil war (?)

1969: Philippines vs the communist Bagong Hukbong Bayan/ New People's Army (40,000)

1969-79: Idi Amin, Uganda (300,000)

1969-02: IRA - Norther Ireland's civil war (3,000)

1969-79: Francisco Macias Nguema, Equatorial Guinea (50,000)

1971: Pakistan-Bangladesh civil war (500,000)

1972-2014: Philippines vs Muslim separatists (Moro Islamic Liberation Front, etc.) (150,000)

1972: Burundi's civil war (300,000)

1972-79: Rhodesia/Zimbabwe's civil war (30,000)

1974-91: Ethiopian civil war (1,000,000)

1975-78: Menghitsu, Ethiopia (1.5 million)

1975-79: Khmer Rouge, Cambodia (1.7 million)

1975-89: Boat people, Vietnam (250,000)

1975-87: civil war in Lebanon (130,000)

1975-87: Laos' civil war (184,000)

1975-2002: Angolan civil war (500,000)

1976-83: Argentina's military regime (20,000)

1976-93: Mozambique's civil war (900,000)

1976-98: Indonesia-East Timor civil war (600,000)

1976-2005: Indonesia-Aceh (GAM) civil war (12,000)

1977-92: El Salvador's civil war (75,000)

1979: Vietnam-China war (30,000)

1979-88: the Soviet Union invades Afghanistan (1.3 million)

1980-88: Iraq-Iran war (435,000)

1980-92: Sendero Luminoso - Peru's civil war (69,000)

1984: Kurds vs Turkey (35,000)

1981-90: Nicaragua vs Contras (60,000)

1982-90: Hissene Habre, Chad (40,000)

1983-: Sri Lanka's civil war (70,000)

1983-2002: Sudanese civil war (2 million)

1986: Indian Kashmir's civil war (60,000)

1987: Palestinian Intifada (4,500)

1988-2001: Afghanistan civil war (400,000)

1988-2004: Somalia's civil war (550,000)

1989: Liberian civil war (220,000)

1989: Uganda vs Lord's Resistance Army (30,000)

1991: Gulf War - large coalition against Iraq to liberate Kuwait (85,000)

1991-97: Congo's civil war (800,000)

1991-2000: Sierra Leone's civil war (200,000)

1991-2009: Russia-Chechnya civil war (200,000)

1991-94: Armenia-Azerbaijan war (35,000)

1992-96: Tajikstan's civil war (50,000)

1992-96: Yugoslavian wars (260,000)

1992-99: Algerian civil war (150,000)

1993-97: Congo Brazzaville's civil war (100,000)

1993-2005: Burundi's civil war (200,000)

1994: Rwanda's civil war (900,000)

1995: Pakistani Sunnis vs Shiites (1,300)

1995: Maoist rebellion in Nepal (12,000)

1998: Congo/Zaire's war - Rwanda and Uganda vs Zimbabwe, Angola and Namibia (3.8 million)

1998-2000: Ethiopia-Eritrea war (75,000)

1999: Kosovo's liberation war - NATO vs Serbia (2,000)

2001: Afghanistan's liberation war - USA & UK vs Taliban (40,000)

2001: Nigeria vs Boko Haram (20,000)

2002: Cote d'Ivoire's civil war (1,000)

2003-11: Second Iraq-USA war - USA, UK and Australia vs Saddam Hussein's regime and Shiite squads and Sunni extremists (160,000)

2003-09: Sudan vs JEM/Darfur (300,000)

2004: Sudan vs SPLM & Eritrea (?)

2004: Yemen vs Houthis (?)

2004: Thailand vs Muslim separatists (3,700)

2007: Pakistan vs Pakistani Taliban (38,000)

2011: Iraq's civil war after the withdrawal of the USA (150,000)

2012: Syria's civil war (320,000)

2013: ISIS in Syria, Iraq, Libya (?)

2013-15: South Sudan vs rebels (10,000)

2014-15: Ukraine's civil war (6,000)

Arab-Israeli wars

- I (1947-49): 6,373 Israeli and 15,000 Arabs die
- II (1956): 231 Israeli and 3,000 Egyptians die
- III (1967): 776 Israeli and 20,000 Arabs die
- IV (1973): 2,688 Israeli and 18,000 Arabs die
- Intifada I (1987-92): 170 Israelis and 1,000 Palestinians
- Intifada II (2000-03): 700 Israelis and 2,000 Palestinians
- Israel-Hamas war (2008): 1,300 Palestinians

(Wars and Casualties of the 20th and 21st Centuries; http://www.scaruffi. com/politics/massacre August 5, 2016)

Never in world history since JESUS spoke those words have there been as many wars, rumors of wars, and preparations for wars as in our generation. Our war-torn, poverty-plagued world will welcome the deceptive promise of peace and prosperity which is the calling card the antichrist will present to the nations.

Surge in Evil

"Because lawlessness will multiply, the love of many will grow cold." Matthew 24:12

Anyone with a passing acquaintance of history knows that evil has been part of the human experience since the fall, as the HOLY SPIRIT testifies in His Word. JESUS states that there will be an observable increase in evil as the last days advance and people lose their love for GOD and one another. Evil multiplies as more people listen to the false voices in our world rather than listening to JESUS' message through His true prophets and apostles.

It's important to recognize that the advance in evil in the last days reflects the evil in the spirits of individuals. It is written:

"But know this: Difficult times will come in the last days. <u>For people will be lovers of self,</u> <u>lovers of money,</u> boastful, proud, blasphemers, disobedient to parents, ungrateful, unholy, unloving, irreconcilable, slanderers, without self-control, brutal, <u>without love for what is</u> <u>good,</u> traitors, reckless, conceited, <u>lovers of</u> <u>pleasure rather than lovers of God, holding</u> <u>to the form of godliness but denying its power.</u> <u>Avoid these people!</u>" 2 Timothy 3:1–5

Because individuals are characterized by self-love rather than loving GOD and others, there will be a corresponding escalation in evil on our darkened planet.

The Index of Evil in the Attack on Children

It is easy to detect the upsurge in evil through the lens of what is happening to the children in our world. Incubated in the atheistic, evolutionary regimes of Communist Russia, then China, the destruction of unborn children has spread across the nations of the world, killing billions within their mothers' wombs throughout the twentieth and twenty-first centuries. Abortion is deceptively portrayed as a woman's right and a choice for life and freedom, but it produces death and slavery to self-centeredness and guilt, often reflected in alcohol and drug abuse. Each year, an estimated fifty million unborn children are ripped out of their mother's wombs and discarded as trash. **The horrendous toll isn't limited to the children lost but includes the destructive impact of abortion on the mother, the medical personnel, the nations that approve of this sacrifice, and the United Nations that promotes it. The communal guilt is shared by all, including many churches, who have accepted, promoted, and tolerated this barbarism.**

An unborn child is not a meaningless blob of tissue, but a developing human being created in the image of GOD. The genetic reality of a new human life is mind-boggling. The nucleus of the single cell created at the time of conception contains approximately three billion base pairs of DNA, intricately coded with approximately twenty-five thousand different genes. There is enough genetic information in one cell to fill the equivalent of several thousand 500-page books of computer code. **Only GOD could create the incredible human genetic code and place it on a speck too small to see.** This is only the beginning of the incredible development of a child in his or her mother's womb. Most of the progression from this single cell to a fully-developed infant is still shrouded in scientific mystery. It is one miracle after another. I encourage you to use the following link to view photos of the unborn as they develop in their mother's womb. If the internet isn't available to you, check out your local library. They may have the LIFE magazine from April 30, 1965. The photos reveal God's amazing handiwork in His creation of children. *(www.bing. com/images/search?q=photos+of+unborn+children&qpvt=-photos+of+unborn+children&FORM=IGRE)*
It is written:

"For it was You who created my inward parts;
You knit me together in my mother's womb.
I will praise You because I have been remarkably
and wonderfully made.
Your works are wonderful, and I know this very well.
My bones were not hidden from You
when I was made in secret,
when I was formed in the depths of the earth."
Psalm 139:13–15

This description of the creation of a new human life was written some 3000 years ago, but the words "remarkably" and "wonderfully" are just as applicable today. From the time of conception, the development of a new human life is miraculous. Already at eighteen days after conception the unborn child has a beating heart. By forty-two days brains waves are detected, and within two months all internal organs are functioning, and the child may develop hiccups and yawn. At three months the child has fingerprints, can feel pain, and can even smile.

Life is GOD's amazing gift. Lamentably, in the culture of violence and death permeating our planet, this gift is often rejected. With a population of over seven and a half billion people on our planet today there is often a very callous and apathetic attitude towards others. We see our own life and the lives of those close to us as valuable, but we often view the lives of others as expendable. Since we do not see unborn children as they grow in their mothers' wombs, many find it easy to dispose of them. **The culture of violence and death has invaded the womb. The sheer number of those being eliminated deadens our senses—but it does not diminish the reality that these are human lives created by GOD.**

The reality of this destruction of our unborn brothers and sisters can be seen in photos on pro-life websites. It's true that "a picture is worth a thousand words". You will not likely find a record of photos of aborted children in politically-correct libraries in our towns and cities, but here are two pro-life websites that expose the truth of abortion. You may want to check them out before the government or the global tech companies remove them:

www.pinterest.ca/FreedomsAusgraphic-images-of-abortion-victims
www.100abortionphotos.com

It is important to express a note of thanks to the faithful spiritual warriors who are defending the lives of the unborn and ministering GOD's grace and truth in JESUS to those who have been affected by or involved in this desecration of human life. The Christian-based pro-life and pregnancy-center ministries are on the frontlines defending the helpless in this war against children, but all believers have a part in lifting up the sanctity of every human life in our daily words, actions, and prayers. It is written:

"Speak up for those who have no voice, for the justice of all who are dispossessed."
Proverbs 31:8

This includes our unborn sisters and brothers.

Until people see with their own eyes the destroyed bodies of these helpless infants, abortion remains camouflaged in philosophical rhetoric divorced from reality. If human life is not considered valuable in its beginning stages, it is not valuable at any stage. Abortion is a sin against not only the unborn, but against our CREATOR Who made all of us in His own image. National and international repentance is needed on the part of all who have succumbed to, promoted, and tolerated this slaughter of the innocent.

As predicted fifty years ago by many pro-life advocates, this culture of death is now inevitably progressing to euthanasia of the incurably-ill and severely-handicapped. The right to choose to eliminate unwanted unborn children has now expanded to include other groups of unwanted people.

Piling evil upon evil, there is a corresponding increase in the violent physical and sexual abuse of children occurring worldwide. The pandemic of child abuse and slavery that has been exposed in our generation is only the tip of the iceberg. The gruesome treatment of little children in our world is symptomatic of the sinful nature of humanity in the last days. Once again, slanderous accusations are being hurled at GOD, blaming Him for this evil. The abuse, however, is carried out by those who turn their hearts away from GOD and His Word and gracious will—including many who camouflage themselves with religious threads.

It is impossible to list all the depravity that permeates our planet today. Only a miniscule fraction is mentioned daily in our newspapers, and on our televisions, smartphones, and computer screens. Anyone with eyes to see and ears to hear is a witness to the horrific evil that is taking place 24/7 around our world. Every heart and every nation is an incubator capable of growing evil in all its manifestations—increasing hatred, violence, idolatry, immorality, lying, racism, disintegration of families, etc. **When CHRIST returns to our world and brings His judgment, it will be justified.** Only His amazing patience and desire to save as many as possible has postponed judgment for a future day— which is coming soon.

Contrary to popular humanistic mythology, human beings are not basically good but are corrupted in mind and heart and desperately in need of forgiveness and transformation. **Only JESUS can transform all who cry to Him for mercy and help through His cleansing blood and the ministry of His SPIRIT and Word in our lives.** Praise the LORD that millions all over our world are repenting of their sins and, through faith in CHRIST, are receiving His forgiveness and salvation and the new birth of their eternal spirits. They are being set free from sin and guilt to live a life of love to the LORD our GOD and to others around them, including the little children.

If you have not yet repented of your sin and received JESUS into your life as your gracious SAVIOR and Returning LORD, today is still a day of salvation. The SPIRIT of JESUS invites you today to come to CHRIST to be cleansed of all sin

and receive a new spirit of faith and love. The alternative is CHRIST's righteous and eternal condemnation in Hell. May all of us cry out to GOD in JESUS' name for His mercy and salvation in these evil days in which we are living.

Escalation in Persecution

JESUS prophesied: *"Then they will hand you over for persecution, and they will kill you. You will be hated by all nations because of My name." Matthew 24:9*

Believers in JESUS have faced varying degrees of ridicule, oppression, and persecution down through the ages. Millions of our brothers and sisters before us have experienced tremendous suffering and death for JESUS and His Gospel. Biblical history contains the record of many who gave their lives for the LORD and His Kingdom.

In many areas of our world today there is a widespread and growing spirit of mockery and hatred for the faithful few. Often people whose first loyalty is to JESUS are perceived as a nuisance and enemy of their nation's agendas and values— and increasingly, the global agendas and values of the elite. Antagonism to GOD's Word and people is one of the common denominators shared by all the world's antichrist leaders— cultural, religious, and political. They look with disdain at the few who still sincerely believe in JESUS and hold to a CHRIST-centered, Biblically-grounded faith. The global administrators look with favor on institutional churches and Christians that are willing to compromise their beliefs and practices and become useful pawns to the prevailing social and political values of the paganized new world order. On the other hand, these officials scorn and seek to silence those who preach and teach CHRIST and His Word and salvation.

The history of persecution, as JESUS pointed out, began with the murder of Abel by his brother Cain in the second generation of the human race *(Matthew 23:35).* Because of jealousy and anger, Cain killed his brother Abel, who by faith was seeking to live a righteous life *(Hebrews 11:4)*. Cain had a nominal religion. Abel had a personal faith and a living relationship with GOD. Instead of repenting of his wrong attitude to his brother and to GOD, Cain let his anger intensify to murderous rage. Those who reject CHRIST often have anger, hatred, and jealousy toward GOD's faithful people. Instead of repenting of their sinful thoughts and hearts, they often allow their hatred to grow to the point of persecuting those who believe.

JESUS frequently warned His followers of the persecution they would face as they obeyed His Word and carried out the mission of His Kingdom. In His Sermon from the Mount JESUS taught:

> *"Those who are persecuted for righteousness are blessed, for the kingdom of heaven is theirs.*
>
> *You are blessed when they insult and persecute you and falsely say every kind of evil against you because of Me. Be glad and rejoice, because your reward is great in heaven. For that is how they persecuted the prophets who were before you... But I tell you, love your enemies and pray for those who persecute you, so that you may be sons of your Father in heaven." Matthew 5:10–12,44–45*

On another occasion He said:

> *"Look, I'm sending you out like sheep among wolves. Therefore be as shrewd as serpents and as harmless as doves. Because people will hand you over to sanhedrins and flog you in their synagogues, beware of them. You will even be brought before governors and kings because of Me, to bear witness to them and*

to the nations. But when they hand you over, don't worry about how or what you should speak. For you will be given what to say at that hour, because you are not speaking, but the Spirit of your Father is speaking through you.

Brother will betray brother to death, and a father his child. Children will even rise up against their parents and have them put to death. You will be hated by everyone because of My name. But the one who endures to the end will be delivered. When they persecute you in one town, escape to another." Matthew 10:16–23

Hours before He was crucified, He reminded those who believed in Him:

"If the world hates you, understand that it hated Me before it hated you. If you were of the world, the world would love you as its own. However, because you are not of the world, but I have chosen you out of it, the world hates you. Remember the word I spoke to you: 'A slave is not greater than his master.' If they persecuted Me, they will also persecute you. If they kept My word, they will also keep yours. But they will do all these things to you on account of My name, because they don't know the One who sent Me." John 15:18–21

Like many other hard-hitting parts of JESUS' teaching, these words are often ignored in soft- cushioned churches these days. It's always easier to fit in with the crowd and enjoy the comfortable life than to be the object of the crowd's jealously, anger, and hatred. **Western-style Christianity is often** obsessed with having fun and being entertained rather than with testifying to CHRIST and being faithful to His Word. Being persecuted for the sake of righteousness is no fun and is therefore removed from the radar screen of many believers. The radar screen is changing.

We have been blessed with religious freedom in many western countries through the sacrifice of believers who preceded us. However, persecution of Christian believers has been spreading and growing dramatically over the past century. Many saints were removed from our planet during the Communist regimes of the Soviet Union, Red China, North Korea, Vietnam, Cambodia, etc. According to organizations that are ministering to persecuted Christians in our world today, an estimated one hundred million Christians face various levels of persecution on our increasingly blood-stained planet. *("PERSECUTION OF CHRISTIANS REACHES HISTORIC LEVELS, CONDITIONS SUGGEST WORST IS YET TO COME"; January 7, 2015 by Daniel; www.opendoorsusa. org; August 20, 2016).*

Believers in JESUS are daily facing verbal and physical abuse, children are removed from homes, property is taken away, women are raped, and increasing numbers are being imprisoned and tortured while others are being executed by crucifixion, beheading, or other methods. **We are often told that we need to live in the "real world". The real world is horrific for many believers in JESUS today—but they live with their spirits, minds, and hearts set on CHRIST and His coming Kingdom.** It is written:

> *"When the Lamb broke the fifth seal, I saw underneath the altar the souls of those who had been slain because of the word of God, and because of the testimony which they had maintained; and they cried out with a loud voice, saying, 'How long, O Lord, holy and true, will You refrain from judging and avenging our blood on those who dwell on the earth?' And*

there was given to each of them a white robe; and they were told that they should rest for a little while longer, until the number of their fellow servants and their brethren who were to be killed even as they had been, would be completed also." *Revelation 6:9–11 NASB*

Persecution of believers is spreading exponentially across the face of our planet. During the coming reign of the antichrist beast, the powers of this world will wage a global war to eliminate all who worship JESUS and desire to obey His commandments. Those who refuse to bow to the antichrist and his new world order will be labelled as enemies. We are on the verge of worldwide persecution of all whose loyalty is to CHRIST and His Word and Kingdom.

"So the dragon was furious with the woman and left to wage war against the rest of her offspring — those who keep God's commands and have the testimony about Jesus." *Revelation 12:17*

No Fear

The LORD doesn't warn us of persecution to create fear in our hearts. JESUS and His SPIRIT tell us repeatedly to not be afraid, but to live boldly in righteousness, sharing His grace and truth in word and deed wherever we have an open door (***Psalm 11***). Instead of fearing or hating those who ridicule, abuse, imprison, torture, or kill us, we are to love them and pray for them as the LORD tells us to do.

Life in this world is short. One day soon we will die, either through disease, accident, or the violent and hateful actions of others. I don't know when or how my journey on this planet will end, but my prayer is that, if the LORD wills, I would prefer to die while testifying to Him. Peter expressed the same sentiment—until he was surrounded by those who hated JESUS. As JESUS said to His students: *"The spirit is willing, but the flesh is weak" (Matthew 26:41).* May GOD's SPIRIT strengthen us for the days ahead.

Whether by disease or persecution, death is nothing to be feared, for the LORD has gone ahead of us to prepare an eternal, glorious paradise for us, and one day soon He will come back for us. **Believe in JESUS and be of good courage. Serve the LORD and His Kingdom for as long as you can, with all your heart, soul, mind, and strength. The best is yet to come!**

Falling Away from Faith in CHRIST

> *"At that time many will fall away and will betray one another and hate one another."*
> *Matthew 24:10 (NASB)*

JESUS' words in this verse should bring great lament into the spirits of all who believe in and love JESUS and His Church. The Greek word that is translated here as "fall away" is transliterated as "scandalon" from which we have the term "scandal". The term in its basic meaning is a trap, or snare, something that results in sin, in falling away or stumbling. The scandal in this verse speaks of those who have heard of JESUS and His Gospel, who have professed faith in Him, and yet in the last days will fall away or give up their faith in CHRIST and end up betraying and hating the faithful followers of JESUS.

JESUS, in His parable of the seed, stated:

> *"and the one sown on rocky ground — this is one who hears the word and immediately receives it with joy. Yet he has no root in himself, but is short-lived. When pressure or persecution comes because of the word, immediately he stumbles." Matthew 13:20–21*

Our brother Paul writes of individuals already in New Testament times who believed but then fell away from JESUS.

> *"I am amazed that you are so quickly turning away from Him who called you by the grace of Christ and are turning to a different gospel — not that there is another gospel, but there are some who are troubling you and want to change the good news about the Messiah."* Galatians 1:6–7

> *"Timothy, my son, I am giving you this instruction in keeping with the prophecies previously made about you, so that by them you may strongly engage in battle, having faith and a good conscience. <u>Some have rejected these and have suffered the shipwreck of their faith</u>. Hymenaeus and Alexander are among them, and I have delivered them to Satan, so that they may be taught not to blaspheme."* 1 Timothy 1:18–20

Further it is written:

> *"For it is impossible to renew to repentance those who were once enlightened, who tasted the heavenly gift, became companions with the Holy Spirit, tasted God's good word and the powers of the coming age, and who have fallen away, because, to their own harm, they are recrucifying the Son of God and holding Him up to contempt."* Hebrews 6:4–6

Without entering the ongoing and often-heated debate as to whether it is possible for someone who sincerely believes in JESUS to fall away from faith in CHRIST, it is clear that many who proclaim faith in JESUS will fall away from their professed faith and end up betraying CHRIST and His faithful followers. History is filled with many examples of individuals and whole denominations that have descended down that path. Many of the false prophets professed faith in the LORD and His Word at one time. In the last days—because of the multiplication of false prophets and worldly saviors, the explosion of evil, and persecution and ridicule of those who believe in JESUS—many who have professed faith will fall into every kind of sin and will turn their backs on Him. These hypocrites will join the world in its scoffing at CHRIST and those who still believe in Him.

Many today argue that the incredible evils in our world prove that GOD either does not exist or is not loving. This rationalization is used for rejecting GOD and CHRIST and, ironically, for supporting much that is evil. Many individuals hypocritically blame GOD for the evil while promoting the ideas and values that have produced the evil. Blindly, they don't recognize that by using this argument to justify their rejection of JESUS, they are tragically fulfilling His prophecy.

JESUS asked: *"when the Son of Man comes, will He find that faith on earth?" (Luke 18:8).*

Will there be any faithful followers of JESUS left on our planet when He comes back? The answer of the HOLY SPIRIT in His Word is yes, there will be some who believe in CHRIST when He comes, and they will meet CHRIST in the air. JESUS said: *"But the one who endures to the end will be delivered" (Matthew 24:13).* Because of the tremendous persecution in those last days and the falling away from faith in JESUS and His Word, only a remnant will remain of what there could have been.

While the darkness deepens, the light of the love and truth of CHRIST shines forth as a beacon of His kingdom, which is already present in our world and will soon come in all its glory. Amen, come LORD JESUS!

Pray!

CHAPTER 15
HE HOLDS THE WORLD IN HIS HANDS

*"The earth and everything in it,
the world and its inhabitants,
belong to the Lord."*
Psalm 24:1

Degeneration of the Natural World

JESUS said:

*"There will be violent earthquakes, and fam-
ines and plagues in various places, and there
will be terrifying sights and great signs from
heaven."* **Luke 21:11**

N ot only do the human events in our world testify to the
LORD's soon return, but all of nature is shouting that it's
time to wake up and prepare for His coming. Ever since humanity's fall into darkness, the material creation, what we call the
natural world, has been deteriorating, producing increasing
suffering and destruction in our world.

It is written:

> *"For the creation eagerly waits with antici-*
> *pation for God's sons to be revealed. For the*
> *creation was subjected to futility — not will-*
> *ingly, but because of Him who subjected it —*
> *in the hope that the creation itself will also*
> *be set free from the bondage of corruption*
> *into the glorious freedom of God's children."*
> *Romans 8:19–21*

Sin is a curse, not on humanity only, but on all of creation. Contrary to the mythology of evolution— but in keeping with the second law of thermodynamics—everything in our material world is in a state of degeneration. From the moment of birth our bodies begin a process of decay. Using experimental and observational science, several researchers are reporting that our entire human genome is deteriorating because of the accumulation of genetic mutations (Dr. John Sanford, *Genetic Entropy and the Mystery of the Genome;* Technical Publisher: Ivan Press 2005). As a consequence of choosing our way instead of the LORD's way, our bodies, designed to be eternal, have an average life span of only fifty to eighty years, depending on what subdivision of the planet a person lives in.

As the cancer of sin spreads and multiplies in our world, so too does the deterioration it produces on the entire created order. This includes not only out-of-control plagues and pestilences, but also the shaking of our planet and changes in the sun, moon, stars, and universe which will all begin to show evidence of decay. These signs will become clearer in the days immediately preceding CHRIST's second coming *(Matthew 24:29–30; Revelation 6–9)*. The universe had a beginning and, because of humanity's evil, it will soon have an end. **Sin is far more destructive than most people realize.**

Plagues

"Authority was given to them over a fourth of the earth, to kill by the sword, by famine, by plague, and by the wild animals of the earth."
Revelation 6:8

The first antibiotic, penicillin, was discovered by Alexander Fleming in 1928.

"He noticed that some bacteria he had left in a petri dish had been killed by naturally occurring penicillium mold. Since the discovery of penicillin, many other antibiotics have been discovered and developed." (www.bbc.co.uk/schools/ gcsebitesize/science/21c_pre_2011/disease/antibioticsdrug-testingrev1.shtml)

Antibiotics, one of the greatest medical advances of all time, have brought improved health and longer lives to literally billions of people during this past century. Nevertheless, because of their overuse, even the most powerful antibiotics are being rendered useless today by antibiotic-resistant bacteria. National and world health authorities have been blowing the trumpet, warning of the coming antibiotic "apocalypse".

"If the 'antibiotic apocalypse' happens, it'll be because our politicians let it." Nick Dearden "We really are facing – if we don't take action now – a dreadful post-antibiotic apocalypse. England's chief medical officer has repeated her warning of a "post-antibiotic apocalypse" as she urged world leaders to address the growing threat of antibiotic resistance. Prof Dame Sally Davies said that if antibiotics lose their effectiveness it would spell "the end of modern medicine". Without the drugs used to fight infections, common medical interventions such as caesarean sections, cancer treatments and hip replacements would become incredibly risky and transplant medicine would be a thing of the past, she said.

(www.theguardian.com/commentisfree/2017/oct/09/ antibiotic-apocalypse-agribusiness-big-pharma)

I recall that when I was in high school, some of our teachers and the media suggested that the scientific revolution taking place would conquer all diseases. They proclaimed that within twenty to thirty years people would be living to be one hundred fifty years or longer. Forty-five years later we are experiencing the advent of many new infectious, genetic, and other disorders, and the resurgence with new virulence of old diseases once considered vanquished. Ebola, aids, zika, malaria, yellow fever, cholera, dengue fever, hepatitis, and tuberculosis are just a few of the increasing number of old and new diseases bringing suffering and death in many nations today. Through international travel, diseases are circulated rapidly to all nations.

What is true of these human plagues is equally true of animal and plant diseases and insect pestilences. Despite powerful pesticides, fungicides, and herbicides being applied to fields, gardens, and orchards, plant diseases and pests continue to spread and destroy crops. JESUS' warnings concerning plagues and pestilences that would be present in various places in our world in the days before His return are being fulfilled. More devasting plagues are yet to come.

Earthquakes and Volcanoes

"Therefore we will not be afraid, though the earth trembles and the mountains topple into the depths of the seas, though its waters roar and foam and the mountains quake with its turmoil." Psalm 46:2–3

Mountains are shaking, and the land is quaking in many sectors of our planet. Despite denial on the part of many, the facts clearly testify to an increase in earthquakes rattling our blue planet in our generation. Here are the statistics on the number of earthquakes from 1970 until now according to the United States Government Service (USGS) National Earthquake Information Center website:

1970-1979: 1132 earthquakes 6.0 or greater (Richter Scale)
1980-1989: 1291 earthquakes 6.0 or greater
1990-1999: 1541 earthquakes 6.0 or greater
2000-2009: 1615 earthquakes 6.0 or greater
2010-2018 (Sept. 14): 1299 earthquakes 6.0 or greater
(www.earthquakes.usgs.gov; Sept. 14, 2018)

These statistics indicate a 20-30% increase in powerful earthquakes over the past half century.

The number of active volcanoes around the globe has significantly increased as well. This escalation in volcanic activity is to be expected, given the upsurge in earthquakes. As the earth's plates move, lava is being forced to the surface. The incredible capacity of some of the newly-discovered super volcanoes, such as the Yellowstone Caldera, pose a grave threat to life on earth. JESUS testifies that, in the last days before His return, as much as one-third of the earth will be destroyed by some cataclysmic event involving fire *(Revelation 8:7–9)*. The eruption of some of these super volcanoes could result in that kind of impact on life on our planet.

The Earth is Shaking. Is the Sky Falling?

Scoffing aimed at followers of CHRIST for their opposition to abortion, euthanasia, and the legalization of homosexual marriage scornfully boasts that the sun is still shining, and the sky isn't falling despite the tolerance and promotion of these practices today. This same shallow argument could also be applied to all the evils of past history. In spite of humanity's sin over the past 6000 years, the sun continues to shine, and the sky has not collapsed in on us yet. The key word here is **yet.** In the last days the sun will begin to change, and the sky will begin to fall, effecting increasing death and destruction. The order in the heavens will be increasingly shaken, just as the earth is being shaken.

Until two years ago, the scientific consensus was that our earth's magnetic field was decreasing in strength by approximately six percent per century.

"Over the last two centuries the dipole strength has been decreasing at a rate of about 6.3% per century." *"Earth's magnetic field: Time dependence" www. en.m.wikipedia.org, July 30, 2016*

Creation scientists have said for many years that the decay of earth's magnetic field is one of the evidences for a young earth. With only a five percent decrease in strength per century, the magnetic field would have been too powerful even 10,000 years ago for human life to have existed on earth. (Jonathon Sarfati, *The Greatest Hoax on Earth?* Creation Book Publishers, Atlanta, GA 2010 pages 208-210)

It's been guesstimated that if the percent of decrease continued at the same rate as in the past, we would have another 1600-2000 years before this would result in any impact on our world. However, one recent study of the earth's magnetic field

indicated that it has decreased in strength by about five percent over the past decade.

("New Study shows how rapidly Earth's magnetic field is changing" www.scien-
cealert.com May 11, 2016; "Earth's Magnetic Field Is Weakening 10 Times Faster
Now" www.livescience.com July 8, 2014; "Earth's Impending Magnetic Flip" www.
scientificamerican.com October 1, 2014)

Most scientific experts are insisting that, although they
don't know what is causing this decrease of the magnetic field,
it's nothing to be concerned about since they believe this has
happened many times throughout their mythical billions of
years of earth's history. Scientists have some theories as to how
our magnetic field works, but don't have a proven explanation
as to why the magnetic field is getting weaker. Using their theories, they certainly didn't predict this increased decay rate. If
this recent study is accurate, and the magnetic field continues
to decrease in strength at this rate, it will impact life on earth
within our life time. No one, however, fully comprehends what
will happen to our magnetic field in the future. It is all specu-
lation based on very limited understanding.

The magnetic field is also our protective sky shield. It is an
invisible screen that shields us from the harmful solar winds
and cosmic radiation of the sun. This is one intricate aspect
of GOD's amazing design for our planet. If this recent study is
verified, and our planet's magnetic shield is indeed decreasing
at a faster pace than previously believed, then in one sense
the sky may be collapsing in on us. For some unknown reason,
this invisible sky dome that surrounds our planet and protects
us from the sun's rays is fading away. I recall a cancer specialist
making a presentation to a group of chaplains a few years
ago in which he stated that they were expecting a marked
increase in the rate of skin cancer from increased exposure to
the sun's radiation, but he did not elaborate as to why. From a
Biblical perspective, we understand the curse of accumulated

human evil is creating this increasing deterioration in all material systems.

Will the LORD let this happen? GOD has been extremely patient with the evil in our world, but His patience will soon end. Our human race is bringing wickedness to its climax of self-destruction. Do not presume that the sun will continue to shine, and that the magnetic field will continue to protect planet Earth. CHRIST will allow our world to reap what it has sown, but He will return before the world exterminates itself with its arrogance and rebellion.

While many in the world may live in fear of these potential catastrophes, all who trust in the LORD know that even if the earth shakes, volcanoes erupt, or earth's magnetic field begins to disintegrate, we have nothing to fear— for He is with us. As it is written: *"Do not be afraid, Abram. I am your shield; your reward will be very great" (Genesis 15:1).* This same assurance which the LORD gave to Abraham is given hundreds of times throughout His Word to all who trust in Him.

The Final Extreme Warnings of the Trumpets

"Immediately after the tribulation of those days: The sun will be darkened, and the moon will not shed its light; the stars will fall from the sky, and the celestial powers will be shaken. Then the sign of the Son of Man will appear in the sky, and then all the peoples of the earth will mourn; and they will see the Son of Man coming on the clouds of heaven with power and great glory." Matthew 24:29–30

We have noted the increase in general signs and warnings that indicate we are getting closer and closer to the return of CHRIST. These events are revealed in the first five of the seven seals of *Revelation 6*. The sixth seal, however, ushers us into much greater destruction, including extremely powerful earthquakes and the shaking of the heavens that occurs just prior to the LORD's coming on the clouds of heaven *(Revelation 6:12–17)*. The seventh seal *(Revelation 8–9)* becomes the seven trumpets which proclaim the final severe warnings before CHRIST comes to rapture His faithful Church.

The trumpets could be direct acts of GOD in judgment on our world. However, the events that the first four trumpets reveal in *Revelation 8:6–13* could also be the result of nuclear, biological, and chemical warfare or extremely powerful natural disasters, including the eruptions of some of the super volcanoes. In Noah's day, a deluge of water fell from above but also came up from the storehouses below the earth's crust. GOD's judgment on the global society of the antichrist beast will likely involve nuclear fire from above as well as the storehouses of molten lava—liquid fire below our planet's surface. The human race will reap what it has sown.

The Final War

The sixth trumpet announced in *Revelation 9:13–19* proclaims the destruction of a third of the world's inhabitants in the last world war before JESUS' return. This war will be with weapons of mass destruction. The apprehension of mutual nuclear destruction has been mounting as the relationships between the United States, Russia, and China have been increasingly strained over the last few years. With the race to develop new and more destructive weapons, the pressure is building. Propelled by both arrogance and fear, preparations for a full-scale war are being developed and will be activated sooner rather than later.

Still Time to Repent?

During the time of the seals and trumpets there is still opportunity for people to repent and come to faith in CHRIST. The seals are signs and the trumpets are warnings to all who will humble themselves and seek the LORD before it is too late. Tragically, most of the world will harden their hearts to GOD and refuse to repent, despite the incredible destruction that human evil is producing in the world.

> *"The rest of the people, who were not killed by these plagues, did not repent of the works of their hands to stop worshiping demons and idols of gold, silver, bronze, stone, and wood, which are not able to see, hear, or walk. And they did not repent of their murders, their sorceries, their sexual immorality, or their thefts."*
> *Revelation 9:20–21*

As it is written: *"Today, if you hear His voice, do not harden your hearts" (Hebrews 4:7).* Since no one knows what tomorrow will bring, we need to humbly repent and turn to JESUS for His Word of forgiveness and grace whenever the HOLY SPIRIT speaks to us of our sin. Do not wait for tomorrow or next week or until you are on your death bed. You may not die in a bed.

The Wrath-Filled Bowls

The trumpets are the final warnings of GOD before JESUS returns to put an end to all evil. GOD is extremely patient and longsuffering, or to use the popular contemporary term, tolerant. But He has set a limit to His tolerance of our corruption of everything which is good. The LORD our Creator does endure evil for a time, but that time is running out and His wrath is approaching. The warnings of the trumpets are followed by the bowls of His wrath in **Revelation 16.**

After the LORD removes the faithful remnant of believers in the rapture **(Matthew 24:30–31; 1 Corinthians 15:50–57; 1 Thessalonians 4:13–18; Revelation 11:15–19)**, He will pour out the seven bowls of wrath on the Antichrist and his corrupted empire. It is CHRIST who authorizes the pouring out of the bowls of wrath. The same JESUS Who created the heavens and the earth and Who died on the cross for the sins **"of the whole world" (1 John 2:2)** will also fulfill His perfect justice in the destruction of the antichrist's global empire. The bowls of wrath are not warnings or calls to repentance, but the implementation of His righteous judgment on the corruption of the antichrist and his followers.

The Angels declare:

> **"You are righteous, who is and who was, the Holy One, for You have decided these things. Because they poured out the blood of the saints and the prophets, You also gave them blood to drink; they deserve it! Then I heard someone from the altar say: Yes, Lord God, the Almighty, true and righteous are Your judgments.'" Revelation 16:5–7**

Amen!
Pray!

CHAPTER 16

PREPARATION FOR THE ANTICHRIST

*"You are of your father the Devil,
and you want to carry out your father's desires.
He was a murderer from the beginning and has not stood
in the truth, because there is no truth in him.
When he tells a lie, he speaks from his own nature,
because he is a liar and the father of liars."*
JESUS, John 8:44

Forewarnings Regarding the Antichrist

E veryone who truly believes in JESUS, the CHRIST, the Son of GOD, believes that He is coming back a second time. When He returns He will not be born of a virgin, nor suffer and die on a cross, nor rise from the dead, but will come to reign as KING of KINGS and LORD of LORDS. He will call His people to Himself, put an end to evil in our world, and judge the living and the dead. He is coming with power and glory, whether people are ready or not.

JESUS and His HOLY SPIRIT have also clearly forewarned us that, prior to JESUS' return, an ultimate antichrist will come and lead our world to its destruction. There is much about this imitation savior of the last days that GOD has chosen not to reveal to us. We don't know his name, when or where he will be born, or countless other details of his life. Until he is transformed into humanity's counterfeit messiah, we won't know who he is. It isn't helpful to speculate about these details prior to his actual appearance. Only after he arrives and begins to exhibit who he is through his words and actions will he be recognized by those who know CHRIST. The LORD has revealed enough about this anti-savior that faithful Christians will be able to identify him when he appears. **Even though he will be camouflaged as a savior, his character and actions will be unmistakable for everyone who believes the testimony of GOD's Word.**

The Satanic Rebellion

GOD has a plan and so does Satan. Before focusing on the LORD's revelation of the ultimate anti-savior, it is crucial to understand the reality of Satan, who will be at work in and through the antichrist. For many in our pre-Christian world today, the devil is mere mythology, a leftover from superstitious ancestors. For those blinded by a materialistic mindset, anything which isn't comprised of material atoms is fairy-tale stuff that exists only in the imaginations of the gullible, foolish, or insane. Tragically, the reality of the evil one is rejected and ridiculed not only by the materialists of the world, but also by many who occupy church pews, pulpits, college and seminary professorships, and church bureaucracies. In 1977, for the first time, I met a seminary professor who openly rejected the reality of Satan and believed that the devil was nothing more than a literary figure used to personify evil. Today there are legions of seminary professors who reject Satan's existence. As JESUS said: *"Blind guides! You strain out a gnat, yet gulp down a camel!" (Matthew 23:24).*

The devil's presence and schemes are manifested in the multiplicity of barbarisms that engulf our world. JESUS taught that the only way of being free from the deceptions and destruction that Satan is hatefully sowing in our world is to know the truth. Those who refuse to listen to JESUS' words, and who reject the reality of the evil one, are opening their minds' door to all the devil's delusions and temptations.

A second error that many in and outside the church make regarding Satan is to believe that he is equal to GOD and is directly involved in everything that happens in our lives and world. We have all heard the saying: *"The devil made me do it."* Satan is frantically active in our world, but he cannot force anyone to do anything. He works through deception, using words to camouflage good for evil and evil for good.

Through JESUS and His Word, GOD has revealed four spiritual forces present and active in our world:
1. the HOLY SPIRIT of GOD
2. the spiritual angels who serve and glorify GOD
3. Satan and his fallen angels and demons who oppose GOD and His plans
4. the spirits of people

The devil is sly and working in our world feverishly, but he is not all-powerful or equal to GOD. Through faith in JESUS and knowledge of His Word, we can know the truth about Satan and be set free from his lies and deceptions. GOD didn't allow Adam and Eve to use the excuse that the devil made them do it, and that excuse is not available to us today either. Satan can deceive and inspire great evil, but he cannot force anyone to believe his lies or to do his will. Those who live by faith in CHRIST need to be wise and understand Satan's schemes around us—but we need not fear him.

The Personification of Evil

Anyone who reflects on the state of our planet recognizes the incredibly complex threats confronting the global village today, and the apparent need for some super hero to lead us out of humanity's death spiral. **Although the antichrist will be the personification of Satan, he will masquerade as an enlightened, benevolent savior.** He will appear as an intelligent and exceptionally-gifted man who projects the image of having both the sincere desire and the singular ability to solve the world's vast and threatening crises, and to create global unity, peace, and justice. Most of the world's peoples and leaders will initially see him as a prince of peace who can rescue our planet from humanity's self-destructive path. The world is waiting for this demigod savior.

The Global Village in Need of a Global Savior

When I first began to learn about the antichrist in the Scriptures and how he would establish a global empire, most people thought it was impossible because the nations of the world were all too nationalistic. That was forty-five years ago. Today, we are living in a global village where national boundaries are being obliterated and propaganda for a new global order is being disseminated to all peoples. The cry for open borders is widespread, and the creation of international economic, legal, and medical systems is advancing by the day. The global village is being prepared for some new messiah to arrive on the scene to solve our problems and bring us to the full self-actualization of the "good" within us. The world is longing for an inspiring, charismatic, powerful, intelligent, super-human to fulfill the dream of a world without religions where humanity is transformed into a global hippie commune of love, peace, and prosperity. John Lennon wrote the following popular song about this dream in 1971—

227

Imagine
-John Lennon

Imagine there's no heaven
It's easy if you try
No hell below us
Above us only sky
Imagine all the people
Living for today...Aha-ah...
Imagine there's no countries
It isn't hard to do
Nothing to kill or die for
And no religion, too
Imagine all the people
Living life in peace...You...
You may say I'm a dreamer
But I'm not the only one
I hope someday you'll join us
And the world will be as one
Imagine no possessions
I wonder if you can
No need for greed or hunger
A brotherhood of man
Imagine all the people
Sharing all the world...You...
You may say I'm a dreamer
But I'm not the only one
I hope someday you'll join us
And the world will live as one

"Imagine" has been one of the theme hymns of pagan humanists in their drive to rid the world of GOD, and to create their own humanistic socialistic paradise.

On 1 January 2005, the Canadian Broadcasting Corporation named "Imagine" the greatest song in the past 100 years as voted by listeners on the show *50 Tracks*.[45] The song ranked number 30 on the Recording Industry Association of America's list of the 365 Songs of the Century bearing the most historical significance.[45] Virgin Radio conducted a UK favourite song survey in December 2005, and listeners voted "Imagine" number one.[46] Australians selected it the greatest song of all time on the Nine Network's *20 to 1* countdown show on 12 September 2006. They voted it eleventh in the youth radio network Triple J's Hottest 100 Of All Time on 11 July 2009.[47]...

Jimmy Carter said, "in many countries around the world—my wife and I have visited about 125 countries—you hear John Lennon's song 'Imagine' used almost equally with national anthems."[48][nb 3]
(www.en.wikipedia.org/wiki/Imagine_%28John_Lennon_song%29, August 3, 2018)

Imagine was performed at the closing ceremonies of the Summer Olympics in London in 2012 and was also part of the opening ceremonies of the 2018 Winter Olympics in PyeongChang, South Korea. In the 1970s, only John Lennon and a few hippies could imagine this world. Today, this is the imagination of the United Nations being propagandized to the children and youth of the world. All that is needed is an antichrist to be the catalyst of this new global order.

The United Nations: Precursor to the Antichrist

We do not have a global government— yet, but the United Nations is quickly preparing the way. Many aspects of the 2030 agenda—the goals of the United Nations governmental organization— reads like the Communist Manifesto. It sounds so humanitarian in its concern for the peoples of the world and for peace and justice in the world, but its implementation will involve the domination of peoples, including the oppression and persecution of those who don't support these universal goals and values or the methods used to achieve them. Those who oppose these values and the transformation into this new global order will be labelled haters, crazies, or religious fundamentalist zealots.

When I was in communist East Germany in 1979, billboards proclaimed: *"Je starker der Sozialismus, desto sicherer der Frieden"*— *"the stronger the socialism, the more secure the freedom"*. Slogans were employed to conceal oppressive dictatorship. At the time, citizens couldn't even move to a different location without government approval, and they were very unwilling to discuss political issues in public for fear of the authorities. Like these communist slogans, the goals of the 2030 UN agenda are vacuous phrases which will require increasing limitations on individual freedoms.

Here is a little taste of the plans for taking control, propagandized as "transforming our world" as promoted by the United Nations:

Transforming Our World
The 2030 Agenda for Sustainable Development

Preamble
This Agenda is a plan of action for people, planet and prosperity. It also seeks to strengthen universal peace in larger freedom. We recognize

that eradicating poverty in all its forms and dimensions, including extreme poverty, is the greatest global challenge and an indispensable requirement for sustainable development. All countries and all stakeholders, acting in collaborative partnership, will implement this plan. We are resolved to free humanity from the tyranny of poverty and want and to heal and secure our planet. We are determined to take the bold and transformative steps which are urgently needed to shift the world on to a sustainable and resilient path. As we embark on this collective journey, we pledge that no one will be left behind. The 17 Sustainable Development Goals and 169 targets which we are announcing today demonstrate the scale and ambition of this new universal Agenda. They seek to build on the Millennium Development Goals and complete what they did not achieve. They seek to realize the human rights of all and to achieve gender equality and the empowerment of all women and girls. They are integrated and indivisible and balance the three dimensions of sustainable development: the economic, social and environmental. The Goals and targets will stimulate action over the next 15 years in areas of critical importance for humanity and the planet.

People
We are determined to end poverty and hunger, in all their forms and dimensions, and to ensure that all human beings can fulfil their potential in dignity and equality and in a healthy environment.

Planet

We are determined to protect the planet from degradation, including through sustainable consumption and production, sustainably managing its natural resources and taking urgent action on climate change, so that it can support the needs of the present and future generations.

Prosperity

We are determined to ensure that all human beings can enjoy prosperous and fulfilling lives and that economic, social and technological progress occurs in harmony with nature.

Peace

We are determined to foster peaceful, just and inclusive societies which are free from fear and violence. There can be no sustainable development without peace and no peace without sustainable development.

Partnership

We are determined to mobilize the means required to implement this Agenda through a revitalized Global Partnership for Sustainable Development, based on a spirit of strengthened global solidarity, focused on the needs of the poorest and most vulnerable and with the participation of all countries, all stakeholders and all people. The interlinkages and integrated nature of the Sustainable Development Goals are of crucial importance in ensuring that the purpose of the new Agenda is realized. If we realize our ambitions across the full extent of the Agenda, the lives of all will be profoundly improved and our world will be transformed for the better....

4. As we embark on this great collective journey, we pledge that no one will be left behind. Recognizing that the dignity of the human person is fundamental, we wish to see the Goals and targets met for all nations and peoples and for all segments of society. And we will endeavor to reach the furthest behind first.

5. This is an Agenda of unprecedented scope and significance. It is accepted by all countries and is applicable to all, considering different national realities, capacities and levels of development and respecting national policies and priorities.

These are universal goals and targets which involve the entire world, developed and developing countries alike. They are integrated and indivisible and balance the three dimensions of sustainable development...

Our vision
7. In these Goals and targets, we are setting out a supremely ambitious and transformational vision. We envisage a world free of poverty, hunger, disease and want, where all life can thrive. We envisage a world free of fear and violence. A world with universal literacy. A world with equitable and universal access to quality education at all levels, to health care and social protection, where physical, mental and social well-being are assured. A world where we reaffirm our commitments regarding

the human right to safe drinking water and sanitation and where there is improved hygiene; and where food is sufficient, safe, affordable and nutritious. A world where human habitats are safe, resilient and sustainable and where there is universal access to affordable, reliable and sustainable energy.

8. We envisage a world of universal respect for human rights and human dignity, the rule of law, justice, equality and non-discrimination; of respect for race, ethnicity and cultural diversity; and of equal opportunity permitting the full realization of human potential and contributing to shared prosperity. A world which invests in its children and in which every child grows up free from violence and exploitation. A world in which every woman and girl enjoys full gender equality and all legal, social and economic barriers to their empowerment have been removed. A just, equitable, tolerant, open and socially inclusive world in which the needs of the most vulnerable are met.

9. We envisage a world in which every country enjoys sustained, inclusive and sustainable economic growth and decent work for all. A world in which consumption and production patterns and use of all natural resources – from air to land, from rivers, lakes and aquifers to oceans and seas – are sustainable. One in which democracy, good governance and the rule of law, as well as an enabling environment at the national and international levels, are essential for sustainable development, including sustained and inclusive economic growth, social

development, environmental protection and the eradication of poverty and hunger. One in which development and the application of technology are climate-sensitive, respect biodiversity and are resilient. One in which humanity lives in harmony with nature and in which wildlife and other living species are protected.
(United Nations A/RES/70/1 General Assembly Distr.: General 21 October 2015
Seventieth session Agenda items 15 and 116 15-16301 (E)
1516301
Resolution adopted by the General Assembly on 25 September 2015
https://sustainabledevelopment.un.org/content/documents/21252030%20Agenda%20for%20Sustainable%20Development%20web.pdf)

The UN agenda is written in the same kind of double-speak as was the Communist Manifesto and other vacuous propaganda pieces of various dictatorial regimes. It sounds so enlightened, progressive, and humanitarian, until you read between the lines, understand what they mean, and how they are planning to achieve their objectives. They have no way of accomplishing any of these goals without being able to control the actions and words of people. To fulfill their plans, they will need to reduce individual freedoms, and criminalize all individuals or organizations, including churches, that don't conform to the politically and socially correct thoughts or actions they will promote for the sake of unity and peace. They will need to control the flow of information through the internet by criminalizing all ideas contrary to their global values and agenda.

Between the lines of their stated desire for improving the welfare, health, and status of women is the increasing promotion of abortion services for all women, to free them from the burden of bearing and raising children. The United Nations has already declared that abortion is a human right for every woman, and they will seek to implement this right everywhere, except in Muslim-dominated nations. If that fails to reduce the increasing populations, they will resort to laws limiting families to one or two children, like the communist regime in China. While they spout democracy, they will be unable to realize their authoritarian schemes without controlling the population and severely limiting freedoms. Their goal of "equality" and "justice" for all includes the promotion of idolatry, sexual immorality, homosexuality, and trans-sexuality, except, of course, in Muslim-dominated nations. An integral aspect of their justice agenda will be the marginalization and persecution of those who do not walk lockstep with their so called "global values".

Most modern societies have social insurance or social security numbers to keep track of their citizens and to facilitate data collection. With the move to global economic, legal, and health systems, a universal identification system using some new high-tech programmed chip or mark will be created to monitor people in all these global programs. Undoubtedly, these global leaders will promise to provide everyone with a guaranteed income above the poverty line, an idea which is already being promoted in numerous nations. The masses will embrace these programs and gleefully look forward to this new socialistic world order where everyone will receive a base income just by registering and receiving the mark or chip. They will foolishly imagine that this will eliminate all poverty.

It is interesting to note that these 2030 goals place no value on the reality of our CREATOR and SAVIOR or the protection of religious freedom to proclaim the truth of CHRIST. This is a strictly secular, humanistic document with no understanding of humanity's fallen condition, no faith in CHRIST and His salvation and coming Kingdom, no seeking of GOD's help—and no hope of realization! The implementation of these 2030 goals will involve the marginalization, oppression, and eventually the persecution of those who proclaim CHRIST, and of others who don't fall in line with their schemes. The agenda goals are a mere camouflage for moving the world towards a one-world authoritarian government.

Without knowing the warnings in GOD's Word and without realizing that the UN is preparing the way for the coming antichrist and a global government, it would be very easy to join the parade and link arms with all who are willing to work towards this humanistic utopia. We all live on the same planet and ought to work together to solve the planet's problems, except there is no human way to save ourselves. Like the proverbial lemmings, people are following the global mob to the cliff's edge. If CHRIST did not intervene, our doom would be sealed. The move to the new global order is humanistic mythology, lacking an understanding of history and the sinful nature of man. Like the creators of all the humanist manifestos of the past century, the UN insanely believes that we can save ourselves, even as they steer the world to its termination point. The prophet Jeremiah testified about the false prophets of his generation:

> *"They have treated superficially the brokenness of My dear people, claiming, 'Peace, peace,' when there is no peace." Jeremiah 8:11*

Those pushing this UN agenda recognize there is no hope of accomplishing these goals without some precipitous global event and a dynamic human savior to propel the agenda forward. A global economic collapse, a limited nuclear war, or some other major disaster is essential to pressure the nations towards this new global order. In addition to some impacting event, the planet requires a demigod leader to arise and guide this planetary government to "save" the world. It's possible that the personification of Satan is already on the scene, developing his schemes to step forward, "save" the world, and usher in his global utopian empire. We don't know the day or the hour of CHRIST's return, or of the appearing of the antichrist. We need to watch and wait.

Pray!

CHAPTER 17

THE ADVENT AND TERMINATION OF THE ANTICHRIST

"Then I saw heaven opened, and there was a white horse.
Its rider is called Faithful and True,
and He judges and makes war in righteousness...
He wore a robe stained with blood,
and His name is the Word of God...
A sharp sword came from His mouth,
so that He might strike the nations with it...
He will also trample the winepress
of the fierce anger of God, the Almighty.
And He has a name written on His robe and on His thigh:
KING OF KINGS AND LORD OF LORDS...
Then I saw the beast, the kings of the earth,
and their armies gathered together to wage war against
the rider on the horse and against His army.
But the beast was taken prisoner,
and along with him the false prophet,
who had performed the signs in his presence...
Both of them were thrown alive into the lake of fire

that burns with sulfur."
Revelation 19:11–20

The Desire for the Antichrist

O ur world desperately needs a savior. When JESUS came into our world to be humanity's SAVIOR over two thousand years ago, He was rejected and continues to be rejected by the masses. As it is written:

> *"He was despised and rejected by men, a man of suffering who knew what sickness was. He was like someone people turned away from; He was despised, and we didn't value Him." Isaiah 53:3*

> *"He was in the world, and the world was created through Him, yet the world did not recognize Him. He came to His own, and His own people did not receive Him." John 1:10–11*

Having rejected the One Who was given the name *"Jesus, because He will save His people from their sins" (Matthew 1:21),* the overwhelming majority of the human race is waiting for a different kind of savior: an antichrist who will give them a humanistic paradise on earth.

The vast majority of the leaders down through history were little antichrists, desiring people to worship and serve them instead of the LORD GOD. Sometimes this was accomplished at the edge of the sword and sometimes by deceiving them into believing that their kings, pharaohs, sultans, or emperors were god-like and would lead them into a utopian society. However, the record of history, as the historian Edward Gibbon wrote, *"is indeed little more than the register of the crimes, follies, and*

misfortunes of mankind." (*www.brainyquote.com/authors/*
edward_gibbon)

People are growing tired of these trivial false saviors, their
self-promotion, and the wreckage they have led their countries or tribes into. The world has had enough of these minor
egotistical leaders and is waiting for a man of real power and
authority to come and unite the world in peace, prosperity,
and justice for all. This is the spirit of the antichrist gaining
ascendancy in all nations today. The world desperately needs
a savior. Tragically, having rejected JESUS, the only true SAVIOR,
they are waiting for a humanistic savior to come and rescue
our world from its trajectory of destruction and give them the
paradise they want.

The Beast

JESUS came into our world as a humble lamb. He was
gentle and humble in heart *(Matthew 11:29).* He came as
a servant to seek the lost, minister to the needy, and bring
the good news of His coming Kingdom to the poor in spirit
who were being oppressed by the world *(Luke 4:18–19).* He
came to suffer and die for our sin, and to conquer sin, death,
the devil, and Hell for all who trust in Him. The antichrist will
promise to save the world from destruction, to help the poor,
needy, and oppressed peoples in our world, and to usher in a
utopian era. He will sound a lot like JESUS. He will promise an
economic system of prosperity for all. He will bring a tentative
peace to the warring nations. He will be called many noble
names, perhaps receive many Nobel prizes, and will soak in the
lavish praise that will be heaped upon him. He will be a false
savior whose heart will be filled with vanity, hatred for CHRIST,
and disdain for humanity, even as sweet words proceed from
his mouth. He will be a beast in sheep's clothing.

Is the Antichrist a Real Human?

Many Jewish rabbis and liberal theologians choose to interpret the clear prophesies to CHRIST's first coming in *Psalm 22* and *Isaiah 52–53* as references not to an actual man but rather to the whole nation of Israel as GOD's suffering servant in this world. In a similar vein, many interpret the prophesies concerning the antichrist as representing a world system and not an individual. Like the prophecies on JESUS' first coming, the prophesies about the antichrist clearly refer to a man.

In Revelation 13 the antichrist is referred to as a "beast":

> *"And I saw a beast coming up out of the sea. He had 10 horns and seven heads. On his horns were 10 diadems, and on his heads were blasphemous names. The beast I saw was like a leopard, his feet were like a bear's, and his mouth was like a lion's mouth. The dragon gave him his power, his throne, and great authority." Revelation 13:1–2*

If this were a literal description of the antichrist, he would certainly be a very strange-looking, beastly creature and not a man. However, most interpreters recognize that this is a symbolic description of the character and power of the antichrist. Although this portrayal certainly could depict a world system, it is clear from the context, as well as from other Scripture passages, that it refers to the coming **antichrist and his global empire.** Later, in exposing the mark of the beast, we are informed that his number is *"the number of a man" (Revelation 13:16–18).*

The Man of Lawlessness

Through the Apostle Paul, the LORD speaks of His return and the coming of the antichrist, who is referred to as *"the man of lawlessness".*

> *"Now concerning the coming of our Lord Jesus Christ and our being gathered to Him: We ask you, brothers, not to be easily upset in mind or troubled, either by a spirit or by a message or by a letter as if from us, alleging that the Day of the Lord has come. Don't let anyone deceive you in any way. For that day will not come unless the apostasy comes first and the man of lawlessness is revealed, the son of destruction. He opposes and exalts himself above every so-called god or object of worship, so that he sits in God's sanctuary, publicizing that he himself is God. Don't you remember that when I was still with you I told you about this? And you know what currently restrains him, so that he will be revealed in his time. For the mystery of lawlessness is already at work, but the one now restraining will do so until he is out of the way, and then the lawless one will be revealed. The Lord Jesus will destroy him with the breath of His mouth and will bring him to nothing with the brightness of His coming." 2 Thessalonians 2:1–8*

The Apostle Paul had spoken often in the churches about CHRIST's return and the coming of the antichrist. He wrote:*"Don't you remember that when I was still with you I told you about this?" (verse 5).* They had previously heard Paul's testimony concerning JESUS' return but had carelessly allowed these truths to be removed from their minds. As JESUS testified in His parable of the sower in **Matthew 13,** Satan loves to snatch GOD's Word away from those who have heard it. The cares, worries, pleasures, and treasures of this world choke out GOD's Word and people soon forget what the LORD has revealed to them.

Paul was also writing to clarify their misunderstanding. Some people were spreading rumors about the Apostle Paul, reporting that he had either said or written that CHRIST had already returned. Based on JESUS' promises, many were expecting His return—but because their understanding was limited, they were easily misled by false teachings which were spreading in the churches. The same scenario is taking place today. Many have heard of the LORD's return but are very con- fused by false prophesies that are circulating regarding His second coming. To avoid being deceived by false teachers, we must pay attention to the LORD's testimony through His apos- tles. For all who will receive these words as GOD's truth, much is revealed here about the antichrist.

The HOLY SPIRIT makes clear the following truths con- cerning the antichrist and JESUS' return:

➢ The LORD will not return to our world until the anti- christ comes.

➢ The antichrist is here identified as **"the man of law- lessness"** and **"the son of destruction"**, and his work is referred to as **"the apostasy".** JESUS came to fulfill the Law, but the antichrist will have no regard for GOD's law and commands but will be a law unto himself. He will do whatever he pleases and will unite our world in a complete planetary rebellion against the LORD GOD and against those who seek to follow CHRIST and His Word.

➢ The antichrist will at some point proclaim himself to be god and have idols of himself set up throughout the world (**Revelation 13:11–15**). Unlike JESUS, Who was accused and sentenced to death for proclaiming the truth that He was the SON of GOD, the antichrist will be worshiped and praised by all nations when he falsely proclaims himself to be GOD.

The Abomination that Causes Desolation

The prophesies in Daniel testify to a prince or ruler who will come in the last seven-year period of world history and set up in the temple area an *"abomination of desolation"* (*Daniel 11:31, 12:11*). Some interpreters suggest these prophesies may have had an earlier foreshadowing when an idol of the pagan god Zeus was set up in the temple by Antiochus Epiphanes circa 168 BC. In *Matthew 24:15,* JESUS referred to Daniel's prophecy when speaking of the last days before His return, and therefore could not have been referring to the event which took place one hundred sixty-eight years before His first coming. The *"abomination that causes desolation"* that JESUS was referring to is generally understood to refer to the time when the final antichrist will proclaim himself to be humanity's god and savior in Jerusalem's temple area. The world will worship him as their god and savior.

Will the Temple be Rebuilt? How? When?

Since numerous interpreters believe that the temple in Jerusalem must be rebuilt to fulfill the prophecy regarding the *"abomination that causes desolation"*, they are convinced that JESUS won't return before its reconstruction. Other interpreters suggest the prophecy will be fulfilled if the antichrist makes his proclamation in the area where the temple was located. Since our understanding is incomplete, we need to always be ready for the LORD's return.

Although preparations for the rebuilding of the Temple have been underway for several years, many assume construction in the near future isn't possible considering the political situation in the Middle East. However, it could happen very quickly during the reign of the beast. The antichrist will have the authority, the world's resources and technology, and the support of the community of nations and religions, including Jews and Muslims. In his scheme to desecrate the temple area by using it to proclaim his divinity and blaspheme GOD, he will have strong motivation to rapidly reconstruct the temple.

The Antichrist as the Messiah of All Religions

Considering the dedication of some religious followers across the planet, how will the antichrist persuade all people to follow him? The World Council of Churches has, over the past seventy years, increasingly propagated the belief that all religions are equal and all lead to GOD. For the noble causes of unity and peace, religious studies courses in most universities around the globe have been indoctrinating the gullible minds of the young with this false teaching. Spiritual leaders gather together in inter-church and inter-religious conferences to promote harmony and common spirituality among all religious peoples. Clear Biblical teachings or doctrines are being thrown out in favor of inner spiritual development and religious harmony. The groundwork for a universal religion and a universal savior has already been laid—all that is needed to cement it is the coming of that false savior.

During his ascent to power, the antichrist will likely claim to be the promised savior each religion is waiting for:
- the Jewish Messiah
- the Islamic Mahdi or the Islamic Jesus
- the Buddhist Maitreya
- the Taoist Li Hong
- the Hindu kalki
- the Zoroastrian Saoshyant
- the reincarnated avatar of new agers

> ➤ the more highly-evolved man for the atheist
> ➤ the returning Christ of the Christians.

(www.en.m.wikipedia.org; Messianism, November 1, 2017)

To win over the Jewish people, the antichrist will claim to be their Messiah. Many Jewish people, having rejected JESUS as the Messiah, are still waiting for their Messiah to come and reign over the Earth from Jerusalem. It's interesting to note that Muslims are also waiting for Jesus to come back and reign, but their Jesus is not the SON of GOD, Who died and rose again. Muslims are also waiting for the Mahdi to come rid the world of evil prior to the day of judgment and the coming of their false Jesus. Like Jews and Muslims, many of the world's religions and new age spiritualities are waiting for some kind of savior to show up and save the world.

Will the antichrist be Jewish or Muslim or arise out of some other religious or ethnic background? Since Jewish prophecy clearly states that the Messiah will be a descendant of King David, **(Isaiah 9:6–7)** the antichrist will likely claim David as his ancestor to convince the orthodox Jews. Although this could simply be a deception, since deceiving others will be his specialty, it is certainly possible that he could be a descendant of David as well as being a Muslim. Some people of Jewish descent are Muslim in their faith and practice. The antichrist, using his power and authority from Satan, will do many signs and wonders **(*Matthew 24:24; 2 Thessalonians 2:9–10*).** Combined with his global agenda of justice and peace, these amazing miracles will convince most religious and non-religious people that he is the savior they are hoping and waiting for. He will deceive all who do not know and love the real JESUS.

Most Christians in our world are nominal or cultural Christians, including many leaders in Protestant, Roman Catholic, Orthodox, Evangelical, Pentecostal, and non-denominational churches. Christian churches today are, in some respects, like the Jewish synagogues of JESUS' day. Even though

Jewish people had the Law, the Psalms, and the Prophets pointing them to JESUS, most didn't recognize or receive Him when He came. Given the choice between JESUS and Barabbas, they chose the lawless Barabbas. Tragically, many who fill the pews, pulpits, stages, and board rooms of Christian churches today will make the same mistake when the antichrist comes. They will choose to follow the man of lawlessness rather than be true and faithful to JESUS.

How will you cast your vote when the antichrist sits on his throne claiming to be God and is worshiped by the peoples of the world, including the majority of those in Christian churches, Jewish synagogues, Muslim mosques, Hindu temples, etc.? If you don't follow the crowd by worshiping humanity's false savior, you will be derided and persecuted. Are you prepared to face the opposition of the world and fallen church, and the hatred of the antichrist beast?

> *"And he was permitted to wage war against the saints and to conquer them. He was also given authority over every tribe, people, language, and nation. All those who live on the earth will worship him, everyone whose name was not written from the foundation of the world in the book of life of the Lamb who was slaughtered. If anyone has an ear, he should listen:*
>
> *If anyone is destined for captivity, into captivity he goes. If anyone is to be killed with a sword, with a sword he will be killed. This demands the perseverance and faith of the saints." Revelation 13:7–10*

Whether we live in those days of the antichrist, or in these days of many antichrists, we must rely on the SPIRIT of the

LORD and His Word to enable us to faithfully endure and give the good testimony to JESUS before our lost world.

No need to be Deceived

Even though the masses of humanity will be deceived by the antichrist when he comes, you do not need to be. The HOLY SPIRIT says through the Apostle Paul:

> *"The coming of the lawless one is based on Satan's working, with all kinds of false miracles, signs, and wonders, and with every unrighteous deception among those who are perishing. <u>They perish because they did not accept the love of the truth in order to be saved</u>. For this reason God sends them a strong delusion so that they will believe what is false, so that all will be condemned — those who <u>did not believe the truth but enjoyed unrighteousness</u>. But we must always thank God for you, brothers loved by the Lord, because from the beginning God has chosen you for salvation through sanctification by the Spirit and <u>through belief in the truth</u>. He called you to this through our gospel, so that you might obtain the glory of our Lord Jesus Christ. Therefore, brothers, stand firm and hold to the traditions you were taught, either by our message or by our letter." 2 Thessalonians 2:9–15*

Those who do not *"believe the truth"* will be deceived, which means that those who believe and hold to the truth will not be deceived.

What is the truth about the antichrist? How can anyone know the truth? JESUS said: *"If you continue in My word... you will know the truth, and the truth will set you free" (John 8: 31–32).* Before going to the cross, He prayed for those who would trust in Him: *"Sanctify them by the truth; Your word is truth" (John 17:17).* If you earnestly read and believe GOD's Word, you will know JESUS and will recognize the anti-Jesus when He comes. The only way of recognizing what is false is by knowing what is true. If you don't know JESUS personally—if you aren't walking and talking with Him continually, if you pay no attention to His Word and don't hold on to His teachings— you won't be able to recognize the antichrist when he comes, and you will be deceived. Do not think you are too smart or too good to be deceived. If you aren't following and trusting in JESUS and His Word today, you are already being deceived.

Listed below is a review of four basic teachings of GOD's Word which will clearly identify the antichrist for those who believe in and love GOD's truth:

➤ **He will not come on the clouds with the saints and angels of Heaven as JESUS will. He will not come to rapture true CHRIST believers out of the world before bringing his wrath on the world.** Now it is in the realm of possibility that he may deceptively claim to some people— he will give different stories to different groups of people—to have arrived on a spaceship from some distant galaxy or even from another universe or dimension. Because evolutionary mythology and science fiction have blinded our generation, many believe that alien humans from another galaxy seeded human life hundreds of millions of years ago and will return to save our world. The antichrist may use this mythology, and any other mythology he can, to deceive the blind and gullible.

➤ **He will be a man who establishes his power and authority in our world through political intrigue and various miraculous signs and wonders.**

> **He will not rule according to the teachings of JESUS and His Word.** He will likely quote a few of JESUS' words, twisting them to encourage lawlessness and rebellion against the commands of GOD. He will make up his own laws and enforce them, just as all the little antichrists have always done.
> **He will persecute all who refuse to worship him, especially those who sincerely believe in JESUS and His Word.**

The antichrist is not JESUS. When JESUS comes, the entire world will see Him, like lightning that lights up the sky *(Matthew 24:27).* JESUS is not coming again through a virgin's womb, but on the clouds of Heaven *(Matthew 24:30; Acts 1:9-11).* He is not coming alone, but with the armies of angels in Heaven *(Matthew 24:31)* and all the saints who have lived in ages past *(1 Thessalonians 4:13–18).* He is not coming to die for our sins, but to gather His people together before He brings His judgment on the world of evil *(Matthew 24:31).* He is not coming to shed His own blood again, but to spill the blood of His enemies *(Revelation 19:11-16).* He is not coming to bring peace to the world, but to wage war against the beast and his global empire.

The antichrist's words will sound enlightened and his actions will seem miraculous—but no one will be deceived who truly knows JESUS, the teaching of His Word concerning His return, and the HOLY SPIRIT's depiction of the antichrist.

The Termination of the Antichrist and His Global Empire

Shortly after the antichrist's declaration of godhood, the LORD JESUS will overthrow him *"with the breath of His mouth" (2 Thessalonians 2:8).* The SPIRIT reveals that the days of the beast will be incredibly difficult for believers in the LORD, but the good news is that the antichrist's global empire won't last long. The LORD has set a limit to his reign; his power on earth will be temporary. **Revelation 13:5** speaks of just forty-two months for the beast to reign and to carry out the most severe persecution of believers. Whether this number is symbolic or literal, the message is that his reign will be limited, and he is doomed. As the LORD says in **Revelation 13:10**, this calls for **"the perseverance and faith of the saints"** during the insanity of those days.

We all know that during particularly difficult circumstances time seems to drag on. The tragic realities of life prior to and during the reign of the antichrist are not going to last forever. Hitler bragged about establishing a thousand-year Reich, but it became a heap of rubble after only a few years. When dictators are in their full strength and power, it appears as if nothing can defeat them. Then a stronger ruler arrives and their power and empire collapse. **During the antichrist's dictatorship it will seem that he has won and that his empire is invincible—but suddenly JESUS will come, and the beast and his empire will be terminated.**

All through the New Testament, the SPIRIT calls believers to persevere in their faith. Revelation is not a book of gloom and doom unless you worship this world and its antichrists. Revelation is a book of hope and encouragement to all who trust in JESUS as SAVIOR and LORD. We know the end is near, and we are called to be faithful to the end. JESUS said: **"But the one who endures to the end, he will be saved" (Matthew 24:13 NASB).**

Only CHRIST can and will defeat the beast and his global empire. JESUS defeated Satan through His death and resurrection and when He comes again He will terminate the antichrist. The LORD's righteous wrath will be poured out on the beast and his followers during the last days of his empire **(Revelation 16-18).**

When CHRIST returns:

"He will also trample the winepress of the fierce anger of God, the Almighty… But the beast was taken prisoner, and along with him the false prophet, who had performed the signs in his presence. He deceived those who accepted the mark of the beast and those who worshiped his image with these signs. Both of them were thrown alive into the lake of fire that burns with sulfur." Revelation 19:15–20

Many signs that JESUS said would precede His return are being fulfilled in our generation. Even though we can't know the exact day or hour of the LORD's coming or the appearing of the antichrist, the realities of life today ought to cause us to humble ourselves and cry out to the LORD for His mercy and help.

Pray!

CHAPTER 18

HALLELUJAH! HALLELUJAH! HALLELUJAH! HALLELUJAH!

"Hallelujah! Salvation and glory and power belong to our God;
BECAUSE HIS JUDGMENTS ARE TRUE AND RIGHTEOUS...
And a second time they said, "Hallelujah! ...
And the twenty-four elders and the four living creatures
fell down and worshiped God who sits on the throne saying,
"Amen. Hallelujah!"
And a voice came from the throne, saying,
'Give praise to our God, all you His bond-servants,
you who fear Him, the small and the great.'
Then I heard something like the voice of a great multitude
and like the sound of many waters
and like the sound of mighty peals of thunder, saying,
'Hallelujah! For the Lord our God, the Almighty, reigns.
Let us rejoice and be glad and give the glory to Him,
for the marriage of the Lamb has come
and His bride has made herself ready.'"
Revelation 19:1–7 (NASB)

The Hallelujah Chorus!

I believe that the Hallelujah Chorus of Handel's *Messiah* is the most powerful chorus of praise ever composed and proclaimed on earth. It will only be exceeded by the Hallelujahs that reverberate through the heavens as JESUS returns. It will all happen very quickly in the end. When JESUS descends to the Mount of Olives (*Zechariah 14:4–9*), the antichrist and his worldly empire will be destroyed, and he will be cast into the eternal lake of fire *(Revelation 19:20)*.

This will be followed by the Day of Judgment *(Matthew 25:31-46; Revelation 20:11–15)* when JESUS will separate those who have lived self-centered, unrepentant lives of sin from those who have trusted, loved and served Him. Those who have lived by faith in Him and His Word– repenting of their sin and seeking to love and serve Him and others in His Name–will receive the eternal life JESUS has won for them. Those who have lived for themselves and for the pleasures and treasures of this world will be condemned by CHRIST to the eternal lake of fire. Evil will be no more. JESUS will reign over His Kingdom of righteousness, peace, love, and joy forever. The Hallelujah celebrations begun in Heaven will continue for all eternity.

The SPIRIT of the LORD tells us many times in His Word to "watch", particularly in reference to the coming of the Day of the LORD. If these are the days that will completely fulfill all the prophecies of His return, today's technology—televisions, radios, computers, iPods, iPads, smart phones, etc.—will enable people world-wide to see the events CHRIST revealed regarding His second coming literally occurring before our eyes and ears.

In these days we all need to keep our eyes on the goal: eternal life with CHRIST in His Kingdom. Whether or not we live during the days of the ultimate antichrist, we will sooner or later face suffering, pain, and death. In these times, through faith in JESUS, we look ahead to the eternal celebrations to come when we will experience joy and peace beyond comprehension.

What Will Our Returning SAVIOR and KING Be Like?

Ultimately, the second coming of JESUS is not about an exact chronology of events that will precede His return. The signs preceding His return are like trumpets calling out to all people to get ready for the coming of the KING of KINGS and LORD of LORDS. For believers, our focus is not on these passing events but on JESUS. We look forward to seeing Him and living with Him in His kingdom. When JESUS ascended into Heaven two thousand years ago, the disciples were all gazing at Him *(Acts 1:9–11)*. It's important that we keep our eyes focused on Him as we wait for His second coming, particularly since those days— which may in fact be these days—are days of much confusion and anxiety around the globe.

When JESUS returns to our world one day soon, He is coming as the eternal KING and LORD of the universe. He is coming in love to rescue His Bride, but in wrath to the nations of the world who have abused His Bride. This is a very different JESUS than the mushy caricatures of Him in many churches today. Numerous denominations and churches have rejected this warrior JESUS because He doesn't fit in with their cheap-grace, universalistic theologies where everyone ends up in a "better place". What they have failed to understand, because they don't believe all of GOD's Word, is that this is the same JESUS who lived and ministered GOD's amazing grace and powerful truth two thousand years ago. The same JESUS who died on the cross for the sin of the world will bring His judgment and wrath on the nations of the world for their rebellion and evil. JESUS has not changed or evolved. As the HOLY SPIRIT testifies, *"Jesus Christ is the same yesterday, today, and forever" (Hebrews 13:8).* Those who reject this warrior JESUS are rejecting JESUS in all His fullness and trying to recast Him in their own twenty-first century, progressive, humanistic image. The HOLY SPIRIT's description of CHRIST returning to our world on the clouds to rapture His people and to bring His wrath on the world is crucial for us. Otherwise, we may be deceived by the antichrist when he comes with his smooth, charismatic appeal to love, peace, and unity, centered on him and his mythical utopia.

Coming for the Elect

JESUS said in **Matthew 24:31** that when He comes His angels will gather **"His elect"** from all parts of the world. Sometimes in wedding announcements the bride is referred to as the bride-elect, the one whom the groom has chosen to be united with for life. Who are the ones that JESUS has elected to be His Bride—to be united with forever? JESUS refers to the elect three times when speaking of His return:

> *"But those days will be limited because of the*
> *elect... False messiahs and false prophets will*
> *arise and perform great signs and wonders to*
> *lead astray, if possible, even the elect... He will*
> *send out His angels with a loud trumpet, and*
> *they will gather His elect from the four winds,*
> *from one end of the sky to the other." Matthew*
> *24:22,24,31*

The Apostle Paul wrote*: "Who can bring an accusation against God's elect? (Romans 8:33).* The Apostle John addresses one of the early Christian churches with the words: "**To the elect lady and her children: I love all of you in the truth" (2 John 1:1).**
The more common word used throughout GOD's Word to describe the elect is "chosen". In His conclusion to the parable of the wedding banquet, JESUS said: "**For many are invited, but few are chosen" (Matthew 22:14).** And in His last hours with His disciples before His arrest and crucifixion JESUS told them:

> *"If you were of the world, the world would love*
> *you as its own. However, because you are not*

of the world, but _I have chosen you_ out of it, the world hates you." John 15:19

The Apostle Peter wrote:

"To the temporary residents dispersed in Pontus, Galatia, Cappadocia, Asia, and Bithynia, _chosen according to the foreknowledge_ of God the Father and set apart by the Spirit for obedience and for sprinkling with the blood of Jesus Christ." 1 Peter 1:1–2

Who has CHRIST elected or chosen to be His Bride to spend eternity with? JESUS and the HOLY SPIRIT are clear that it is **those who sincerely believe in Him, who have had their sins forgiven through His blood, and who are seeking to love and obey Him and to serve others in His Name.** The elect are those who know JESUS, and who will not be deceived by the false prophets or the antichrist. They are waiting for their SAVIOR and KING and LORD to return and take them home.

Are you one of the elect? Have you sincerely repented of your sin before GOD and placed your faith and trust in what JESUS has done for you on the cross? Do you love Him—and are you seeking to honor and glorify Him and share His grace and truth with our lost world? It is time for all who know and love CHRIST to stand up for the KING of KINGS and LORD of LORDS, to get ready to meet their Creator and Savior, and to proclaim His salvation to all nations.

"He who testifies about these things says, "Yes, I am coming quickly." Amen! Come, Lord Jesus!" Revelation 22:20

Hallelujah!
Pray!

CHAPTER 19

COMING WHEN THE MISSION IS COMPLETED

"But the one who endures to the end will be delivered.
This good news of the kingdom will be proclaimed
in all the world as a testimony to all nations.
And then the end will come."
Matthew 24:13–14

The Last Days of Mission

The end is near. But for those who have repented and are trusting in JESUS, the end is not something to fear. It is a call to greater zeal for completing the mission the LORD has given us. Apart from the LORD's return or a world-wide revival, nothing can prevent the world's self-destruction by antichrist leaders, weapons of mass destruction, and scientists determined to mess with the foundations of the universe and life. Only through a massive revival happening in the majority of nations, bringing CHRIST-centered leadership and sanity to our world, can our world exist for a few more decades. As followers of our LORD JESUS we need to dedicate ourselves to sharing His Word and salvation, so more people will be brought into

His eternal Kingdom before He returns. Given the apocalyptic realities today, the time given to complete the mission is short.

"So when they had come together, they asked Him, 'Lord, are You restoring the kingdom to Israel at this time?' He said to them, 'It is not for you to know times or periods that the Father has set by His own authority. But you will receive power when the Holy Spirit has come on you, and you will be My witnesses in Jerusalem, in all Judea and Samaria, and to the ends of the earth.'" Acts 1:6–8

The **"last days"** is the Church age, during which CHRIST gave His HOLY SPIRIT and His authority to His followers to bring the good news of His life, death, resurrection, return, and coming Kingdom to the nations of the world. Beginning with JESUS' apostles in the first century AD, His faithful followers have been taking His Gospel and Word from Jerusalem to the ends of the earth for almost two thousand years.

"All authority has been given to Me in heaven and on earth. Go, therefore, and make disciples of all nations, baptizing them in the name of the Father and of the Son and of the Holy Spirit, teaching them to observe everything I have commanded you. And remember, I am with you always, to the end of the age." Matthew 28:18–20

In the last chapter of the Bible JESUS proclaimed:

"Both the Spirit and the bride say, 'Come!' Anyone who hears should say, 'Come!' And

> *the one who is thirsty should come. Whoever*
> *desires should take the living water as a gift."*
> **Revelation 22:17**

The fulfillment of the outpouring of GOD's SPIRIT on CHRIST's followers began on the Day of Pentecost and will end at the time of His return. Today, every single day is like Pentecost *(Acts 2)* as people in all ends of the earth hear the Good News of JESUS' life, death, resurrection, ascension, and coming return in their own language. Despite ridicule and persecution, people are coming to faith in JESUS in increasing numbers in these apocalyptic days. Every day thousands are coming to repentance of their sin and faith in CHRIST as their SAVIOR and LORD. The angels in Heaven are rejoicing over everyone who comes to repentance and faith (*Luke 15:7,10*).

GOD's SPIRIT is doing amazing things in and through His faithful servants. CHRIST, the Word of GOD, is touching and affecting the lives of countless numbers of people through evangelism, prophecy, education, healing, and mercy. Hundreds of thousands of CHRIST-centered congregations and ministries across our planet's landscape are spreading the pleasing aroma of JESUS to all peoples. As it is written:

> *"But thanks be to God, who always puts us*
> *on display in Christ and through us spreads*
> *the aroma of the knowledge of Him in every*
> *place. <u>For to God we are the fragrance of</u>*
> *<u>Christ among those who are being saved and</u>*
> *<u>among those who are perishing. To some we</u>*
> *<u>are an aroma of death leading to death, but</u>*
> *<u>to others, an aroma of life leading to life.</u>"*
> *2 Corinthians 2:14–16*

The Sign of the Gospel in Every Nation

This is the age of mission. CHRIST testified that He will return when this mission is completed *(Matthew 24:13–14)*. One of the significant signs of the last days will be the proclamation of the Gospel of CHRIST and His Kingdom to all nations. Most of the other signs which JESUS testified would precede His return result from the evil instigated by the devil, the antichrist, and the unbelieving world, and it's terrible consequences reflected in nature. This sign of the Gospel in all nations is the fruit of the love and commitment of His faithful followers to the mission the LORD has given to us.

Today, for the first time in history, this prophecy is on the verge of being fulfilled. Only the LORD knows when it will be completely fulfilled, but we are living in the age when, through a multitude of people and ways, GOD's SPIRIT and faithful church are bringing the good news of CHRIST and His salvation and kingdom to the ends of the earth. Praise the LORD that His Name and salvation are being proclaimed throughout our world today. JESUS, however, has not yet returned and therefore, the mission has not yet been completed. As JESUS taught:

> *"The harvest is abundant, but the workers are few. Therefore, pray to the Lord of the harvest to send out workers into His harvest."*
> *Matthew 9:37–38*

More people still need to hear about CHRIST, and the LORD is giving us a little more time to complete our mission. The needs and the opportunities to testify to JESUS have never been greater.

A Life of Mission

As we wait for CHRIST to return to end evil and to take us into His eternal Kingdom, we have a mission to fulfill. The evening before He was crucified, JESUS prayed on our behalf:

> *"I am not praying that You take them out of the world but that You protect them from the evil one. They are not of the world, as I am not of the world. Sanctify them by the truth; Your word is truth. As You sent Me into the world, I also have sent them into the world. I sanctify Myself for them, so they also may be sanctified by the truth." John 17:15–19*

JESUS' prayer for all who believe in Him isn't that we would be removed from this present earthly sphere before our work here is completed. He prays that each of us will be sanctified or committed to Him through the truth of His Word. Once we know Who JESUS is, what He has accomplished for us, what He is doing now and will soon do when He returns, and once we have received His HOLY SPIRIT into our lives, He sends us to be His witnesses in these last days to our lost and despairing world. As JESUS says: *"Peace to you! As the Father has sent Me, I also send you" (John 20:21).*

Every true believer in the LORD has an important part in His kingdom work to be occupied with until He comes. The Apostle Paul, in light of JESUS' resurrection and ours, writes:

> *"Therefore, my dear brothers, be steadfast, immovable, always excelling in the Lord's work, knowing that your labor in the Lord is not in vain." 1 Corinthians 15:58*

The LORD knows that we can't accomplish the mission He's given us by our own strength or wisdom. Therefore, He has given His HOLY SPIRIT to enable us to be His witnesses. We are inadequate and weak and will never perfectly reflect JESUS to our world, but through the power of His SPIRIT in us we can point others to CHRIST as the HOLY LAMB of GOD Who can and will save all who come to Him in repentance and faith. The LORD sends us to go In His Name knowing that He is with us and will use us for His glory and the salvation of His people.

We are thankful for the saints before us who have shared the good news of the LORD JESUS and His Kingdom with others and with us, but we recognize that all of them, like us, have fallen short. As the Apostle Paul wrote concerning himself:

"When I came to you, brothers, announcing the testimony of God to you, I did not come with brilliance of speech or wisdom. For I didn't think it was a good idea to know anything among you except Jesus Christ and Him crucified. I came to you in weakness, in fear, and in much trembling. My speech and my proclamation were not with persuasive words of wisdom but with a powerful demonstration by the Spirit, so that your faith might not be based on men's wisdom but on God's power."
1 Corinthians 2:1–5

Some are tempted to worship the saints of the past. If they were here they would tear their clothes and tell us not to worship them, but to give all our worship and praise to GOD-to CHRIST *(Acts 14:8–18)*.

The HOLY SPIRIT and the saints throughout the past two thousand years have testified to Who JESUS is, what He has done, what He is doing, and what He will soon do. It's time now for all of us who have come to CHRIST in our generation to add our lives and voices as a testimony to JESUS to those around us and to the ends of the earth, wherever the LORD calls and sends.

Are you willing to commit yourself, as the LORD enables you, to helping to complete this incredible mission? The harvest of souls is His!

Glory be to the FATHER, SON, and HOLY SPIRIT! Amen **Pray!**

LIVING THE FINALE
WITH JESUS

"I am the Alpha and the Omega,
the First and the Last, the Beginning and the End."
Revelation 22:13

JESUS IS! He IS the Beginning and the End, Who WAS and IS and IS to Come! He IS GOD and Man, Creator, Savior and Counselor! He IS the Rock of All Ages, the Bright Morning Star, the Lily of the Valley! He IS the Bread and Water of Life! He IS the Good Shepherd Who lay down His life for His Sheep! He IS the Risen LORD and Victorious, Returning KING! He IS the Eager Bridegroom and Faithful Husband! He IS the Light that shines in our darkened world! He IS Grace and Truth! He IS love, joy, peace, and the abundant and eternal Life!

He IS with Us!

JESUS said: *"And remember, I am with you always, to the end of the age" (Matthew 28:20).*
JESUS is with all who sincerely trust in Him in this very broken and dying world. We are all part of the broken and

dying, but He is with His people to save, speak, teach, rebuke, forgive, correct, train, comfort, and encourage. He will be with us to the very end. Only the LORD knows if we will be present on this planet when JESUS descends with the saints and the holy angels, or if we will be coming with Him and them. Present or coming, we will see Him, and will see His promises fulfilled. Every word and letter will be accomplished before our very eyes.

As we face the challenges of the conclusion of life on this planet, His Body and Blood are our food and drink, His SPIRIT is our Helper and Guide, and His Word is the information we need to propel us to pick up our cross and follow Him on the path of faith. Soon our faith will be sight, but even as we wait to see Him in all His glory, our minds and hearts are focused on Him. As it is written:

> *"But we do see Jesus — made lower than the angels for a short time so that by God's grace He might taste death for everyone — crowned with glory and honor because of His suffering in death." Hebrews 2:9*

> *"You love Him, though you have not seen Him. And though not seeing Him now, you believe in Him and rejoice with inexpressible and glorious joy, because you are receiving the goal of your faith, the salvation of your souls." 1 Peter 1:8–9*

A Life of Faith

Everyone lives by faith in something—the only difference is what our faith is in.

Secularists live by faith in atoms and in their intellectual ability to perceive and understand the material universe. From the outset, their faith is a contradiction because reason is not a material reality. The ability to reason and to perceive that you are reasoning is a clear indicator of the presence of mind and spirit. For you or me to understand anything there must be a you or me to do the understanding! Mineral molecules do not think, or feel, or delight in anything. Although materialism is used to rationalize away moral accountability, it is a bankrupt paradigm that begins and ends in futility.

Every day, in every way, everyone lives life in this world by faith. Our lives are directed by faith in ourselves, our feelings, our intuitions, our reasoning, and our philosophies, as well as in family members, teachers, medical doctors, nurses, carpenters, plumbers, political leaders, engineers, airline pilots, and technological systems. From experience we have come to trust in some of these people and systems, and from experience we know that none of these, including ourselves, is ultimately trustworthy. We all fail ourselves and others. We were not created by any of these people, and none of them can save us or give us the abundant and eternal life. Many people can be trusted to a limited extent at certain times, but in the whole scheme of life they cannot give us any purpose or hope. Would you trust all the important decisions of your life into the hands of anyone else? We are all human, sinning and failing GOD and others more frequently than we are willing to admit. We need to learn to forgive one another as GOD in CHRIST forgives us *(Colossians 3:13)*. Some may think they are perfect, but it is written: *"If we say, 'We have no sin,' we are deceiving ourselves, and the truth is not in us" (1 John 1:8).*

There is only One Who is worthy of our faith and trust, and that is the LORD our GOD—Creator, Savior, and Counselor. It is written:

"Trust in the Lord with all your heart,
and do not rely on your own understanding;
think about Him in all your ways,

and He will guide you on the right paths."
Proverbs 3: 5–6

Who else should we trust in except the One Who made us? Who else can save us except the One Who died and conquered death for us? Who else can guide our lives except the One Who loves us and desires to lead us on the path to the abundant and eternal life? There is an unbridgeable gulf between CHRIST and all other people. CHRIST alone has risen from the dead and His SPIRIT continues to enlighten and save people in all nations.

We were not there at the time of JESUS' virgin conception. We didn't hear the angels proclaiming His glory on the evening of His birth. We didn't hear Him preach or teach. We weren't there when they crucified Him or when He rose from the dead or ascended into Heaven. We haven't seen His resurrection body. Yet we can know all these truths concerning JESUS through His HOLY SPIRIT Who has powerfully testified to Who JESUS is, to all He has accomplished, to what He is presently doing, and to what He will soon do. Through the amazing ministry of the HOLY SPIRIT over the past two thousand years, people from all walks of life—children, youth, adults, senior citizens, locals and nationals from all tribes and nations, religious and non-religious, politicians, athletes, many poor and unknown, and a few rich and famous—have come to repentance of their sin and faith in CHRIST and into a new life of grace, truth, joy, peace, hope, and love.

To place our faith in JESUS doesn't mean to just have a nice feeling toward JESUS, but to place Him at the center of our lives. It is crucial for us to be wise, and to listen, believe, and put into practice all that His SPIRIT teaches us in His Word, without adding or subtracting to it based on our own personal or cultural prejudices. He is the Teacher and we are His students. He has so much to reveal to us, so much for all of us to learn. We all need to *"grow in the grace and knowledge of our Lord and Savior Jesus Christ" (2 Peter 3:18).*

We all choose whom we are going to believe in, but there is only One Who is *"called Faithful and True" (Revelation 19:11)* and worthy of our complete trust. We encourage everyone to take His nail-pierced hand and let Him lead.

A Life of Repentance

To believe in JESUS implies acknowledging the guilt of our sin and our undeniable need of His sacrificial death on the cross to save us from the power of death and Hell and for eternal life with Him. JESUS preached to all people: *"Repent, because the kingdom of heaven has come near!" (Matthew 4:17).* Repentance of sin isn't a one-time experience, but a continual coming to His cross for cleansing from our selfish thoughts, arrogant attitudes, deceptive words, and destructive actions. JESUS and His SPIRIT call all people to confess our own sin, not the sins of our neighbors. **Part of our daily exercise needs to be treading the well-worn path to His cross in sincere contrition for our sin, and to rejoice with praise for His mercy, forgiveness, and salvation.**

A Life of Holiness

To believe in JESUS is not to just to confess our sins, but to seek His help to transform our lives, thoughts, words, and actions to reflect His grace and truth. Repentance is not just acknowledging our sins, but, with the help of His HOLY SPIRIT, to reject them and live a life of holiness, obeying GOD's will, and serving others in His Name.

The Apostle Paul, moved by the HOLY SPIRIT, wrote:

"For those who live according to the flesh think about the things of the flesh, but those who

live according to the Spirit, about the things of the Spirit. For the mind-set of the flesh is death, but the mind-set of the Spirit is life and peace. For the mind-set of the flesh is hostile to God because it does not submit itself to God's law, for it is unable to do so. Those who are in the flesh cannot please God. You, however, are not in the flesh, but in the Spirit, since the Spirit of God lives in you. But if anyone does not have the Spirit of Christ, he does not belong to Him. Now if Christ is in you, the body is dead because of sin, but the Spirit is life because of righteousness. And if the Spirit of Him who raised Jesus from the dead lives in you, then He who raised Christ from the dead will also bring your mortal bodies to life through His Spirit who lives in you." **Romans 8:5–11**

Note the clear testimony to the triune nature of GOD in these verses. The HOLY SPIRIT is the SPIRIT of GOD and the SPIRIT of CHRIST Who lives with all who sincerely trust in JESUS as their SAVIOR and LORD. Only by relying on the HOLY SPIRIT through His Word and through prayer can we live a holy life which honors CHRIST and leads to the abundant and eternal life.

It is written:

"In fact, all those who want to live a godly life in Christ Jesus will be persecuted. Evil people and impostors will become worse, deceiving and being deceived. But as for you, continue in what you have learned and firmly believed. You know those who taught you, and you know that from childhood you have known the sacred Scriptures, which are able to give you

__wisdom for salvation through faith in Christ__
__Jesus__. __All Scripture is inspired by God and is__
__profitable__ for teaching, for rebuking, for cor-
recting, for training in righteousness, so that
the man of God may be complete, equipped
for every good work." 2 Timothy 3:12–17

The world rejects and persecutes those on the path of the
godly life in CHRIST, just as it rejected and persecuted JESUS.
But if we continue in His Word we will always have the assurance of salvation and will be trained and equipped to live a
holy life that will glorify Him and help others to know Him. It
is crucial to live in harmony and peace with His will and purposes for our lives, seeking the help and inspiration of GOD's
SPIRIT through prayer and actively listening to His Word. As it
is written: *"I have treasured Your word in my heart so that I*
may not sin against You" (Psalm 119:11).

GOD's general will, which is the same for all of us, is clearly
revealed in His commands and teachings in His Word, and lived
out perfectly by JESUS. Although none of us can ever live the
holy life CHRIST lived, His Word and His example are presented
to us as the goal for which we must aim.

A Life of Love

A holy life of faith in JESUS is a life lived in love for JESUS
and for others. Love is at the center of the Holiness of the
FATHER, SON, and the HOLY SPIRIT. The greatest command of
GOD which illuminates His heart is to love Him and others as
He loves us. As it is written:

"This is My command: Love one another as I
have loved you... This is what I command you:
Love one another." John 15:12,17

"If I speak human or angelic languages but do not have love, I am a sounding gong or a clanging cymbal. If I have the gift of prophecy and understand all mysteries and all knowledge, and if I have all faith so that I can move mountains but do not have love, I am nothing. And if I donate all my goods to feed the poor, and if I give my body in order to boast but do not have love, I gain nothing....

Now these three remain: faith, hope, and love. But the greatest of these is love."
1 Corinthians 13:1–3,13

"God's love was revealed among us in this way: God sent His One and Only Son into the world so that we might live through Him. Love consists in this: not that we loved God, but that He loved us and sent His Son to be the propitiation for our sins. Dear friends, if God loved us in this way, we also must love one another."
1 John 4:9–11

Dear friends, the LORD makes it crystal clear that the holy life He calls us to live by His SPIRIT is a life of love for GOD and love for others, including those who despise and persecute us. This is the love of JESUS in us. Our greatest sin is our lack of love for the LORD and for others. Our self-centered nature always desires to look after "me". We all need to learn to die to ourselves and to live for CHRIST and others. JESUS deserves first place in our lives for He is our CREATOR, SAVIOR, and COUNSELOR. Others are just as important as me and mine. Only GOD's love through CHRIST can put our selfish nature to death and empower us to live in His love for Him and others, beginning with our brothers and sisters in GOD's family and extending to all we have contact with.

JESUS is love. As we focus our lives on Him, His love will flow into our lives and through us into the lives of others. As JESUS said: *"You have received free of charge; give free of charge" (Matthew 10:8).*

A Life of Hope

We live in a world of despair, where people increasingly turn to drugs or alcohol to make it through another day, or to suicide to end their emotional and spiritual pain. Without JESUS, life is a hollow, futile enterprise. Everyone needs JESUS. JESUS gives hope to all who come to Him.

Through faith in JESUS we receive forgiveness, holiness, love, and a life of hope—the most astonishing hope that anyone could ever receive. This life In CHRIST begins with His SPIRIT's presence with us amid the brokenness of our present world, but is brought to complete fulfillment in the new Heaven and new Earth where we will live with Him in the new eternal bodies that He will resurrect for our spirits to live in. This resurrection hope is presented throughout the Scriptures, but it was manifested and gifted to all sincere believers through CHRIST's resurrection. As the Scripture says:

"What eye did not see and ear did not hear, and what never entered the human mind —
God prepared this for those who love Him."
1 Corinthians 2:9

Although we cannot fully grasp the fullness of this eternal life with JESUS, we know Who JESUS IS, the reality of His power and wisdom, and the incredible promises in His Word—so we know that it will be greater than anything we could ever ask or imagine. This is the eternal home that He is preparing for His Bride, His people, His children. When we realize the incredible beauty, wisdom, and power that is manifested in this world to bless our brief lives here, we cannot begin to imagine how marvelous this new eternal Heaven and Earth will be that He has been creating for two thousand years.

The LORD doesn't give us all the details of our eternal life with Him. What we do know is that it is a holy city of righteousness, peace, love, joy, and continual worship and celebration. There is no sin or evil, suffering or death. There is GOD: FATHER-SON-HOLY SPIRIT, the holy angels, the saints, and whatever else the LORD in His wisdom and love creates and places there. It is our eternal home which we look forward to with great and joyful anticipation.

JESUS' last words:

"He who testifies about these things says, 'Yes,
I am coming quickly.'
Amen! Come, Lord Jesus!
The grace of the Lord Jesus be with all the
saints. Amen." Revelation 22:20–21

Pray!

GOOD NEWS FROM OUR SAVIOR

1. GOD created us in His own image to be His children. He loves us and desires that we should love and obey Him, and love and serve others. (Matthew 22)
2. All of us have sinned against GOD and others. Through sin we are destroying everything and heading towards death and eternal judgment. (Romans 3; Revelation 20)
3. GOD, in His love and amazing grace, sent His SON, JESUS CHRIST, into our world. JESUS gave His life on a cross for all of our sin. He rose again from the dead to give eternal life to everyone who sincerely believes in Him. (John 3; Romans 3; 1 Peter 1)
4. GOD the FATHER, SON, and HOLY SPIRIT, calls upon each of us to repent of our sin and trust in Him. *(Matthew 4:17; Luke 24:45–47; Acts 20:21)*
5. CHRIST will soon return to judge our planet and establish His new eternal world for His people. (Matthew 24–25; Revelation 21)

"For God loved the world in this way: He gave His One and Only Son, so that everyone who believes in Him will not perish but have eternal life." JESUS (John 3:16)

If you believe this, you need to ask GOD to forgive your sins, and place your faith in CHRIST and what He has done for you. GOD can and will forgive all your sins and give you the gift of eternal life. JESUS promises you that!
May it be so! Come LORD JESUS!

JESUS, Still Lead On

JESUS still lead on, Till our rest be won;
And although the way be cheerless,
We will follow, calm and fearless;
Guide us by Thy hand to our Fatherland.

If the way be drear, If the foe be near,
Let not faithless fears o'er take us,
Let not faith and hope forsake us;
For through many a foe to our home we go.

When we seek relief from a long felt grief,
When temptations come alluring
Make us patient and enduring;
Show us that bright shore where we
weep no more.

JESUS, still lead on, till our rest be won;
Heavenly Leader, still direct us,
Still support, console, protect us,
Till we safely stand in our Fatherland! Amen.

- "JESU Geh Voran"
Nicolaus Ludwig von Zinzendorf 1700-1760
translator Jane L. Borthwick, 1813-97